ALSO BY EDWARD I. KOCH:

MAYOR

POLITICS

HIS EMINENCE AND HIZZONOR:
*A Candid Exchange (with John Cardinal O'Connor)*

# All the Best

## *LETTERS FROM A FEISTY MAYOR*

---

# EDWARD I. KOCH

WITH

LELAND T. JONES

SIMON AND SCHUSTER

NEW YORK · LONDON · TORONTO · SYDNEY · TOKYO · SINGAPORE

SIMON AND SCHUSTER
SIMON & SCHUSTER BUILDING
ROCKEFELLER CENTER
1230 AVENUE OF THE AMERICAS
NEW YORK, NEW YORK 10020

DESIGNED BY EVE METZ
MANUFACTURED IN THE UNITED STATES OF AMERICA

1 3 5 7 9 10 8 6 4 2

LIBRARY OF CONGRESS CATALOGING-IN-PUBLICATION DATA
KOCH, ED, DATE-
ALL THE BEST : LETTERS FROM A FEISTY MAYOR / EDWARD I. KOCH WITH
LELAND T. JONES.
P. CM.
1. NEW YORK (N.Y.)—POLITICS AND GOVERNMENT—1951– 2. KOCH, ED,
1924– —CORRESPONDENCE. I. JONES, LELAND T. II. TITLE.
F128.55.K63 1990
974.7'1043'092—DC20                                90-31606
                                                    CIP

ISBN: 1-4164-8518-4
ISBN: 978-1-4165-8518-3

THIS BOOK IS DEDICATED TO FOUR PEOPLE WHO HAVE HELPED ME ENORMOUSLY OVER THE YEARS:

To STANLEY BREZENOFF, who served as my First Deputy Mayor. Without him, this government could not have functioned. And without his constant intellectual and emotional support, I could not have survived the daily assaults made upon me by the press and others seeking to end my career as Mayor.

To DIANE COFFEY, who worked with me in my congressional office and served as Chief of Staff in my mayoral administration. In addition to performing superbly, she too provided daily intellectual and emotional support, never losing her marvelous sense of humor.

To MARY GARRIGAN, who served as my secretary and assistant during my congressional days and through the twelve years of my mayoralty. I never had to worry about something getting done. I knew that if I left it in her hands, it would be taken care of. She made it possible for me to perform my duties as Mayor, both in and out of City Hall.

To ALLEN SCHWARTZ, my former law partner, appointed by me as Corporation Counsel to the City of New York, and my closest friend, for all his sage advice.

# CONTENTS

CONTENTS

# Dear Reader,

This book is a collection of some of the more interesting letters I have written over the years, primarily about controversial matters, in many cases in response to attacks made upon me for things I have done or said.

My willingness to speak out is, I think, well known. I have been castigated not only by those hostile to me politically, but also by friends who believe I am too candid in my remarks. Candor is both my strength and my weakness, but on balance, I believe, it has proved more a strength than a weakness.

Some have also criticized me for being too confrontational, citing my letters in particular as illustrations of needless combat. I don't agree. I have always believed that as Mayor I had not only a right but a duty and an obligation to speak out, and I have never been persuaded that I would be more effective working behind the scenes with a lower voice and less charged pen. I have fought what I have always believed to be the good fight—protecting the hapless, upholding the truth, and where appropriate, defending myself and my administration. That sometimes I erred in judgment and protested too much, I will concede. But when you consider the number of written statements I have issued over the years, as well as extemporaneously voiced opinions and responses to questions or attacks, it is amazing how few times I have put either one or both feet in my mouth.

Among my favorite letters are two that I cannot find in my files. One was written by me and one was written to me.

The letter from me was to a woman who wrote to me sometime after my election to Congress. Her letter said, in effect, "You won the election. You are my congressman. I don't like what you stand for, but I am going to begin corresponding with you with the thought of seeking to change your mind on particular issues."

I recognized the woman's name, checked it out, and found that she was, in fact, the widow of an American Nazi. I make it a rule to answer every letter, no matter how hostile and no matter from whom. But in this case I made an exception. The woman bombarded me with letters, which were polite at first but then quickly degenerated into very hostile anti-Semitism. So whereas I normally reply letter-to-letter within a few days, I began to store up her correspondence; when I'd accumulated three or four of her letters, I'd respond by simply writing, "I received your last three letters and I have placed them in the loony bin, where they belong." After receiving a few of my replies, she stopped writing.

One day sometime later, Peter Peyser, a Republican member of Congress from Westchester, came into my office and said, "Ed, I got a letter from a woman who lives in your district and who says she's going to consider me her congressman. She's going to begin corresponding with me." He handed me the letter and asked, "What should I do?"

The letter, of course, was from Madame Nazi. "Peter," I said, "I will take care of this." I sent the following letter, which is embedded in my memory verbatim:

*Dear Madame,*

*The letter you sent to Congressman Peter Peyser has ended up in my hands. You may ask, how is it possible that a letter sent by you to Congressman Peter Peyser would end up in my hands? You should know that every letter you send, no matter to whom, ends up in my hands.*

While I can't vouch for it, I doubt that the woman ever sent another letter to anybody.

The second letter I referred to was sent to me from a criminal, although when I met him he was simply a detainee in the federal house of detention on West Street in Manhattan. His name was Sam Melville. As a member of Congress, I had paid a visit to the federal house of detention in the aftermath of a prison riot. Tear gas had been used to subdue the prisoners. I asked the federal warden if I could tour the jail and, in particular, visit the maximum-security area. He said yes.

When I arrived, the smell of tear gas was still in the air. It was about noon and prisoners were being fed on tin plates shoved beneath the bars of their cells. While talking with the warden I heard someone say,

"Congressman, may I speak with you?" I asked the warden if I could speak to the prisoner alone. "Yes," he said.

I walked over to the cell. The prisoner, a white male probably in his thirties, said to me, "Congressman, I need your help. They don't let me exercise. They don't let me shower but once a week. Will you help me?"

I asked why he was being detained. "For bombings," he answered.

"What's your name?" I asked.

"Sam Melville," he said.

"I know you," I said. "You're the Village One." I was referring to posters that radicals had put up all over Greenwich Village bearing the simple slogan, "Free the Village One—Sam Melville."

I returned to the warden, told him of Melville's complaints, and asked him, Why the restrictions? "It's for his safety," the warden said. "The other prisoners don't like bombers. That's why we don't allow him to exercise or shower with them."

When I returned to my Washington office, I wrote a letter to the director of federal prisons, Norman Carlson, bringing the matter to his attention and asking for his intercession. About three weeks later, I received a letter from Melville. As I recall, it read as follows:

*Dear Congressman Koch:*

*There is a new adage at the prison: "It takes a visit from the brass to get the warden off your ass." I am now allowed to shower and exercise every day, for which I thank you. And now, I would like to talk to you about the library.*

*Sincerely yours,*

*Sam Melville*

*P.S. Sorry about the bombings in your district. I will try to have them moved elsewhere.*

Melville ultimately was convicted and incarcerated at Attica, where during a major prison riot, he and thirty-one other prisoners were killed. I am not sure whether he was shot when the guards retook the prison or, as rumor has it, was killed while making and throwing bombs.

Since then, I've written thousands of letters. Some people say I write too many—and maybe that's true. But they are not written just so I can see my name in print. I believe that my letters have always played an important role in educating the public and, in other cases, correcting the record. The letters which appear in this book are a small sampling of those that I have written over the last twelve years. I hope you enjoy them.

*All the best,*

*Ed Koch*

# PART
# 1

## "A LIBERAL WITH SANITY"

---

### Feminism

The National Organization for Women—NOW—has done an enormous amount of good work. But despite all of that good work, sometimes, regrettably, NOW has dedicated all of its energies to picking fights with me over proposals it should have supported. For example, in late 1983 Barbara Rochman, then president of the local chapter of NOW and a friend of mine, took strong exception to a bill that had passed the City Council and was on my desk for signature.

As passed, the bill required all establishments selling or serving alcoholic beverages to post in a highly visible place a sign which read, in big black letters, "Warning—Drinking Alcoholic Beverages during Pregnancy Can Cause Birth Defects." If I signed it, New York City would become the first municipality in the land to require bars, liquor stores, and restaurants serving alcohol to post the signs.

Barbara Rochman didn't disagree with the wisdom of the warning. By then, after all, virtually all of the scientific and medical evidence clearly linked the consumption of alcohol by women during pregnancy to low birth weights, impaired mental and motor functions for the baby, and even a higher incidence of infant mortality within the first year of life.

"To single out pregnant women as a class is not only not fair, but may well violate New York State law against sex discrimination in places of public accommodation," she wrote to me in advance of the public hearing at which I would decide whether to sign the bill. "We anticipate that posting of these notices will lead to cases of harassment of pregnant women in bars and restaurants.

"Moreover," she continued, "we are most uneasy about the step that this legislation takes toward protecting the unborn at the expense of women's freedom. The bill may seem innocuous, but it does establish a precedent on women's reproductive freedom in the future." However "well intentioned" the bill, she asked that I veto it.

"Such a nice person," I thought when I read her letter, "but such a foolish comment." I replied:

*I received your letter of November 30 urging at the request of NOW that I veto the City Council legislation which requires that warnings of the dangers of alcohol to pregnant women be posted in public places that sell alcoholic beverages.*

*I am truly shocked by your statement, "Moreover, we are most uneasy about the step that this legislation takes toward protecting the unborn at the expense of women's freedom." This bill, which I intend to make law, does not impose any sanctions. It's a warning in the same way that we warn pregnant women about various medicines which can have special side effects on the unborn. Should we stop doing that? I hardly think so.*

*I have doubts about the bill simply because I don't believe many, if any, will read the poster, in the same way that I don't think the warning on cigarette packages deters many. If I had my way, I would put a skull and crossbones on the poster and cigarette packages as well but, regrettably, I don't have my way.*

*Please do rethink your position. I intend to sign this legislation and make it law.*
*All the best.*

I signed the bill as promised, and, three months later, I went to Le Zinc Restaurant, near City Hall, to post the first warning. "The warning is as valuable to men as it is to women," I said at the time, conscious of Ms. Rochman's concerns. "All of us are concerned for the health of the city's children. It really does not matter who reads this sign, only that it is read and understood."

And that really is all that does matter. It's not a question of threats to a woman's constitutional rights but of threats to a child's health. While I always have protected and always will protect a woman's right to choose to have an abortion under *Roe* v. *Wade,* I will also seek to protect the right of a child a mother decides to bring to term to enjoy good health and a long life, while warning every mother of the dangers to her health and that of her fetus when, as the saying goes, she drinks for two.

Regrettably, the kind of militant feminism sometimes practiced by organizations like NOW can tend to polarize our society, forcing the public debate into essentially irrelevant issues when there are so many more legitimate issues they have raised that are still to be resolved.

On one side of the polarity are the "yahoos" who seek to portray every feminist issue—whether at the fringe or at the core of our society—as one more gripe from the "bra burners." On the other side are those who seem intent on eliminating any difference whatsoever between the sexes.

Consider the case of Alair Townsend. She currently is the publisher of *Crain's New York Business.* I brought her into my administration in 1981 as Director of the Office of Management and Budget, the person responsible for keeping the books of the fourth-largest public budget in the country in balance. She performed superbly. Then in 1985 I appointed her Deputy Mayor, Finance and Economic Development, the third woman I had named a deputy mayor. Again, she performed superbly.

Selecting Alair, in other words, was one of the best appointments I made in the course of my twelve years as Mayor. Tremendous energy, intelligence, wit—and, it so happens, a great pair of legs. I happened to mention that in an interview with Harvard University's *Governing Magazine.*

Not surprisingly in this age of androgyny, my observation brought howls of protest from one Arlene D. Bjorkman. One's legs, she argued, have nothing to do with one's abilities to serve in government. I of course responded:

*I read Arlene D. Bjorkman's letter in the July issue of* Governing *and was surprised that she was upset with my comment concerning Deputy Mayor Alair A. Townsend—that she "combines extraordinary intelligence with great legs. It helps to have both."*

*Was it wrong for me to comment on that? I don't think so, and I don't believe that Alair was upset by my comment. Is Ms. Bjorkman offended when people discuss the combination of the Kennedys' charisma, wit, and handsome appearance? Does she find that derogatory?*

*I also don't believe that women are less aggressive or combative or that their judgments may be made more on an instinctive level. I have met aggressive and passive men and women, and I prefer the former in both genders when making appointments. No one can tell me that Alair Townsend makes her judgments on instinct alone.*

*I would make the same statement about the other women in my administration who hold positions of high visibility and importance. They are all tough women when it comes to carrying out their obligations of office. However, their toughness in that category in no way reduces, nor should it, their physical attractiveness.*

Great legs or not, I personally believe that there's not a single job in government that women cannot do. As my mayoralty has demonstrated, they are just as able as men to be superb police officers, fire fighters, and sanitation workers. And one day soon I hope and I am sure that a woman will be elected Mayor of the City of New York.

There certainly are many talented and able women to fill the position. I know because I've appointed many of them to the highest positions in my government.

# Welfare

When first established by President Franklin Delano Roosevelt, federal welfare programs were seen as a temporary measure necessary to help thousands upon thousands of families get through the darkest days of the Great Depression. There were very real risks associated with welfare, FDR thought, not just for the government financing it, but also for those receiving it.

"Continued dependence upon relief," he told Congress in January 1935, "induces a spiritual and moral disintegration fundamentally destructive to the national fiber." He was right.

What began as a temporary measure is now, fifty years later, a permanent system. And, among too many families, generation after generation sees welfare as an acceptable style of life and, indeed, the best the future holds in store for them.

It is, I believe, a human tragedy. Regrettably, but inevitably, our society will always have people too ill, too disabled, or too aged to work and maintain financial independence. They will need food and shelter and medical care. Particularly where children are involved, society must always be generous and caring enough to provide them with the sustenance they require.

In June 1989, some 815,000 men, women, and children received public assistance in New York City—more men, women, and children than live in San Francisco or Honolulu, Phoenix or Baltimore. Of those on public assistance, the overwhelming majority—up to 80 percent— are children. Obviously, these children should be in school, not at work. Of the adults, many have children under the age of three at home or are not able-bodied enough to hold a job. They shouldn't be required to work either.

The rest should be seeking a job or be engaged in job training. I believe, for example, that able-bodied people who are on public assistance should be required to go back to work and should lose their benefits if they refuse. If they can't find a job, we should help them find one. If they don't have the skills to hold a job, we should teach them the skills. And if they simply don't want to work, they should be cut off from a public assistance check. In 1989, in fact, the City of New York levied sanctions against some 23,500 able-bodied public assistance recipients who failed to enter job training or go to work.

Just ask the working poor what they think. In many instances, the paychecks they bring home each month are smaller than the combined public assistance, shelter allowance, food stamps, and Medicaid benefits a public assistance family receives each month. The working poor resent that. But they keep on working. As FDR might say, it's testimony to their fiber.

Clearly, there are and should be limits to government's generosity to and society's responsibility for able-bodied people on public assistance. The question of how generous and how responsible was raised for me one day in the winter of 1988 when I visited a city-owned apartment—one of 12,000 we'd rehabilitated for homeless families—occupied by a once homeless family which, until shortly before my visit, had lived in one of the city's welfare hotels.

By all accounts, our program had been a tremendous success, and I'd expected to end my visit enthusiastic. As I wrote to *The New York Times*, I didn't:

The number 19 recently became more than a number to me for reasons that are both different and related.

Not long ago, I visited a family in a once abandoned apartment building that is now owned by New York City. The city rehabilitated it at a cost of about $65,000 per apartment as part of a program that provides permanent homes for homeless families living in temporary shelter in welfare hotels. The city rehabilitates almost 4,000 such apartments a year. This particular apartment building is in the Bronx, in an otherwise blighted neighborhood. It's the best building on the block.

The family I visited—a mother and three children—live in a tastefully furnished apartment. When I walked in, the children were sitting on the couch watching a very large television set with the volume turned up loud. On top of the set was a VCR. A member of my staff went over to turn down the volume so we could talk. The mother said: "Don't touch it. You have to use the remote control to turn down the volume." Which she then did. I asked her how she liked the apartment.

She said, "It's wonderful." And it is. I asked her where she lived before. She said she'd been living in one of the welfare hotels. I asked her how long she had been there. "Five years," she replied.

I was shocked. About 30 percent of families living in welfare hotels leave within a month, and approximately 60 percent within six months. Other, usually larger families that are more difficult to place remain for a longer period, bringing the average stay up to thirteen months. But I'd never heard of anyone living in a hotel for five years. I was aghast.

I said, "Five years—and we never offered you an apartment?"

She said: "Oh no, Mayor. Of course you did. Your people showed me nineteen apartments."

"Why didn't you take one?"

"I didn't like any of them. Either they weren't located in nice build-

6

ings or nice neighborhoods or they weren't in the borough I wanted to live in."

Again, I was shocked. Here was a person who was bringing up her children under difficult, squalid circumstances in a welfare hotel and she'd turned down nineteen apartments until she got the one she wanted. I thought to myself, people who are part of the working poor, and who are perhaps either doubled up or living in substandard housing, would be furious if they knew they'd been denied the opportunity to take one of those nineteen apartments this woman had turned down.

Something has gone wrong when people on public assistance have more choices than people who are making it on their own. However, when I sought to place restrictions on the number of apartments any recipient could turn down, welfare advocates denounced me as "Attila the Hun."

When I persisted in trying to bring about this reform, the New York State Commissioner of Social Services, Cesar Perales, cited the requirement known as fair hearings, which allow welfare recipients to reject apartments for reasons that boggle the mind.

Welfare should be treated as a response to a temporary emergency, not as a permanent way of life. Our goal should be to get people off welfare, not to encourage them to remain on public assistance by giving them options working people don't have.

Welfare clients should not be allowed to turn down apartments that have no hazardous violations. We should not permit more than three apartments to be rejected. At a time when housing is in short supply, questions of neighborhood or borough preference should not be accepted as valid reasons for turning down a place to live.

A few days ago, the number nineteen caught my attention a second time. A newspaper article told the story of a man named Calvin Watkins, who lives in a welfare hotel. He is thirty-one years old. He told the reporter he has had nineteen children—they range in age from fifteen years to a few days old—with four different women, who are scattered among two welfare hotels and an apartment in Harlem. The article reported that Mr. Watkins lives with nine of his children and two of their mothers in a welfare hotel in Brooklyn. Three other children live in a hotel in Manhattan.

Mr. Watkins was in the news because one of his children, Calvin Jr., fourteen, was arrested at the Hotel Bryant on a robbery charge. The article went on to report that another child, James, was placed in the

Jamaica Arms, a welfare hotel in Queens, when he was eight years old. The article said that this was where James first "learned how to hustle." On February 3, James was stabbed fourteen times in what the police called a drug-related robbery. According to the news article, "the boy, who survived the assault, was carrying $1,000 in cash and a quantity of crack when he was attacked by three teen-agers in Room 907 of the Bryant, at 230 West 54th Street."

Again, the number nineteen prompts me to say that something has gone terribly wrong. It has become painfully obvious that there is only so much that government can and should do for those it seeks to help.

Is it really government's responsibility to provide Mr. Watkins, the mothers of his children, and those nineteen children with shelter? Shouldn't we be asking ourselves how much responsibility has to be required of Mr. Watkins and the mothers of his children? Is it wrong to raise the question of their responsibility for the things their children do? Is it the responsibility of the city to take those children into custody as their protector? I don't know.

But I do know this: When rights without responsibilities become the order of the day, we encourage a social breakdown that will harm us in ways yet unimagined. There is a limit to what government can and should do in a democracy. No city or state can be expected to protect adults from themselves. If that is the course we choose for our society, then nothing can protect us from each other.

My op-ed piece did not sit well with the advocates or columnists, provoking screams of outrage that I was "welfare bashing." They said it never happened and demanded that I give up the name of the mother who'd refused nineteen apartments so that they could check and confirm the facts I'd reported. But if a reporter's names, dates, and sources are privileged and confidential, why aren't mine? More relevant, I would have been violating confidentiality and the state law if I had released the name of a person on welfare. All I can say is that the visit occurred, the conversation took place, and, yes, witnesses were present.

My critics charged me with blaming the victims when I ought to be blaming the system. But who is the real victim? The woman who turned down nineteen apartments until she got the one she wanted, all the while forcing her children to spend five years—that's more than 1,800 nights—in a welfare hotel? I don't think so. Or is the victim Mr. Watkins, who, according to the press account, is a husband of four and

8

father of nineteen, including James, a hustler, a thief, a drug dealer, and a stabbing victim? Again, I don't think so.

No, the victims of these scams are to be found elsewhere. Among the thousands of public assistance recipients who do not abuse the system and are trying to get off welfare and onto their own two feet. Among the thousands of working poor families who choose to work two or three jobs so that they'd don't have to go onto relief. And, yes, among the thousands of other families whose taxes go to a public assistance program that they hope will help people who genuinely need help and will leave those who are running a scam to their own devices.

None of us any longer believes that welfare is a temporary measure. Fifty years have taught us otherwise. By now it is a permanent, if imperfect, feature of our society. But if we are unable to talk honestly and openly about its imperfections, the imperfections will persist. And if they do persist, the issue will not be whether to have a permanent welfare system or a temporary system, but whether to have one at all. The American public will support relief. But it will not willingly support rip-offs.

# The Drug Epidemic

By now it's virtually impossible for any public official—from the President on down—to ignore the drug epidemic. Whether the official's a liberal or a conservative, Democratic or Republican, from a big town or small, he or she is almost certain to say that what this country really needs is a good old war on drugs. Regrettably, few seem to have the will to do what's necessary to win that war.

I believe, for example, that the stiffer the penalties against drug dealing and drug use, the less drug abuse there will be. If we're serious, we may want to do what was done in Malaysia and Japan. In Malaysia they put drug dealers to death. And you don't see many drug dealers in Malaysia anymore. In Japan they put—"stuffed" is probably a more accurate description—drug users of any and every sort into jail. And you don't see many drug users in Japan anymore.

Too tough, you say? I say, "Not tough enough." Won't eradicate the problem, you say? I say, "It'll certainly reduce it." Too barbaric, you say? I say, "What about the barbarism of those who steal, rob, even murder to feed their habits?" I would allow drug users to go into treatment, but those who break treatment should go directly to jail.

Drug dealers are a very tough, very barbaric breed. They have, after all, wiped out what seems to be half the government of Colombia. And they're still not finished. If we don't have the will to beat them, they most certainly will beat us.

In 1984 I was invited to address the Democratic National Convention, then assembled in San Francisco. The topic was mine to choose. I spoke about drugs, which I called "the scourge of America." I said then:

> I have never pleaded a public cause with more conviction and urgency than I now bring to the utterly desperate problem of the narcotics traffic in American cities. I am here to enlist our party's moral indignation and support for a strategic program to deal with it honestly and effectively. I propose that we draw on our enormous military resources in this time of peace to secure our own borders and curtail the flow of dangerous drugs into this country.

And I pointed out that "if the Russians were doing this to us, we would be in a state of war. As it is, something even worse is happening: by our government's own indifference it has raised the flag of surrender."

In 1989 Governor Mario Cuomo, who gave what many at the time said was the most moving speech of the entire convention, said that my speech was the more important, though less appreciated.

I must admit, however, to having been surprised at the reaction from the floor of the convention to what I said. Sitting in the front row were a number of members of the New York State delegation, including Gloria Davis, a black woman who represents the Bronx in the State Assembly. Assemblywoman Davis and some of her fellow delegates hooted and howled, laughed and booed as I spoke. "Why is Koch talking about drugs?" I recall them screaming. "Drugs are a local issue, not a national one."

Well, Assemblywoman Davis isn't laughing anymore. Nor, for that matter, is anyone else.

Where are we today, more than five years after I spoke at the Democratic National Convention? Well, drugs are hot, at the center of our national consciousness. People talk knowingly about interdiction. They discuss treatment options. They understand the need for more prisons and stiffer penalties. They ponder how to improve drug education and prevention. And they know drugs are a worse problem today than five years ago.

After weeks of leaks promising a tough stance and even tougher actions, President Bush chose drugs as the topic of his first televised address to the American people from the Oval Office. He promised more than he delivered. While he seems to recognize that drug abuse is a serious threat to our national security, unfortunately, he has not called for nearly enough money to prosecute the so-called war on drugs, nor does he advocate all of the tough measures available.

Make no mistake about it. Right now we are losing the war. Hence I wrote to James R. Stewart, the Director of the National Institute of Justice:

*In a speech to the United States Conference of Mayors on September 18, 1989, I criticized the federal government for failing to do its part to help us stop the scourge of illegal drugs and drug-related crime. I noted that in 1986, state and local authorities made 690,000 of the 711,000 drug arrests in the United States, which means that the federal government contributed only a disgraceful 3 percent of the arrests.*

*According to a report the following day in New York Newsday, you accused me of "clearly overstating the lack of performance" by the federal government, and you argued that in the absence of "a national police force," these arrest figures were to be expected.*

*While these facts may not be surprising, they are still unacceptable. This record surely raises critical questions about what the Drug Enforcement Administration, the Federal Bureau of Investigation and other federal agencies are doing about the drug problem. How many arrests have these agencies, including the Customs Service and the Coast Guard, contributed to the fight against drugs? Have the federal agencies done their job in stopping the flow of illegal drugs and apprehending the drug dealers? Has the Administration given them the resources, support, and commitment they need? I do not think so, and the country's anti-drug efforts have suffered as a result. . . .*

*Those of us in communities throughout this country, including New York, have been left to wage this most crucial war with little or no federal help. The Administration's new strategy does not substantially change this, and we are still waiting for Washington's resources and commitment to match its rhetoric.*

*There is no better evidence of the federal government's feeble anti-*

drug policy than its failure to arrest a substantial number of drug dealers. Most, if not all, of the drug offenses prosecuted in state and local courts are also federal crimes. The prosecution in the federal courts of a fair share of these cases would do much to ease the burden on crowded state and local court dockets. It would also speed the conviction and sentencing of drug dealers, and thereby speed the reclaiming of our neighborhoods.

That is not what is happening today. According to the Statistical Report of the United States Attorney's Office, for federal fiscal year 1988 federal prosecutors throughout the country convicted only 11,158 defendants in drug cases last fiscal year. In the past five fiscal years, all of the United States attorneys together filed only 31,357 drug cases (involving perhaps 40,000–45,000 defendants), while hundreds of thousands of drug arrests were being made nationwide each year. In contrast, New York City prosecutors filed 21,000 drug indictments and obtained more than 15,000 felony drug convictions in 1988 alone.

The two federal prosecutors in New York City combined in federal fiscal year 1988 to send only 728 defendants to federal prison for drug offenses, while our local prosecutors sent more than 7,000 drug defendants to state prison and 28,022 to City jails last year. In fact, these two United States attorneys, whose jurisdiction includes all of New York City plus several other counties, have sent only 2,700 drug defendants to federal prison in the past four years. That is clearly not enough to protect the public from the drug plague gripping our communities.

As these figures demonstrate, it is impossible to "overstate" the lack of federal performance in the war on drugs. Whether or not there is a federal police force, that is no excuse for the failure of the Administration and its National Drug Control Strategy to take some simple, practical steps to redress this shocking imbalance, like making drug cases the number one priority of the United States attorneys; setting up special federal courts to handle drug cases; instituting "federal days," whereby United States attorneys would prosecute street-level drug cases; and treating most drug-related homicides as federal crimes, so that the federal death penalty can be applied.

Moreover, the federal government should stop its foot dragging and finally make surplus military bases available for state and local correctional facilities. There are well over 60,000 inmates in New York State prisons and New York City jails, far more than the approximately 50,000 inmates in the entire federal system. In your position as the

*Director of the National Institute of Justice, instead of defending the status quo, you can be an important advocate for a meaningful federal role in helping us to take back our streets.*

*Unless the Justice Department and the Administration make the kind of fiscal and programmatic commitments necessary to wage a real anti-drug effort, the scourge of drugs will continue to overwhelm us and threaten our national survival.*

*All the best.*

The snail-like progress we have made since 1984 is disheartening. I compared the drug invasion then to an onslaught of Soviet missiles. We have not defended ourselves adequately, and the devastation wrought by drugs is apparent for all to see.

In the age of glasnost, we may have less to fear from Soviet missiles. But the cocaine bombs and heroin rockets continue to fall. We are talking more than ever about fighting back. That's good. But as I said in San Francisco, "the casualties mount, the destruction continues, and the threat grows." When will we once and for all find our national will to fight back?

# Building Prisons in Alaska

I have always tried to get along well with my fellow mayors, regardless of whether they are Republicans or Democrats, from a big city or small, veterans or newcomers to what arguably is the toughest political turf of all—city hall. From personal experience, I know how hard mayors work, how many problems they face, and how often a good night's sleep can be ruined by a telephone call reporting a crisis, disaster, or tragedy which requires a mayor's immediate response.

So when one of my colleagues is upset by something I've said or done, I'm upset too and immediately try to clarify any misunderstanding and reconcile any differences we may have. Such was the case in June 1988, when I delivered a speech before the annual meeting of the U.S. Conference of Mayors in Salt Lake City, "an historic and very clean city," I told my hosts. "All it needs is a few more trees."

No, that's not what caused the trouble. What did was a suggestion made half-seriously and half-jocularly in my speech. The topic was drugs, the plague that threatens every city, town, and village in the land. One manifestation of the drug problem is the overcrowding of city jails and state prisons by persons convicted of drug crimes.

I reminded my audience that a drug crime that is a violation of state or local law is also a federal crime. But the federal government—a government that has failed so miserably at sealing off the borders across which illicit drugs must flow before flooding the streets of our cities— has also failed miserably in assuming its fair share of the burden of incarcerating drug criminals.

It's well past the time, I told my audience, for the federal government to start expanding its prison system. If it does, I promised, cities like New York would even be willing to contribute to the costs of constructing and operating the federal prisons. And I even had a way to keep down building costs. "Build minimum-security prisons in the deserts of Nevada or the tundra of Alaska," I proposed. "What's a prisoner going to do if he does escape? Hail a cab?"

That brought smiles to the faces in the audience. But 469 miles away in Las Vegas, Nevada, Mayor Ron Lurie was enraged by my comments. I heard from him a couple of days later. "Your comments that drug dealers should be incarcerated in tent prisons located in the Nevada desert were insulting to the citizens of our state," he wrote. "We are not a wasteland for the dregs of cities who cannot handle their own social problems."

I replied:

*I received your letter of June 10, 1988, and I have no desire to engage in a dispute with you. Mayors are part of an endangered species and should be treasured, not assailed verbally or otherwise.*

*. . . My reference to jails is not limited to Nevada. I have also suggested Utah and Alaska as areas where the federal government could build jails that would hold the drug pushers and the drug users who do not want to go into treatment centers.*

*In the City of New York, we have doubled our jail space. In five years, we have gone from 7,500 to 15,600 jail cells or other beds. The State of New York has 40,000 cells or a maximum jail population of 55,000 prisoners. Today we are at full capacity. Our jails are actually above 100 percent occupancy capacity and we are building more of them.*

*I have stated that if a jail is located in the middle of the desert and a prisoner escapes, where can he/she run? Because of its location, it could be a minimum security jail and therefore cheaper. If you don't want the prison in Nevada, and surely I am not seeking to force it on you, I suspect that there are other counties throughout the country that desperately want the jails and the jobs that go with them.*

*Let's not fight. We have too many joint enemies.*

*All the best.*

I hope Mayor Lurie and the good citizens of Las Vegas now understand that I was not trying to insult them but, instead, was trying to find a solution to a problem which, I am sure, afflicts even the Sagebrush State. Drugs are killing people in every state and every city, and unless the federal government starts carrying more of the load, we'll all be overwhelmed.

By the way, I never got any angry letters from Alaska about my idea. They probably would enjoy having a few more people way up north— referring of course to prison guards and their families, not the prisoners themselves. Then again, the first Europeans to settle in Australia were convicted prisoners. They didn't do so bad a job of transforming a continent. Just imagine what they could do for Alaska.

# Why I Don't Race Camels

I often receive invitations from mayors of other cities and governors of other states who want help in calling attention to a particular activity in their jurisdiction. No wonder. New York is the media capital of the world. So if their community's event "plays" here, there's a good chance it'll play everywhere.

When an invitation comes in, I always try to respond, even if it means having to recall a not-so-comfortable ride in 1980 on a not-so-cooperative camel in the shadows of the Great Pyramids of Egypt. Consider my RSVP to the mayor of Indio, California:

*I was delighted to receive your invitation to participate with you in a camel race. As you know, I recently returned from Egypt, where I had gone to look into the question of whether camels could be introduced into New York City. I had tried bicycles and had even created special bike lanes, but that venture failed miserably. As I drove by those lanes one Sunday, I found only four bikers and one of them was going the wrong way. Those lanes were quickly removed. Unfortunately, camels are not the answer either. Let me tell you of my findings in Egypt.*

*Camels are mean, smelly, and try to bite. I know that for a fact, because I asked for the toughest camel they had. Its name, by the way, was California. I hope that my camel's disposition did not result from Californian ancestors. I asked the camel drover to send me the pedigree of this camel as quickly as possible, but I have yet to receive it. When it does arrive, I will send it on to you.*

*Nevertheless, notwithstanding the vile disposition of the camel—which is in contrast with the sweet disposition of our mass transit riders, particularly those using mass transit at 7:30 A.M.—I publicly stated that I was considering building a camel walk on Fifth Avenue, our most prestigious thoroughfare. Would you believe, when I got back, I found that some smart Wall Streeter had cornered all of the camels available in the Northeast? Had I gone forward with the camel walk, he, because of his corner on the camel market, would have made a bundle. And the SEC would have begun an investigation, which I certainly don't need since this City now has an unblemished record. Even worse, the expectation was that every chic person would want his or her own camel, which would bid the camels out of sight of the common person. So I announced I would not allow the camel walk to be built and camel futures tumbled.*

*I tell you this story to explain why I cannot accept your offer to camel race. If I were to accept, camel futures would immediately go right back up again.*

*Perhaps you might invite Mayor Jane Byrne. I don't know her stand on camels, but I do know that she has an open mind.*

*All the best.*

Some mayors might "walk a mile for a camel" or a camel ride if it meant a little free publicity. Not this mayor. I haven't smoked cigarettes in thirty-five years and I haven't ridden a camel in ten. In both cases, there's no reason to resume now.

# "A Liberal with Sanity"

To be elected President of the United States, a candidate must win a majority of the popular vote in enough states to garner 270 votes in the Electoral College. These days, Democratic nominees aren't even coming close. Add Jimmy Carter's 49 electoral votes from 1980, Walter Mondale's 13 votes from 1984, and Michael Dukakis's 112 votes from 1988, in fact, and the Democratic Party is still 96 electoral votes short of winning the White House. Even once.

So long and dismal a Democratic dry spell doesn't require a particularly long explanation. Americans like mainstream Presidents. Go too far to the right, like Republican Barry Goldwater in 1964, or too far to the left, like Democrat George McGovern in 1972, and you'll go nowhere fast on Election Day.

Regrettably, the Republicans have been quicker to learn the lesson than the Democrats—even though some Democrats, like myself, have sounded the warning for years. Our warnings caused angry criticism from some of our more radical colleagues in the Democratic Party.

Election after election, they've argued that the farther to the left our party goes, the better the chances for victory. In election after election, however, they've been proven wrong.

Some conservative political observers suggest that I am a Democrat at odds with my own party, a liberal who takes strong exception to liberal traditions. I've always been proud of the fact that I am a liberal.

In responding to columnist Joseph Sobran in the *New York City Tribune* in 1985, I tried to explain exactly what kind of a liberal and what kind of a Democrat I am—a liberal with sanity:

> First and foremost, I don't mean that the Democratic donkey ought to start acting like a Republican elephant. We came to modern-day power under the banner of Franklin Roosevelt, not Herbert Hoover.
>
> Democrats shouldn't turn our backs on the very important issues which we've addressed and the very important constituencies we've represented in the past forty years. We must remain committed to ending racial and religious discrimination by helping to advance the progress of minorities into the economic mainstream of this country.

We must continue addressing the issue of nuclear escalation and seeking the reduction of armaments, both nuclear and conventional. We must keep working to secure equal rights for women and protecting their rights with respect to abortion provided for by the U.S. Supreme Court. We must resist government and private sector intrusions into the bedrooms of this nation by prohibiting discrimination based on sexual orientation. And we must be willing to address other issues that do not necessarily interest or affect the largest number of people in this country but are nevertheless exceedingly important to those who are affected.

If the concerns of these Americans are not addressed, it would deny the Democratic Party its *raison d'être*, its very sense of self and morality. In the interest of our party and of all Americans, let's let the Republicans keep Herbert Hoover all to themselves.

While every one of these issues must be addressed, at the same time the Democratic Party must also make clear that it is likewise not only interested in but also advancing the causes and addressing the concerns of mainstream America. Democrats don't have to and shouldn't reject hard work and the economic rewards that come from it, drug-free and disciplined classrooms, or patriotism and love for our country. Nor should we drop our opposition to the dictatorships of the left as well as those on the right; our faith in religious and moral values of the Judeo-Christian traditions and the contributions made by all of the world's great religions; our opposition to those who seek only to protect those charged with crime while ignoring the legitimate rights of the victimized; or our understanding that, notwithstanding its calls for disarmament, the Soviet Union remains the greatest threat to the free world, as evidenced by its intervention in Hungary, Czechoslovakia, Poland and, most recently, Afghanistan.

. . . And, we must reject the notion that merely throwing the government's money—your money and mine—at problems will solve those problems. Our compassion must be guided by an intelligent mind with respect to expenditures both for social services and for military. Government alone did not build America and government alone will not solve all of its problems.

I believe that the 1980 debacle should have steered Democrats back to the mainstream course. Judging from the 1984 debacle, it didn't. Now, more than ever, the Democratic Party must return to its traditional representation of mainstream America. Otherwise, like a bad Hollywood movie, the 1988 elections will be labeled Debacle III. . . .

Because I've challenged some of the long-held shibboleths as they relate to how a city or a nation is best governed, I've lost a lot of my erstwhile friends. I speak candidly, for example, to every person and group with whom I have a conversation. And if I believe their interests do not responsibly relate to the interests of the City as a whole, I do not support their cause or request of me.

As mayor and congressman, I've treated every group equally and without discrimination. I've said, for example, I do not believe in group rights based on race, religion, or sex. I've said if we had given to the poor all of the money that we had appropriated for their benefit over the last twenty years, they'd be rich instead of still poor. Instead, they've been victimized by the misuse of some of our social programs intended to help, but flawed in their execution or philosophy.

Finally, ever since 1971, I've made it clear that I am indeed a liberal, but a liberal with sanity. I believe in the Democratic Party. I believe in liberalism. I also believe in common sense and traditional values. Taken together, these beliefs constitute what I mean by liberalism with sanity. Taken together, they also represent the path the party must take if it is to regain mainstream America.

Regrettably, the Democratic Party paid my warnings no mind three years later. While it did not nominate the most liberal candidate—the Reverend Jesse Jackson—it did nominate someone perceived as more liberal than mainstream Democrats—Governor Michael Dukakis.

Prior to the April 1988 primary in New York, I had met at Gracie Mansion with both Governor Dukakis and U.S. Senator Albert Gore of Tennessee, at that time his main rival for my endorsement. No, the Gracie Mansion meetings were not a courtesy call, but a no-holds-barred discussion of a whole host of issues.

The very knowledgeable and very frank answers of Senator Gore deeply impressed me. Not so those of Governor Dukakis. A nice enough man. But every time I'd ask a tough question, out would come another catchphrase, some more litmus tests. Senator Gore, I would later tell the press in endorsing him, had "the possibility of being a great President." My feeling about Dukakis was that he was acceptable as a candidate, but would not turn on the American people.

And he most certainly didn't. Coming out of the convention in Atlanta with an eighteen-point lead over George Bush, on Election Day Dukakis was beaten and beaten soundly, as I had feared. Debacle III!

Governor Dukakis, by the way, called me after I was defeated in my own bid for reelection to a fourth term as Mayor. Having tasted defeat himself, he thought he knew how I felt. I thanked him for his call, but told him there was no need to feel sorry for me. I'd had a wonderful twelve years and I now felt a tremendous burden had been lifted from my shoulders. Someone else could now carry it.

We also talked a bit about his own troubles in his own state. Since the presidential election, it appeared, the much vaunted "Massachusetts Miracle" had gone sour. State spending had to be cut. Taxes raised. Tough, unpopular decisions had to be made. It's not the kind of problem any politician wants to face. I wished him luck in dealing with it. I've been there too.

The bad news for Democrats is that we've lost three straight presidential elections. The good news is that we've got a number of middle-of-the-road officeholders who could lead us to victory in 1992—people like Senator Gore, Senator George Mitchell of Maine, former Governor, now Senator Charles Robb of Virginia, Senator Sam Nunn of Georgia, Governor Mario Cuomo of New York, and Senator Bill Bradley of New Jersey. If we resist the temptation to go radical left and we stay mainstream with any of these, we can win.

Whenever I've argued for a mainstream Democratic Party, inevitably I've been attacked. Such is the price paid by the politically prescient if they are not on the radical left of my party. Fortunately, my view is finally coming to be shared by more liberal members of the party. "There are three not-sa-pos-tas that have hurt liberals," the very liberal Congressman Barney Frank of Massachusetts told *The New York Times* in December 1988. "You're not supposed to say that the free enterprise system is wonderful and has worked better than any other. You're not supposed to say that in our era, certainly since the fall of Hitler, Communism has been by far the worst system of government in the world, or that most people who are in prison are bad people." Hear, hear. I only wish people like Congressman Frank had come to the conclusion sooner.

# PART
# 2

# THE WORLD
# ACCORDING TO KOCH

_____

## To Presidents Ortega and Reagan on Nicaragua

In Congress I was a member of the Foreign Operations Subcommittee of the House Appropriations Committee. Along with Don Fraser, now the Mayor of Minneapolis, I led the fight to cut off U.S. aid to brutal military dictatorships in Latin America. At our urging, aid to Uruguay was cut off. "Next year, on to Nicaragua!" I promised at the time.

I left Congress to come to City Hall in 1978, and military aid to Nicaragua was cut off by President Carter. It was the beginning of the end for the Somoza family, which had ruled with an iron fist and robbed the country blind for more than fifty years. I am proud to have played a role in deposing them.

But it also marked the beginning of the rise to power of the Sandinistas. While I joined many Nicaraguans in welcoming their revolution, I ultimately concluded that the smart and charming Daniel Ortega, leader of the Sandinistas, was merely a Communist version of the smart and charming fascist Anastasio Somoza. Both engaged in the torture of their own citizens and deprived them of their basic human rights.

In 1987, I had a chance to see for myself whether my fears were founded. Charles Robb, the former Governor of Virginia, asked me to lead a delegation to Central America under the auspices of his newly formed Peace and Democracy Watch. He knew of my interest in the region and felt I could serve as a reliable witness as to how well the five nations were complying with the terms of the peace accord crafted by President Oscar Arias of Costa Rica and signed by the five presidents in Esquipulas, Guatemala. On November 5, 1987, the nations were scheduled to observe the first phase of the accord by declaring an amnesty for political prisoners, entering cease-fire agreements with insurgent forces, and lifting censorship.

It was an invitation I couldn't refuse. I asked seven distinguished New Yorkers to join me. After speaking with each nation's ambassador to the United Nations and meeting with Contra leaders during a stopover in Miami to get their side of the story, we left the United States on November 2 for a trip that would take us to the capital cities of Tegucigalpa in Honduras, San Salvador in El Salvador, Managua in Nicaragua, and San José in Costa Rica. On board were reporters from five television stations, three newspapers, two wire services, and three radio stations.

It was an exciting trip. As we drove into Tegucigalpa for a meeting with President Azcona, we were struck by the overwhelming poverty of the people. The soldiers escorting us opened their van doors when traffic slowed to show their carbines as a deadly warning to any who might want to make trouble for our caravan. We arrived in San Salvador the morning guerrillas had brought transportation to a halt with a national strike, and we had to fly in an army transport plane escorted by helicopters to the capital to meet with President Duarte.

And then there was Managua, a city which still had not recovered from the December 1972 earthquakes that damaged 80 percent of the capital's buildings and left 10,000 Nicaraguans dead. We paid our respects at the grave of Pedro Joaquín Chamorro, whose assassination by Somocistas had sparked the overthrow of Somoza, and visited Violeta, his widow, at *La Prensa,* the newspaper he'd founded but which, because of its opposition to the Sandinista revolution, had been shut down by Ortega for more than a year.

We spoke with Lino Hernandez, chairman of the independent Human Rights Commission in Nicaragua, who'd been jailed and tortured by both Somoza and Ortega. Every visitor, he said, was interested in the twenty or so human rights complaints lodged against the Contras. But no one cared about the hundreds that had been brought against the Sandinistas.

"How can you continue to do this?" I asked, given the danger he must be in. "Don't you have a son?"

"It is because I have a son that I do this," he said.

And then there was the November 5 rally celebrating the return to Managua of President Daniel Ortega, back from a mission to Moscow. At the rally on the Plaza of the Revolution he intended to announce whether and how the Sandinistas would comply with the Esquipulas Accord.

A half-day national holiday had been decreed. Buses were transporting thousands of peasants from the countryside around Managua. The entire city was festooned with banners denouncing Reagan, hailing Ortega.

Everyone in our delegation wanted to attend. The U.S. embassy could offer no help. "Your bus won't get within a mile of the plaza, and you'll have to walk the rest of the way," its staff advised us. "With Las Turbas Divinas"—a very militant and sometimes violent Sandinista youth group that resembled Hitler's Brownshirts and Mussolini's Blackshirts—"on the road, we cannot guarantee your safety. And even if you do get there, Ortega will only use you for propaganda purposes."

We went anyway. When we arrived at the plaza, already more than 100,000 Sandinistas had assembled, a crowd stretching all the way to the shores of Lake Managua. To the left of the stage where Ortega would speak was the grave of Carlos Fonseca, a founder of the revolution. To the right was the empty shell of the eighteenth-century National Cathedral, destroyed by the 1972 earthquake.

History was in the making. The international press corps was on the scene. Moises Hassan, the Mayor of Managua, who had graciously greeted us at Sandino International Airport, waved to me and gestured to nine empty folding chairs on the stage. They'd been reserved for our delegation. I declined.

Then Miguel D'Escoto, the Foreign Minister, whom I'd known when I was in Congress, caught my eye. I walked over to the steps leading up to the stage to greet him. We embraced. He too invited me up, promising that Ortega intended not only to comply with the Esquipulas Accord, but to go beyond it. "If he does," I replied, "I might join him on the stage afterward." I never did.

The crowd began to chant. Ortega had arrived. "¡Allí, allá, Yanqui morirá! ¡Allí, allá, Yanqui morirá!" Translated it meant, "Here and there, the Yankees will die." As it seemed we were the only Yankees in a crowd of 100,000, you might say we were a bit put off.

Ortega quieted the crowd and singled me out as not being the type of Yankee that they had been referring to in their chant. He said I'd helped the Sandinistas by leading the fight to cut off aid to Somoza. I was a friend, he said, and safer in Managua than I was on Forty-second Street in New York.

Ortega said he would grant amnesty to about 980 people. "That's ridiculous," I said to the press standing near me. "There are eight to ten thousand political prisoners in jail." Ortega said he'd declare a broader cease-fire and provide a greater amnesty, but only after verification that the other Central American nations had done all that they were required to do. That, I noted, violated the terms of the accord, which had called for simultaneity.

"He obviously hasn't given you a whole loaf," said Vic Miles of WCBS-TV, "but has he given you a half?" I said, "Not even a mouthful."

After his speech, we left the plaza, boarded our bus, and headed back to the Intercontinental Hotel. During our ride the passions and positions each of us had been developing on our tour momentarily boiled over. A heated discussion ensued. Some thought Ortega's speech marked a turning point for peace. Others, including me, thought that it didn't go far enough in complying with the accord.

In the best tradition of democracy North American style, we had what one delegation member described as a "revolution on the bus." Bloodless, of course. We agreed to issue a joint statement the next morning. "Central America's future," we said, "is for Central Americans to decide. . . . The interests of all will be served by an end everywhere in the region to poverty, violence, totalitarianism, human rights violations, and external interference."

Friday was our last full day in Nicaragua. We wondered if we'd meet with Ortega. All day long we'd been told, "It looks good," then, "It looks bad." At about five we heard there would be a meeting. But we didn't know when or where. We went across the street from the hotel to Los Antojitos, an open-air restaurant. Service was terrible. The food was even worse. But I ate everything.

By nine-thirty we still hadn't heard anything. "It makes no sense for us to wait here," I said. "Let's go back to the hotel." An hour later, we were invited to the president's house for a meeting. Into the bus we went, the press following behind us.

Within minutes we were in a neighborhood with big homes and manicured lawns, reminiscent of Great Neck, Long Island. We hadn't been to this section of Managua before. It stood in marked contrast to most other sections of the city.

We entered a large ranch-style home. Ortega, dressed in military fatigues, appeared. He had a very warm handshake. I presented him with the two New York Yankees jerseys George Steinbrenner had given to me.

"Mr. President," I said, "I know you like baseball. Here are two Yankees jerseys, six Yankees caps, as well as six Mets caps for you and your kids."

He said, in English, with a big smile, "I like the Yankees."

"You didn't last night, Mr. President," I immediately said.

He laughed and said, "Well, I mean the Yankees team."

The television cameras were taking all of this in. They wouldn't leave. "Send in the Turbas, Mr. President," I said. "Then they'll leave." He laughed again and the press left.

I sat down next to him. "Mr. President, we've been here four days," I said. "We have a lot of questions. Rather than you opening with a statement, why don't you just allow us to ask some questions and then, in the course of answering, you'll tell us whatever it is that you want us to know." I didn't want him to preempt our discussion with a long speech à la Castro.

"I have three questions," I continued. "My first is about El Chipote. The world believes, and I do too, that it's a place in which people are tortured. Maybe it's not true. Maybe this is a libel against your government. But the fact remains that you have never allowed an on-site inspection, and I've met people who have said they were tortured there. Some said they were beaten and some claimed they were deprived of food. One man told us that he was without food for twenty days. That's torture."

"We do not torture anyone there," he replied. "I would not allow it."

"Mr. President," I responded, "maybe it's taking place and you're not aware of it. Isn't it true, Mr. President, that you were in El Chipote and you were tortured under Somoza?"

He lifted his hand to his forehead, put a finger to a scar, and reflectively said, "That is true."

"Why don't you and I go there tonight and see?" I said.

"No, that wouldn't make sense," he said. "Even if we did go and found nothing, people would say I'd called ahead."

"You're probably right. Why don't you agree to have the International Red Cross or Americas Watch go in to see the prisoners?"

"I'll consider it," he said. I pressed him to make such a decision in the next thirty days. He said he would.

My second question related to four Nicaraguan prisoners. Their names had been given to us by their families, who were asking for clemency. I told Ortega we didn't know anything about any of them, but the delegation felt an obligation to present their names for his consideration.

He looked at the list. "You wouldn't want this first individual released," he said right away. "He's a murderer and he killed children."

"I told you that we couldn't vouch for these people," I replied, "but I'll tell you his mother thinks he's a good boy."

"So did Adolf Hitler's mother," he said. It was a terrific response. Then he looked at the other three names.

"One of them looks okay," he said. "The other two I am not sure of."

"If I were Jesse Jackson," I said, "you'd give me all four."

"Jesse Jackson was here," he answered, "and I didn't give him any. But I may give you two." Everyone laughed.

"My third question relates to the Soviet presence in Nicaragua," I then said.

"There are no Soviet bases or soldiers here," Ortega interrupted. "There are no Cuban soldiers here. There are Cuban advisors here who train our military."

In the course of the discussion he also said, "I have no problem with American soldiers being in Honduras or American ships off our shores, so long as their guns are not pointed at my country."

After almost two hours with Ortega in which all delegation members had a chance to ask questions, we went out to respond to press questions for about thirty minutes. It was close to one-thirty in the morning when we left! We had an early plane to catch for a meeting with President Arias in San José, the final leg of our journey.

A month after our return to New York, I happened to read in *The New York Times* that Ortega had permitted El Chipote prison to be visited by Senators Claiborne Pell and Larry Pressler. I sat down and wrote the following letter to President Ortega:

*I was very pleased to read in this morning's* New York Times *that Tomas Borge, your Interior Minister, had permitted U.S. Senator Claiborne Pell, U.S. Senator Larry Pressler, and representatives of the International Red Cross, Americas Watch, and Amnesty International to visit El Chipote in Managua.*

*During the conversation the New York City delegation had with you in early November, you may remember that I requested that you and I visit the facility that very night. While you did not consent to that request, you did agree to decide within thirty days whether to allow internationally respected organizations such as the Red Cross to visit. I am pleased that, after consideration and within the thirty days, you and Minister Borge saw the wisdom of allowing access to such groups.*

*Denying access only lends credence to the allegations of torture and brutality at El Chipote, which, you assured us, are unfounded. If that is true, permitting regular and full inspections would provide confirmation to the world. Now that you have allowed one group of visitors to El Chipote, I hope that you will allow others to do the same.*

*You may also recall that during our conversation you indicated that the reason you were hesitant to permit the delegation to visit El Chipote was because your critics would only charge that conditions had been improved in advance of our inspections. Interestingly, Lino Hernandez, director of Nicaragua's Permanent Commission for Human Rights, made that very same criticism of the visit by Senators Pressler and Pell.*

*Of course, there is a way you can refute even that charge. First, you can make sure that the visits are scheduled on days when El Chipote* is not empty of detainees, as it reportedly was the day the Senators visited. Indeed, I would hope you would give inspection groups the opportunity to talk with those detained at El Chipote.

Second, you should invite Mr. Hernandez or representatives of the Permanent Commission to participate in these visits. I was very impressed with Mr. Hernandez's sincerity and credibility. So were all of the other members of our delegation. Obviously, if you can persuade him that torture and brutality are not permitted at El Chipote, you will have gone a long way toward convincing the rest of the world.

Again, I am very pleased that you and Minister Borge have taken this first step in attempting to demonstrate that the reprehensible practices of the Somoza regime at El Chipote are not being employed by your government. Now that you have gone this far, however, I would again encourage you to allow regular inspections by respected organizations.

The only thing your government has to lose are the allegations that the terrible ghost of Somoza still haunts El Chipote prison. Now is the time to put that ghost to rest.

All the best.

P.S. What about the two prisoners you thought you might release to me? Can we have them home for Christmas?

Ortega never answered my letter. I don't know what happened to the two prisoners whose release I'd sought. I hope they made it home for Christmas. But I suspect that they did not.

Back home, my trip to Central America had stirred up controversy. Some people thought I should have gone. Some didn't. Here is my response to Jim Wood, a resident of North Babylon, New York, who thought I should be a "stay-at-home" mayor:

Thank you for your recent letter. I must admit I'm a bit puzzled by your reaction to my trip to Central America.

Every Mayor of New York is asked to speak out on international issues because this city is the international capital and home to representatives of all the world's peoples. Every citizen should praise decency and condemn indecency in official behavior wherever it occurs.

In this case, Charles Robb, former Governor of Virginia, asked me to put together a delegation of prominent New Yorkers to go to Central America to monitor the inauguration of the Arias peace process. Others are making similar trips. Incidentally, if you were unaware, the entire trip was financed by private donations.

I believe our mission was useful because it showed American interest *in encouraging the peace process and, most importantly, because it shone a media spotlight on the process and the leaders who must make it work. The thirty-person press entourage we brought with us gave an unprecedented amount of attention to an area and a process that need it.*

*My previous history as a well-known opponent of Somoza helped me talk openly and candidly with the Sandinistas. But I developed a similar relationship with Contra leaders. I regard both groups as patriots. It is my hope that President Ortega and his adversaries will be further encouraged by the Reagan administration to seek a political settlement.*

*I did not volunteer for this task, but when called on, I was happy to help. I don't think anyone who knows my round-the-clock schedule as Mayor could reasonably say that a week out of the country means that I was neglecting the difficult problems of the city. In any case, I was in regular phone contact with First Deputy Mayor Stan Brezenoff, who is a superb administrator.*

*The truth is, where peace is in the balance, we should all do what we can, however modest. Don't you agree?*

*All the best.*

In the years since my visit, some real progress has been made in Central America. The guerrillas and the government in El Salvador now at least occasionally talk about the possibility of negotiating a settlement to end the bloodshed there. The insurgency in Honduras does not appear to have picked up steam. Though shaky, the democratically elected government of Guatemala still holds power. The Contras seem to have put down their guns, and in Nicaragua, closely watched elections will soon be held, although Ortega has threatened to break the truce and resume his offensive against the remaining Contras. Peace might be at hand and it might not be. But after years of violence and thousands of deaths, at least it's on the table.

Which means, of course, that the role of the United States in the region must be reconsidered. As our delegation's visit came to an end and we rode in an air-conditioned bus along a freeway from the San José airport to our meeting with President Arias, I believe every member of the delegation had the same impression.

Honduras, El Salvador, Guatemala, Nicaragua—all are so very, very poor. But Costa Rica—a country which eliminated its armed forces in 1948 and embraced a capitalist economy—is so prosperous. If the region has a model for its future, it's probably Costa Rica. These thoughts prompted my March 1988 letter to President Reagan:

*It would be naive for anyone knowing the recent history of Central America to believe that the events of the past week have cleared the way for a true and lasting peace. Regrettably, the internecine problems of the region, as well as foreign influences, work against any such optimism.*

*What has become abundantly clear to the American people since the signing of the Guatemala Accords last August is that for every action in Washington there is a reaction in Managua and a reverberation that is felt throughout the entire region. Now that progress has been made, a truce has been signed and, finally, the Contras are negotiating directly with the Sandinistas. All those interested in peace for this region are looking to you to see what comes next. More than ever the world will be looking toward the United States to play a constructive role. Mr. President, it is time for the carrot rather than the stick.*

*Last fall when I visited Central America with a delegation of prominent New Yorkers, we proposed that the United States, in cooperation with the five countries of that region, and other concerned nations of the free world, develop an aid program for Central America along the lines of the Marshall Plan. As you well know, the most formidable enemy in that part of the world is not communism or capitalism, Sandinista or insurgent; it is poverty. Costa Rica represents what could be the future for Guatemala, Honduras, Nicaragua, and El Salvador. America and its partners throughout the free world should lead the effort to help us realize that potential. The aid you proposed for the Contras last year and the military assistance we gave to the other nations of that region amounts to more than $500 million. We should invest it in a Marshall Plan for Central America instead. And we should challenge the Cubans and Soviets to convert their military assistance into economic and humanitarian aid as well. If we could ensure that such monies were spent on reconstruction, as opposed to being drained by graft or mismanagement, the latest peace initiative would have a genuine chance to succeed.*

*There are many reasons to be skeptical about the workability of a Central American Marshall Plan. But considering the options, this may well be the best and least expensive alternative to decades more of grinding poverty and bloody civil wars.*

I believe that our delegation played a constructive role. I am told the State Department thought so too. In November of 1989, Mrs. Violeta Chamorro, now the presidential candidate of fourteen political parties for a scheduled 1990 election, came to visit me at City Hall. It was a privilege and a pleasure to welcome her, and I wish her all the best and Godspeed.

# On Anti-Semitism in Poland

Waldemar Lipka-Chudzik, Consul General of the People's Republic of Poland, sent me a letter on October 26, 1989. It is probably a copy of the same letter he'd sent to hundreds, perhaps thousands of Jewish leaders. Attached was a letter he'd sent to the *New York Post*, responding to Alan Dershowitz, who had argued that anti-Semitism continues in Poland.

"To most Poles the notion of anti-Semitism is hard to understand," the Consul General said. "These people know that Poland was their homeland for ages, that over 80 percent of the entire Jewish people lived there. It was Poland where Jewish culture, art, and religion flourished, making its way to the rest of the world. Neither of our peoples, Jewish and Polish, has been pampered by history. The fate of both our peoples clearly shows how much we need each other."

I could not refrain from responding to his letter, so offended was I by it:

*While I know that there were many Poles who risked their lives in assisting Jews by concealing them from the Nazis, there is no question but that thousands of Jews were delivered to the Nazis by Poles. Indeed, thousands were killed by the Poles when they escaped from concentration camps and ghettos and were looking for assistance in the Polish Christian community, where they went to hide. Even worse, there were pogroms and killings of Jews by Poles after the Poles were liberated by the Soviet Union and the Nazis had surrendered.*

*So for you to say, "To most Poles the notion of anti-Semitism is hard to understand," I say that either you led a most sheltered life in Poland or you have blocked out a sad but important part of the history of*

*Poland. In either case, no American Jew who has ever discussed this matter with Jews or anyone else who survived the Holocaust in Poland can accept your statement.*

*However, I certainly do admire the renaissance of Poland under Solidarity and Lech Walesa. On the other hand, in earlier times, the recent comments of Cardinal Glemp would have been a call for a pogrom.*

*All the best.*

I've never met a Jew of Polish extraction—that is to say whose parents or grandparents were born in Poland—or who came here as a refugee or an immigrant who thinks of Poland as his or her homeland or who describes him- or herself as Polish.

Why is this? Talk to Poles who are Christians, in Poland or here in the United States, and they'll not refer to Jews born in Poland or to their descendants as Poles. They'll call them Jews. So far as most Poles are concerned, it seems, you are a Pole only if you're a Christian born in the country or are descended from one.

The history of the Jew in Poland is unique. Violent anti-Semitism existed long before Hitler. Indeed, Hitler built his concentration camps in Poland precisely because he believed the Poles would not resist the idea of gathering up the Jews into concentration camps.

Of course, there were Poles who risked their lives to save Jews. Jerusalem, in fact, has more monuments to righteous Christian Poles who saved Jews than for any other nationality. There are about three thousand of these heroes. But, for the most part, Poles either did nothing to save Jews or turned them over to the Nazis. To be a Jew-catcher in Poland wasn't unique.

What is shocking is that anti-Semitism still lives in Poland. And in the highest circles. Consider a recent sermon at Mass by Jozef Cardinal Glemp, the Roman Catholic Primate. He was commenting on the controversy over a Carmelite nunnery established in 1984 at Auschwitz, the concentration camp where more than three million Jews were imprisoned, then killed with zyclone B gas and cremated at Birkenau, the adjacent camp.

I have visited both of these camps. I wept at the scene of the brutality used against the Jews. Others were killed there who were not Jewish, but the overwhelming majority, more than 75 percent, were Jewish. The feeling among most survivors was that housing a Christian religious institution in the very building in which the zyclone B containers had been stored was an abomination. In 1987 an agreement was signed by four European archbishops and Jewish leaders to have the convent removed early in 1989.

In his sermon, however, Cardinal Glemp clearly indicated that it would not be moved. "I would like to say, dear Jews, do not talk with us from the position of a people raised above all others, and do not dictate conditions that are impossible to fulfill," he said. "Do you, esteemed Jews, not see that your pronouncements against the nuns offend the feelings of all Poles, and our sovereignty, which has been achieved with such difficulty?" And he said, "Your power lies in the mass media that are easily at your disposal in many countries. Let them not serve to spread anti-Polish feeling."

Prior to this sermon, several Jews, including one from New York, Rabbi Avi Weiss, went to Poland. They were outraged that the Polish Catholic church hadn't kept its commitment to move the nunnery. They picketed the nunnery and, in apparent frustration, leaped over the gates and entered the grounds. They were ejected by Polish workers, subjected to anti-Semitic epithets, and some were beaten.

"Recently, a squad of seven Jews from New York launched attacks on the convent," said Cardinal Glemp. "In fact, it did not happen that the sisters were killed or the convent destroyed, because they were apprehended." That was an outright lie. While Avi Weiss and the others shouldn't have forced their way onto the convent grounds, they certainly were not bent on assaulting the nuns. The Cardinal's suggestion that they were was intended to incite the Christian populace.

When I heard these comments reported, I thought to myself, "That is exactly what a priest would have said during the many pre–World War I pogroms that occurred. And maybe it was also said after World War II, when 5,000 Jews were killed in Kielce when they returned to their homes, having been liberated from concentration camps."

Cardinal Glemp's statement sparked angry reactions around the world among both Catholics and non-Catholics. New York's own John Cardinal O'Connor said he was "shocked" by Cardinal Glemp's comments and publicly urged Polish church officials to honor the 1987 agreement. I am convinced that privately he made his position known to his brother cardinals and used his closeness to Pope John Paul II to encourage him to make sure the agreement was honored and the convent moved.

Particularly heartwarming was the response of Lech Walesa and Solidarity to Cardinal Glemp's sermon. A front-page editorial in its newspaper said his words had caused "real and not artificial or paper pain. The expressions used by the Primate, even if contrary to their intent, threaten to wound deeply the feelings of many of those who are descendants and brothers of Holocaust victims. The words were heard with regret and pain, and particularly on the eve of commemorations marking the fiftieth anniversary of the outbreak of World War II."

I wish the Polish people the best. I admire their courage. They were the first to stand up to the Soviet Union and achieve the right in modified form to govern themselves and elect a non-Communist government. It was an extraordinary feat!

It is just sad that the Poles have never viewed the Jews among them, who fought in the Polish army and died in defense of Poland and who contributed so much to Poland's culture and commerce, as fellow citizens. Indeed, on occasions through the ages they haven't even seen them as fellow human beings. And as of this moment, although the church has agreed to move the convent, nothing has happened yet.


# To Mikhail Gorbachev about Raoul Wallenberg


One case that has particularly troubled me is that of Raoul Wallenberg, the young Swedish diplomat who saved tens of thousands of Hungarian Jews from Nazi death camps.

When Soviet troops liberated Budapest in 1945, Wallenberg was taken into custody. For all intents and purposes, he disappeared from the face of the earth. Historically, the Soviet Union had always denied any knowledge of his whereabouts and always denied that he was ever in a Soviet prison.

The rest of the world knew better. Every year since I have been Mayor, there has been a special ceremony to honor the memory of Raoul Wallenberg and to keep that memory alive by putting pressure on the Soviet Union in the world press to find out what happened to him. Over the last several years, he has allegedly been seen by other prisoners in Soviet jails.

In 1985, after Mikhail Gorbachev's elevation to the job of General Secretary of the Communist Party, I wrote to him asking him to intercede. Clearly he had become the boss of all Soviet bosses. Maybe he could get to the bottom of the story:

34

*I congratulate you on your elevation to your new position of General Secretary. As the new leader of the Soviet Union, you are no doubt aware of the present atmosphere conducive to having nations of the world join together in special efforts to reduce international tensions and to address problems such as hunger, oppression, disease, and poverty that, regrettably, exist across the globe. There is also a heightened awareness that, throughout history, there have been brave and dedicated people who have sacrificed so much for the cause of justice and freedom that they are perceived as international martyrs by citizens of all nations. Among them are Mahatma Gandhi, Dr. Martin Luther King, Jr., and Nelson and Winnie Mandela.*

*This year commemorates the fortieth anniversary of the disappearance of another such martyr, Raoul Wallenberg. As you undoubtedly know, Raoul Wallenberg, a Swedish diplomat during World War II, was unequivocally responsible for saving the lives of 100,000 Hungarian Jews from the Nazis, although he himself was not a Jew. It is clear that, without Wallenberg's help, these Jews would have been sent to the death camps and exterminated by the Third Reich.*

*We here in New York are participating in the international celebration of the anniversary of Wallenberg's disappearance. As part of a world-wide ceremony, New Yorkers from all walks of life joined together on the steps of the City Hall Rotunda to ring a symbolic liberty bell forty times, once for each year since he disappeared. In addition, I recently signed legislation enacted by the New York City Council naming part of the roadway which the United Nations faces—First Avenue from East 42nd to East 49th Streets, in Manhattan—"Raoul Wallenberg Walk." I formally unveiled the signs noting this new designation at a ceremony in his honor on April 9th.*

*In past years, your government has answered inquiries about Raoul Wallenberg by stating that he died in July 1947. Nevertheless, there have been persistent and continuing reports that he is, in fact, alive and in the Soviet Union. In the spirit of common humanity and in recognition of the need to do full honor to those martyred in the name of freedom and justice, I beseech you to direct your government to take a fresh look at Wallenberg's status. If, indeed, he is alive and living in your country, I further urge that you permit him to return to his native Sweden.*

*You know as I do that many governments throughout the world have committed actions violative of human rights which they later have regretted. As the new leader of the Soviet Union, you come to your position unencumbered by the past and able to examine this question backed by the full resources of your government. I hope you will take advantage of this unique opportunity.*

*Moreover, I believe that if you discover that Raoul Wallenberg is, indeed, alive, and, further, if you set him free, you will endear yourself personally to millions of people around the world. Such a compassionate act would earn you and the Soviet Union the plaudits of every nation and every individual around the world committed to the very causes that the experience of Raoul Wallenberg epitomizes.*

*I appreciate any efforts you may make in this matter.*

*All the best.*

General Secretary Gorbachev never responded to my inquiry. The Soviets have consistently maintained that Wallenberg, then a healthy young man of thirty-five, was arrested by Soviet troops in 1945 and transported to Moscow's Lubyanka Prison, where, Soviet officials said, he died of heart failure just two years later, on January 17, 1947.

In October 1989 the Soviet Union invited Wallenberg's half brother and half sister to Moscow to receive what it called "recently discovered" personal effects, including Wallenberg's notebooks, some money, and his Swedish diplomatic passport.

While describing Wallenberg's arrest as a "tragic mistake which has never been corrected," Gennadi Gerasimov of the Soviet Foreign Ministry said the documents, uncovered after a search of KGB archives, do not change the "irrefutable fact that Raoul Wallenberg died in 1947."

The belongings, said Mrs. Nina Lagergren, his half sister, "do not prove that Raoul is dead." Indeed, Wallenberg's family provided Soviet officials with a list of some twenty witnesses who say they have seen Wallenberg over the years. "They only prove that the Soviet authorities have been lying to us all these years when they said they had no more information on Raoul," said Mrs. Lagergren, "and it only strengthens our belief that Raoul is alive today."

While it was extraordinary that the Soviet Union made this gesture toward his family, we who commemorate Wallenberg's memory will not give up. We will continue to believe that he may still be alive.

Unless and until the Soviet Union identifies the grave site and a qualified person from the Free World examines the remains and certifies them to be those of Wallenberg, in the words of Jesse Jackson (used in another context but appropriate here), "Let's keep hope alive!"

# About South Africa

In the face of rising opposition, the apartheid government of South Africa imposed a state of emergency in September 1984. Police and security forces were given broad powers. Thousands were arrested. At least 160 blacks were killed in just three months.

"What is taking place in South Africa rivals what took place in Nazi Germany," I said. "The question we face is this: what can and should the world do when confronted by states which destroy the lives and crush the fundamental freedoms of their own people and then claim that other states have no right to interfere?" Nazi Germany, too, used this "flimsy, false, and immoral argument . . . when other nations questioned the outrages being perpetrated against the Jews." New York City, I stated, "will not give aid and comfort to the enemies of human rights."

In the months that followed I proposed, and the city began to make use of, a number of means to bring pressure against apartheid, including a phased divestment of city pension-fund holdings in companies doing business in South Africa. My strong support for the measures brought a strongly worded rebuke from the mayors of seven South African cities—Bloemfontein, Cape Town, Durban, Johannesburg, Port Elizabeth, Pretoria, and Soweto.

"Having read your book *Mayor*, I have difficulty in associating the Mayor Koch that I got to know from the publication with your present initiative on the question of disinvestment," wrote Mayor Eddy Magid of Johannesburg. "Should you subscribe to the ideology of peaceful change" in South Africa, "please desist from the present misguided and irresponsible campaign."

But with 160 people already dead and thousands more detained by South African security forces, the only way to achieve such change, I believed, was to bring the city's economic resources to bear against apartheid.

I replied to the mayor and his colleagues:

*I read with great dismay your letter urging me to oppose the divestment of City pension funds and advocate what you term "the ideology*

37

of peaceful change." I cannot accept the view you and the other six mayors expressed in your joint statement for one simple reason: apartheid is an unconscionable evil that defies any explanation or justification.

Apartheid is not a new or transitory phenomenon in South Africa. It is not the whim of one particular administration or leader, but rather, a system of laws and regulations that embodies the wholesale disenfranchisement of the majority of the South African people. It is the longstanding overt policy of the South African government, and there is no indication that diplomatic or other strategies have in any way influenced the government to abandon apartheid or even reform this reprehensible system of complete racial separatism.

Therefore, I have endorsed a program of divestment of City pension funds and initiated legislation to restrict City involvement with banks and corporations that do business with South Africa. The adoption of this course of action is not "misguided and irresponsible" as you suggest. Regrettably, I believe it is the only way to bring pressure to bear against your nation's leaders and lawmakers and to make clear that complicity with the proponents and institutions of apartheid is intolerable to me and to the citizens of the City of New York.

I believe that public servants have an obligation to speak out against injustice, and that is why on many occasions I have criticized the Soviet Union, Libya, Iran, Argentina, South Africa, and other nations whose leaders and styles of government fail to respect the sanctity of human life and the inherent equality of all people. I have spoken out on behalf of Nelson and Winnie Mandela as well as other international martyrs who are relentlessly persecuted because they cherish the ideals of freedom and liberty. And, I will continue to do what I can to draw world public attention to those pariah nations whose governments practice oppression and discrimination.

It is only in rare cases that a city should formulate a policy restricting its deposits and purchases in deference to political and social conditions abroad. In the case of South Africa, I believe it is appropriate for the City of New York to act materially. I reject the notion of so-called peaceful change in South Africa because I will not embrace what I believe amounts to tacit acceptance of apartheid.

On a final note, while I was pleased to learn that you read my book, I disagree with your observation. My record indicates that I speak out on issues, regardless of what is politic. I believe my book shows I am *committed to justice and equality. I will continue to oppose apartheid and support measures consistent with this belief.*

*At this juncture in the terrible history of apartheid, I believe that South Africa is in very much the same position as ancient Babylon was when King Belshezzar saw a warning of the end of his reign inscribed on a palace wall in a dream: "Mene, mene tekel upharsin (God has numbered the days of your kingdom and brought it to an end; you have been weighed in the balance and found wanting; your kingdom has been divided and given [to others])." Belshezzar did not heed the handwriting on the wall. That night he was killed, his sovereignty ended, and the next day his kingdom was conquered. South Africa still has time. Seize the opportunity and end apartheid.*

South African interests weren't the only ones to oppose my efforts to bring economic pressure against a system which I had called "evil incarnate." Closer to home, New York City was advised by some to stay out of the business of foreign affairs.

The most unbelievable attacks on what my administration did to press for change in South Africa, however, came from those who I would have thought supported what we were doing and, therefore, would have applauded me. But leave it to Charlie Rangel, the Congressman from Harlem, to treat an ally in a fight as though he were a foe.

Rangel and I go back a long way. In the sixties both of us were district leaders. In the seventies both of us served in Congress. And in the eighties both of us played major roles in the political life of our city—I as the Mayor and he as a ranking member on the House Ways and Means Committee.

Sometimes we've been on the same side of the issues. We joined forces, for example, in an unsuccessful fight to renew General Revenue Sharing, a federal program of critical importance to over 39,000 cities, towns, villages, and even Indian tribes. More successfully, we have joined to push, prod, and otherwise try to persuade Washington to assume its rightful place at the front lines in the war against drugs.

Other times, however, we've been on opposite sides. Personally, I believe he bristles at the fact that, as Mayor, I've refused to grant to the black political leadership of Harlem, and to him in particular, the right to decide which housing contractors will work on city contracts in his district. When they were allowed to make the selections on four contracts, they selected the same contractor for three of the jobs. It smacked of favoritism. And I stopped it.

During the 1988 New York Democratic presidential primary I'd taken on Jesse Jackson. My criticisms were substantive, and to this day no one has refuted their accuracy. But, in hindsight, I realize that my tone was too strident for those Jackson supporters who had invested so much emotion and hope in his candidacy.

Jackson was and still is a sacred cow. But I was the one butchered by columnists and editorial boards for having taken his candidacy seriously enough to criticize him on substantive grounds. "Too strident," the columnists said; "too divisive."

The stridency of others, however, never sparked similar rebukes. When Rangel, for example, said I was trying to be "the King of the Jews," he offended me and many other Jews. But not a peep was heard from any editorial quarter criticizing Rangel for his rhetorical excesses, arguably worse than but certainly equivalent to anything I'd said about Jackson. What I'd said, after all, was factual. What Rangel said was not.

But Rangel doesn't let the facts get in his way. During a nationally televised news show—*The MacNeil/Lehrer Newshour*—on the eve of the vote in New York, Rangel misstated my record in opposing apartheid to go on the attack. "We haven't heard from Mayor Koch," he charged, "on the issue of South Africa."

I was furious and responded with the following letter:

*I watched your recent appearance on* The MacNeil/Lehrer News-hour *and your discussion of concerns I've expressed about Reverend Jackson's still vague positions on the federal deficit, defense preparedness, and the resolution of the tragic conflict between the State of Israel and her neighbors.*

*From a personal point of view, I am pleased that you were "angry" with yourself for making comments offensive to Christians and Jews. But I must assume you did not intend this as an apology for your remarks, just an acknowledgment that you were caught by an off-the-cuff remark and are embarrassed. The acknowledgment may make you feel better because it, as the saying goes, "covers your political butt," but I'm sure that most of those offended would not and will not consider it to be the apology that is due. When the heat of the primary season cools, I hope that too will be forthcoming.*

*After watching the show, I'm sure most viewers agreed that your reputation for cleverness is well deserved. Particularly impressive was your deftness in portraying me, rather than Reverend Jackson and his policies, as the issue in the New York primary. After all, by shifting the focus to my comments, Reverend Jackson is again able to avoid providing clear and substantive answers to questions which many of us, including some of his supporters, have been asking since he ran in 1984.*

*Sometimes, though, you're too clever, with both inaccurate and distressing results. When you "talk about Botha," you told the interviewer, "he should know . . . that my President Reagan and my State Department has been embracing this white racist for the last seven years. And we haven't heard from Mayor Koch on that issue."*

*Hold it, Charlie. You know you know better. Just check the public record and you'll find I've spoken out again and again in opposition to the Reagan-Bush administration's failed policy of constructive engagement, its refusal to support meaningful sanctions or corporate disinvestment and, thereby, its tacit support for the cruel, repugnant system of apartheid. . . .*

I then went on to outline a whole list of statements I'd made and actions I'd taken in opposition to apartheid:

*I find it inexplicable and unacceptable, then, for you to have suggested to a national audience that I have not been vocal in my opposition to apartheid or to the Reagan-Bush administration policies which lend it support. Not only have I been a proud partner in efforts by the Council, Board and Pension Funds to cut our ties with South Africa, but I have also marched, attended rallies, written about, and spoken out again and again in opposition to apartheid and the President's policies.*

*I think you know that to be true, no matter what you said last week. If you have the temerity to say you haven't heard from me on South Africa, Charlie, I hope it's because you've not been listening or . . . paying attention and not because you're deliberately distorting the record. Though over the years we've had our disagreements, they've never been based on distortions of each other's record. We've known each other too long and worked together too well to start the practice now.*

*The struggle against apartheid in South Africa has involved hundreds of thousands of people of all races, religions, ethnic groups, and political persuasions. Appreciation, not denigration, is due each and every one of these people for the contributions they've made and dedication they've shown. Anything less only . mpairs the chances for success of a just cause in which both of us believe and for which both of us have fought.*

*All the best. Love to Alma.*

After drafting the letter I showed it to a coterie of my advisors. "It would be harmful," they said, to send this letter.

So I didn't send the letter. At least not right away. A couple of weeks later, Charlie was at it again. Again he attacked me. Again he misstated my record. "I really think the Mayor has been an embarrassment to the city and its citizens," he said, indicating that he might run for mayor.

I'd had enough. "Stop talking and put your body on the line, Charlie. Run, Charlie, run," I told the press. "It's like he lives on his own little planet, can say anything he wants and gets away with it. I'm sick of it."

So sick, in fact, that I instructed my press office to release my unsent letter to reporters in City Hall. "As the Mayor said this morning," a note I had dictated to attach to the letter read, "in April he prepared the following letter to be sent to Congressman Rangel to express his distress at comments he'd made on *The MacNeil/Lehrer Newhour.* On reflection, however, the Mayor chose not to send the letter so as to avoid adding to any tensions prior to or following the New York primary. He's now sorry he didn't send it."

Despite the lie behind his charge of not having "heard from the Mayor" on South Africa, Rangel got away with it again. And, again, not a peep was heard from a single editorial board or columnist. Thus emboldened, Rangel was at it again in the 1989 Democratic mayoral primary.

"The Mayor is a sick man and I'm not talking physically," he said to reporters on a campaign swing with David Dinkins. Described by his admirers both in and out of government as a decent man, David uncharacteristically "chuckled as Rangel spoke," the press said, and referred to Rangel as "my mental health commissioner." At one point "Rangel turned to a toothless and shirtless man wearing soiled pants and walking along 125th Street. 'He and Koch went to the same school,' the Congressman said."

If I'd said or done that, of course, I would have been lambasted by every editorial board as, at worst, racist and, at best, insensitive. But I knew no one would hold Rangel accountable for his outrageous language or his impolitic and inappropriate taunt of a homeless man. "I will not respond in kind," I said to reporters. "I, for one, will turn the other cheek and I will not be provoked." But Rangel got away with it. Again.

What's happening in South Africa is a horror story. And for columnists who are either lazy or at wit's end for a new and interesting metaphor, it's always easy to allude to the terrible plight of blacks in Soweto or in the homelands when writing about continuing racial injustice in the United States. My own view, however, is that overworking the comparison to apartheid only exacerbates tensions here while diminishing the struggle there.

And using the analogy can yield outrageous columns masking a murderous intent. Consider the views of Les Payne, a columnist for *Newsday*. "South Africa must surely be studying how America, without untidy apartheid laws, has managed to sustain a more efficient homeland policy," he wrote in a column entitled "Local Real Estate Agents Enforce a U.S. Apartheid." In "our republic, the real estate brokers, finally, represent the demented will of the white majority they serve."

The only way it would be changed, he suggested, is through the use of "exterior force." It was a clear call for violence, an action I could not allow to stand unchallenged:

*I was shocked to read Les Payne's column entitled "Local Real Estate Agents Enforce a U.S. Apartheid," which appeared in the December 22, 1985,* Newsday. *Payne talks about real estate agents who practice racial discrimination and compares [their methods] to the former policies of former Governor George Wallace of Alabama. Payne then goes on to write, "A bullet in a Maryland shopping center has moved Wallace, now in a wheelchair, to a straighter and narrower path." The clear implication is that Wallace, who has changed his position on civil rights and equal rights for black citizens, was moved to do so because he was shot. Payne continues, "The discriminatory Long Island housing system is no more capable of changing itself than George Wallace was capable of changing himself—without being acted upon by exterior force."*

*The "exterior force" that struck Wallace was a bullet fired by a would-be murderer. In my judgment, Payne's statement is a clear call for violence, comparable to the threats made by Louis Farrakhan against David Dinkins and others. I am convinced that* Newsday *would never permit a journalist other than Les Payne to make such despicable comments with impunity. It is not clear why Payne stoops to such depths, but he seems to be losing touch with reality. In the December*

43

*23, 1985, issue of New York magazine he writes that the worst thing about New York City is "Mayor Koch," and concludes: "A city's mayor should be judged on how he treats its poor and its minorities, who in this city happen to be in the majority." Les Payne has fallen behind the people he claims to represent. Apparently, the poor and minorities think I'm treating them well. Payne is unwilling to face the fact that I was reelected with huge majorities in the black and Hispanic communities. According to a poll released on December 18th, my popularity is at an all-time high, with "favorable" ratings from 63 percent of blacks and 81 percent of Hispanics. The voters did more than say "yea" to my administration. They said "hooray."*

As usual, Payne never apologized for his outrages, never denied that his definition of "exterior force" included violence. And *Newsday* berates me for being divisive? Unbelievable.

The simple fact is that there is a remarkable difference between the apartheid government in South Africa and our democratic government. It is true that one still finds instances of injustice in the United States, but they are far less numerous, of course, than in South Africa.

The fundamental difference ignored by Payne, an allegedly intelligent journalist, is that the laws of South Africa enforce apartheid and discrimination. The laws of the United States and of New York City are intended to prohibit both. Recognizing that fact might force Payne to search elsewhere for his analogies. And it might ensure that violence is not used and lives are not lost in our efforts to solve the kinds of problems his column identified.

# On My Visit to Ireland

In July 1988 His Eminence John Cardinal O'Connor announced that he would lead a pilgrimage for peace to the Shrine of Our Lady of Knock in Ireland.

I learned of his plans when I was marching in the St. Patrick's Day parade. Members of the parade committee asked me to go. When I stopped at St. Patrick's Cathedral to greet the Cardinal, I asked him if I could join the pilgrimage. He said he'd love to have me.

"I am honored to be a Jewish soldier in the Cardinal's Christian army," I later told the press, as one of only a handful of public officials making the journey. "Any press conferences that will be held, if I can restrain myself, will be conducted by him and I may just add ditto, ditto, ditto," I said.

I didn't expect to make much news, if any, during my five days on the Emerald Isle, which was to include visits to Knock, Dublin, and Belfast. While I was gone, after all, Governor Michael Dukakis would be trying to fight off a last-minute challenge from the Reverend Jesse Jackson at the Democratic National Convention in Atlanta. Since I had not been chosen as a delegate, I did not plan to attend. But I was sure their race for the party's nomination would dominate the front pages while I was overseas.

And, at first, I didn't make much news, prompting Kevin Flynn of *Newsday* to call it "the miracle of the Shrine of Our Lady of Knock. Mayor Koch has spent four days without offending anyone, saying the wrong thing, or creating an international incident."

So much for "miracles," for I soon made news of a sort that I wish I had never made. In the course of a visit to Northern Ireland, I took note of the recent improvements made there by the British government in the areas of civil rights, housing, and employment for Catholics. I think that even critics of British rule—and for more than twenty-five years I most certainly have been one—will agree that there have been at least modest improvements.

Foolishly, however, I went too far in my assessment of those improvements. "I thought that the British had a good attitude. I do not believe that the British are occupying forces," I told reporters over breakfast the morning I was scheduled to return to New York. "I think they're here more from the point of view of safeguarding the peace and preventing what, if these people were Jewish, would be called a pogrom."

Believe me, my comments were more than enough to bump the Democratic National Convention off the front page in at least two New York tabloids. "Koch Barb Riles Irish," blared the *Daily News.* "Eddie Go Blah!" screamed the *New York Post.* "Koch Praises British Rule in N. Ireland."

Maybe the prominent front-page play given my comments was the result of a circulation war between two papers competing for Irish readers. Moments after I'd made my comments, in fact, I'd said to Doug Feiden of the *Post* that "I don't want you to write a headline that says I love the British." Feiden went ahead and did so anyway.

But the ensuing furor was even more the result of my own failure to acknowledge that a few years of modest improvements couldn't make up for eight hundred years of oppression. I should have said in conclusion on that beautiful Dublin morning what I had been saying for twenty-five years—"And above all else, Brits out of Ireland!"

I knew I was in trouble when I returned to City Hall and two close friends who are Irish and were current or former members of my staff, Rosemary Ginty and Paul Crotty, said, "Mayor, how could you have said that about the British?"

And that meant I was in a lot of political hot water with Irish voters in New York City. They'd given me overwhelmingly favorable support in my 1981 and 1985 reelection bids. I hoped that they would do the same when I sought a fourth term in 1989. But I obviously had a lot of explaining to do if I expected to regain their support.

Adding to my woes were comments made by British Prime Minister Margaret Thatcher. "I do indeed welcome Mayor Koch's remarks and I admire his forthrightness in making them," she told the House of Commons. "I'm glad he took time to come to Northern Ireland and, with an open mind, to see what is happening."

"I need that," I told the press after hearing of her remarks, "like I need a hole in the head."

So I wrote a column about the situation in the *Staten Island Advance* just a few days after my return from Ireland:

Contrary to what some newspapers would have you believe, nothing that I observed or was told during my visit has in any way altered my resolve to someday see a withdrawal of British troops, a unified Ireland, and, just as important, an end to the discrimination against Catholics in the North.

I hope this column brings back into context my remarks and my aspirations for peace and unity for the Irish. . . .

Nothing can remove the stain of eight hundred years of British oppression in Ireland, which is an immutable fact of history. There can be no Irish reunification without the withdrawal of British troops. Real progress toward reunification cannot be made without a timetable for this withdrawal. Logically, the British are in the best position to set a credible schedule for withdrawal. The provisions of the Anglo-Irish Agreement make such a declaration highly unlikely in the immediate future. In the alternative, even a declaration by the Republic of Ireland

46

could serve to focus public attention on the problem and produce pressure on the British for a change.

Certainly, the British have been oppressors in Ireland, and their troops serve as an occupation force there. I never intended to convey forgiveness of the British for their ongoing occupation. But today, after thousands of deaths and billions of dollars, it seems to me that the British are looking for a solution that would extend the Irish government's role in Northern Ireland and open the door to a dignified withdrawal.

It would be a mistake to turn away from these indications of a British accommodation simply because the historical record is so bad. Those of us who support the Irish cause must proceed with caution, but we must also take our lead from the Irish government, which is moving toward a new relationship with the British in Northern Ireland.

For twenty-five years I have stood on platforms with Irish-Americans demanding an end to British rule in Northern Ireland and condemning Great Britain for what it has done. I stand by everything that I said. I hope it doesn't take another twenty-five years to see our fervent hope become reality.

More than voting blocs had been put at risk by my having rushed to be an expert about something I did not fully understand and by not having fully appreciated all of the nuances involved in so complex an issue. I endangered personal friendships and professional relationships.

"I can't agree with that," said Cardinal O'Connor when asked about my statements upon his return from Ireland, "and it wouldn't be the first time the Mayor and I have disagreed." It was a very difficult time for me.

I knew I had a great deal of work to do if I was to redeem myself in the eyes of Irish-Americans, who had given me so much support over the years. Over the next three months I probably participated in more Irish events than I'd attended in the prior three years.

Fortunately, many of my friends in the Irish-American community came forward and offered to help. One was Adrian Flannelly, a noted local radio personality who, I would say later, "taught me everything I should have known about Northern Ireland." Adrian's support culminated in my being named the 1989 Honorary Irishman of the Year at the Great Irish Fair and Festival in the Rockaways. It is an honor I will always cherish.

Another friend was John Thornton, publisher of the *Irish Echo.* I had asked to see him as soon as I returned from Ireland. He graciously consented to my request, listened sympathetically as I explained what I had meant and not meant to say, and, over the next year, made it possible for me to remind his readers of my long-standing support for a reunified Ireland and for an end to the British occupation.

Following my defeat in the 1989 Democratic primary election, the *Irish Echo* published an editorial summarizing my mayoralty. "The Koch era will end in a few months," it said. "It has been a fantastic era—these twelve years. Perhaps no figure in this city's tumultuous era was more suited to the post. Ed Koch could amaze, anger, agitate, and uplift friend and foe alike.

"Ed Koch," it.continued, "has always been a man of controversy and he probably always will be. But he has also been a marvelous Mayor. History will decide exactly what his place will be. But from here it seems clear that when they decide who was the best Mayor of New York, Ed Koch's name will be very near the top—if not at the top of the list."

How could I not express my gratitude for this show of support?

*I just want to thank you from the bottom of my heart for all of the many kindnesses that you extended to me over the years, particularly when through a failure or nuance, and some might say stupidity, I erred in some of my comments after returning from Northern Ireland last year. You helped me overcome that difficult period, and I am grateful.*

*I also want to thank you for your lovely editorial of September 23, which I will always treasure.*

*All the best.*

Given the mistake I had made and the trouble I had created for myself as a result of my trip to Ireland, John's editorial was remarkable. Even though I had said something dumb which could have caused a permanent rift in our friendship, he was willing to meet, to listen, and ultimately to forgive me.

The same was true, I should add, of Irish-American voters in general. While I did not win the Democratic primary, according to one poll I received 60 percent of the Irish-American vote. It was not as well as I had done in earlier elections, but in those elections I hadn't made the fundamental mistake of foolishly implying that a few years of modest change could make up for eight hundred years of British oppression.

# PART
# 3

# PEN PALS

---

## Mayor Chen Xitong of Beijing

"We do not believe that there was any tragedy in Tiananmen Square" in Beijing, the newly installed General Secretary of the Chinese Communist Party, Jiang Zemin, told reporters in 1989 at his first press conference, three months after the tanks had rolled and the blood had flowed. "What actually happened was a counterrevolutionary rebellion aimed at opposing the leadership of the Communist Party."

The Free World saw it differently. Hundreds, some estimate even thousands, of peaceful protesters gunned down in the square by their own army. A nationwide manhunt for leaders who, when apprehended, were bound, then paraded before television cameras like prisoners of war or, worse, common criminals, forced to read confessions, and then summarily executed, a bullet in the back of their necks.

It was, most definitely, a tragedy. Not just for the Chinese people, but for anyone who loves freedom.

The events in Tiananmen Square shocked the world. But they didn't shock me. Many had come to believe that the Communist government of the People's Republic of China was somehow different, somehow more benign than the Communist government of the Soviet Union.

I have always believed that no matter what promises they make, no matter how they package themselves, Communist governments stand ever ready to stamp out any and all signs of dissent, any and all democratic tendencies, at the slightest provocation. Tiananmen Square is only the latest example.

It is in the much-heralded age of glasnost and perestroika, after all, that we have heard reports of Soviet soldiers using shovels to kill demonstrators in the Soviet republic of Georgia and spraying poison gas in the republic of Azerbaijan.

Like the Soviet bear, the Chinese panda has a brutal side to its nature. I knew the City of New York had to act, if only symbolically, to express our outrage at the massacre in Tiananmen Square and its aftermath. So I sent the following letter to Mayor Chen Xitong of Beijing, a man I had previously met and liked:

*It is with great sadness and concern that I write this letter. I have always held you in high regard and I am dismayed to hear reports that you are in support of the military action against the freedom demonstrators. We in New York have many friends in Beijing; we fear for their safety and well-being.*

*Notwithstanding concepts of sovereignty and international law, I must still protest the actions taken by the People's Liberation Army against the people of China. For over two hundred years the American experiment has taught that, no matter how unsettling, only by permitting the free expression of ideas does a government establish its legitimacy. Governments based upon the rule of force will inevitably fail.*

*Our two cities have made significant strides in the last ten years since we established sister city relations. Cultural exchanges, increased business activity and the visit of the pandas improved the level of understanding and the sense of cooperation between our people. I fear that all the good will we worked to create may have been destroyed in a few violent days.*

*From all reports that we have received here, both written and broadcast, there was no student provocation involving violence of any kind that would have required the use of violence against them. Indeed, what we saw and heard was that students and their supporters welcomed the first troops who marched on the square with flowers, food, and entreaties, and the soldiers withdrew. Clearly, a subsequent decision was made, and it is my understanding that you supported that decision, to unleash power to teach these students a lesson and, by the use of violence against them, intimidate others. The action of the People's Republic of China against its own innocent people can only be described as shameful.*

*The people of New York, Chinese and non-Chinese alike, are outraged at this brutality. I know I speak for my fellow citizens when I express profound feelings of solidarity with the freedom demonstrators and their goals. Therefore, I have ordered a suspension of all sister city activity with Beijing until further notice. Surely you realize that your government's actions leave people of good conscience no option.*

*Mayor Chen, I urge you to search your soul and to use your influence to bring about a change of policy. Your government must find a more humane response to the current political situation or history will condemn you.*

There was a second symbolic action we could take. To protest Soviet oppression, I had proposed and the City Council had passed local legislation naming an intersection near the Soviet mission to the United Nations as Andrei Sakharov–Yelena Bonner Corner. To protest South African apartheid, we'd designated a site near the South African mission as Nelson Mandela–Winnie Mandela Square.

To protest Chinese oppression, I proposed renaming a site near the Chinese mission Tiananmen Square Corner. Our plans called for a replica of the "Goddess of Democracy" statue which had graced the square in Beijing to be erected at the Manhattan site.

# Weng Fupei, Consul General of the People's Republic of China

When the bill reached my desk for signature, so did a letter from Ambassador Weng Fupei, Consul General of the People's Republic of China. "China brooks no interference in any form in its internal affairs," he wrote. "Such proposed scheme of naming Tiananmen Square as well as erecting monument to the so-called 'Goddess of Democracy' are an out-and-out interference in China's internal affairs and are bound to seriously hurt the feelings of the Chinese people."

I of course replied:

*I have your letter of September 16. It is not my intention to use this letter for the purpose of diatribe. You do know the position of the people of the City of New York vis-à-vis the oppressive actions taken by the government of the People's Republic of China against its own people in Tiananmen Square.*

*There is, I believe, universal support for continuing to show our condemnation of those actions by a memorial. It is that memorial to which you object, but it is my intention to sign the legislation. I think you know that the anger felt by the people of the City of New York and by our legislators is duplicated in the United States at large and in the Congress itself. Obviously, all of this can change if the People's Republic of China would respect the human rights of its own citizens. I look forward to that day.*

*All the best.*

Ambassador Weng responded a few days later, giving his official version of what had happened in Tiananmen Square. "The situation in those days in Beijing had become increasingly serious, with anarchism viciously spreading nationwide and many areas sinking into complete chaos and white terror," he wrote. "The martial law forces, having suffered heavy casualties and been driven beyond forbearance, were forced to fire to open the way forward after repeated warnings."

In smashing "the rebellion," he reported, "more than 6,000 martial law soldiers and policemen and more than 3,000 civilians were wounded, and several dozens of soldiers and policemen and over 200 civilians including 36 college students died. This was because bad people mingled with the good. . . .

"I am obliged to point out to you," he said in closing, "that any condemnations or sanctions against our government in this regard are unwise and in the long run will rebound on those imposing them, and you will be no exception."

I wrote back:

*I would like to acknowledge your letter of September 28.*

*I can appreciate your distress at what we in the City of New York are doing to voice our objections to the incident that occurred in Tiananmen Square on June 4. However, according to all independent reports, your government murdered students who had been engaging in peaceful protest.*

*The subsequent television news stories authorized by your own government showed that the students were hunted down like rats and forced to confess to crimes which most people in the West don't believe they committed. Some of them were summarily shot, which has further increased the anger not only of the people of this city but around the world against the People's Republic of China.*

*Those actions, in violation of basic human rights, have turned the People's Republic of China into a pariah government. We in the City of New York will never lose our affection for the Chinese people, whom we admire and respect. But we will not reestablish our sister city relationship with Beijing until your government changes its course of action, opens the prisons, frees political prisoners, and punishes those in government and in the army who ordered and committed murders against the very people whom they are intended to serve.*

*Your letter, the booklets and the statement you enclosed from Chinese government officials are similar to what Orwell predicted in 1984—the use of double speak—war is peace, nonviolent student acts become violent, murderous acts taken by the People's Army against students become murderous acts of students against the army.*

*There were, however, too many witnesses to what happened for the lies to take hold. The atrocities were shown around the world on television, which was there to cover the visit of President Gorbachev, when the government of the People's Republic of China decided to show its true colors.*

*I urge you to defect and seek asylum here in the United States and then to tell the truth.*
*All the best.*

Ambassador Weng did not take me up on my invitation. "Your letter of October 6, 1989 is hereby rejected on account of the insulting language used in its last paragraph. As Mayor of the City of New York, you have gone so far as to brazenly urge me to defect. This is a gross insult to the dignity of Chinese diplomats and an unreasonable provocation against the Chinese people. Thus," he concluded, "I express my indignation and lodge my protest against such an imprudent act on your part."

In diplomatic terms, Ambassador Weng's letter could be considered a demarche, one step below a declaration of war. I responded:

*I read your letter of October 20, and I am sorry that you are turning this matter into a personal one. I am speaking on behalf of most Americans, and certainly most New Yorkers, when I say that what your government has done in violating the human rights of its own citizens is shocking and unacceptable and must be changed.*

*Obviously, we are not going to war with the People's Republic of China over this matter. Therefore, the only way we can influence the actions of your government is through public denunciation. Let me cite what is reported in today's paper regarding the actions that your government took in Tiananmen Square on June 4 and subsequently in punishing so many young people.*

*New York Newsday reports, "More than 1,000 civilians died in the military's assault on Tiananmen Square, according to many diplomats and major Western human rights organizations, who say that an accurate death toll isn't likely, at least not until after a major political change in China."*

*Indeed, the International League for Human Rights has put the number in excess of 3,000. Your own Chinese branch of the International Red Cross stated in early June that "2,600 people were killed in the Tiananmen onslaught." Yes, it is true that the Chinese Red Cross subsequently retracted under orders from the government, but that is just another illustration of the force and pressure used so unfairly by your government.*

*An equally shocking statistic, according to Asia Watch, is that "at least 6,000 people have been arrested in a nationwide effort to crush*

54

*dissent" and that "many more people, perhaps 30,000 in all, have been seized secretly."*

Let me reiterate the affection and respect that I, all New Yorkers, and most Americans surely have for the Chinese people. But we distinguish between the people who are being oppressed and the government that is oppressing them.

All the best.

## Prime Minister Margaret Thatcher

While I was distressed by what was taking place inside China, I was just as concerned about what might happen just beyond the Bamboo Curtain, in Hong Kong. A British crown colony since 1841, it is scheduled to revert to the People's Republic of China on June 30, 1997. Under the 1984 "One Country, Two Systems" agreement with the British, the Chinese have promised to maintain Hong Kong's capitalist system for at least fifty years.

The events in Tiananmen Square, however, caused many of Hong Kong's 5.7 million residents to have grave doubts about China's good intentions. Understandably, many expressed the desire to emigrate to Great Britain to avoid the consequences of Chinese rule. However, Prime Minister Thatcher's government publicly stated that it would not allow them to emigrate to Great Britain even though they held valid British passports.

So I wrote the following letter to Mrs. Thatcher:

*I hope you and your family are well.*

*I am writing in reference to a report in* The New York Times *on June 7 concerning your government's apparent decision that "the 3.5 million Chinese holders of British passports in the colony (i.e., Hong Kong) would not be granted the option of seeking refuge in Britain." I am disturbed by these comments and would urge your government to reconsider the policy.*

*The "thinking behind ruling out immigration," the* Times *cited one of your ministers as explaining, "was that a cold, overpopulated island of 57 million people was no place for a sudden influx of Chinese from the tropics." The comment is ludicrous.*

*Mrs. Thatcher, the premise is both offensive and absurd. Are we really to believe that, given a choice, the people of Hong Kong or any other land prefer warm temperatures and gentle breezes to democracy? Ridiculous.*

*In recent weeks, the spirit of democracy has risen up in China, only to be met by repression and state-sponsored violence. The issue for the people of China and of Hong Kong is not the opportunity to enjoy fair weather but the right to enjoy fundamental freedoms.*

*Under separate cover, and in the spirit of a nation built upon the contributions of immigrants from every corner of the globe, I have today written to President George Bush to encourage him to begin an immediate and comprehensive review of our nation's immigration policies in order to ensure that the maximum number of people from Hong Kong holding valid British passports who wish to leave the Crown Colony when it comes under Chinese control in 1997 will be able to seek refuge in the United States. I would encourage Britain, as one of the world's oldest democracies, to conduct a similar review.*

*We simply cannot abandon the people of Hong Kong or of China to the mercy of the repressive government in power in Beijing. The hundreds, perhaps thousands who have been brutally shot or injured by the government there in recent weeks clearly demonstrate that the Chinese government has no concept of mercy or of the democratic impulse now in full bloom in Beijing, Shanghai, and, I am sure, many other cities, towns, and villages in China.*

*Again, I urge you to reconsider the course of action your government now has under consideration. Holders of valid British passports ought to have the right to emigrate and to seek refuge in your country, especially when a brutal state-sponsored repression is biting at their heels, endangering their lives, and denying them fundamental freedoms.*

*As two of the world's great democracies, the United States and Great Britain should open, not close, their doors to people yearning to be free.*

*All the best.*

Prime Minister Thatcher replied a few weeks later: "I am particularly conscious of the impact which these events have had on the people of Hong Kong. I understand why they want to secure some form of ultimate assurance for themselves and their families. But there would be overwhelming practical difficulties for this country if we were to take on the massive new immigration commitment you suggest.

"We would simply be unable to cope with it," Mrs. Thatcher said. "You may be assured that Britain will not shirk her responsibilities towards Hong Kong: our commitment to Hong Kong and to its people is firm." She indicated that "a Bill of Rights for Hong Kong will be introduced as soon as possible."

I was still troubled and not sure that would be enough to protect the citizens of Hong Kong from the kind of oppression the Chinese had proven they could unleash. So I wrote again to 10 Downing Street:

*I greatly appreciate your response to my letter concerning Hong Kong. I was remiss in not making myself sufficiently aware of the significant details of British policy for the final decade. Your preparation of the people of Hong Kong for the future, beginning with the institution of a Bill of Rights, is obviously of crucial importance. But a Bill of Rights derives its force from a government's willingness to respect it. At this moment in history, it challenges [the] imagination to believe that the Government of China is capable of embracing more than the most modest degree of political enlightenment.*

*Things may change radically, but it seems that the world will have one more refugee problem. I agree completely with you that the burden must be shared by the international community. I hope that Britain will take the leadership role, and have the United States by its side prepared to make the requisite sacrifices. However, I believe that Britain as well as the other Commonwealth nations have a particular obligation to open their doors to the Chinese people of Hong Kong who wish to emigrate.*

*For what it is worth, it is very important that you press, as you are doing, for the strongest commitments from the Chinese government for at least modified democracy in Hong Kong.*

*It is understandable that the Chinese people of Hong Kong who are British subjects have complained that the decision not to accept them into Great Britain in the event they need sanctuary is a racist decision. I'm sure they believe that if Argentina had won the war in the Falklands, every British subject on those islands would have been given unrestricted entry into Great Britain. Indeed, the Concorde would probably have been sent to bring them home as quickly as possible.*

*From the point of view of Hong Kong residents and their supporters, like myself, it could understandably appear that the decision was made on the basis of skin color. I believe the experience of the United States establishes that having the sons and daughters of every nation in the world has made us a unique and thriving democracy. We are a better nation as a result of drawing on the talents of all races, religions, and nations. We are all citizens of one country—Americans in the United States.*

*Whether or not one accepts this point of view, there is always the lingering question of betrayal. Can you in good conscience deliver the British subjects of Hong Kong into the hands of the Communist Chinese with their clear ability to engage in the vilest of oppression? I think not. I hope not.*

*People with a taste for freedom should not be expendable. The Chinese people have shown that they have the taste.*

*All the best.*

To my surprise, Mrs. Thatcher responded again. "I emphatically do not accept your assertion that our decision not to give the right of abode to all 3.28 million Hong Kong British Dependent Territories citizens was taken on racial grounds. It is simply a matter of practicalities," she said. "We are nevertheless determined to do what we can to help, within the limits of what is possible," she added, indicating that exactly what the British would do would be announced shortly.

It was not long in coming, and when it did, I was very pleased. Of course I wrote to the Prime Minister to tell her so:

*I was overjoyed when I read that your Foreign Secretary, John Major, stated in a speech to the United Nations General Assembly that the British government would be extending the right to immigrate to Great Britain to a number of Chinese-British subjects in Hong Kong after the territory is returned to the People's Republic of China. As you know from our extensive correspondence, I feel very close to this subject.*

*I just want to congratulate and thank you for having taken this action. Other countries, my own included, should follow your lead in this matter.*

*All the best.*

Throughout my correspondence with Mrs. Thatcher, I was particularly pleased that she always took the time to reply personally and always at great length. After all, I was small potatoes. And I'm sure she had many other things on her mind.

I have met, spoken, and corresponded with five Presidents of the United States—Nixon, Ford, Carter, Reagan, and Bush. None has ever responded so directly, at such length, and so respectfully of my position.

# Katharine Hepburn

New York City's a great town, not the least because any movie made anywhere in the world is almost certain to be shown in our theaters. Making it here, of course, doesn't mean a movie will pass the Peoria test and make it everywhere. Sometimes, after all, New Yorkers' tastes are too cosmopolitan, sometimes too parochial. But if a reviewer I respect gives a movie a thumbs-up or three stars, I'll try to see it.

I'm an avid moviegoer—always have been, always will be. Every Friday afternoon I take five minutes to read through the *Times*'s weekend entertainment section. Usually there's an abundance of film reviews. On Saturday night, generally with friends, I'll go to the movies and an Italian restaurant after the show. It's my favorite form of relaxation.

I've even been in a few movies. I played opposite Kermit the Frog and Miss Piggy when the Muppets took Manhattan. I had a speaking role in a made-for-TV movie, *Terrible Joe Moran*, starring the late Jimmy Cagney. In *New York Stories* I played the Mayor. Typecasting, I'd say. I even went to the Everglades in Florida one weekend to play a New York tourist in a movie that never opened in the theaters but went straight to the video stores.

And an animated short subject—"Sundae in New York"—made by the very talented Jimmy Picker, won an Academy Award. One of the "claymation" figures was me, singing the song "New York, New York" in a voice clearly mine in inflection but not totally mine since the person singing could actually carry the tune.

For me, one of the most memorable movie stars of all time is Katharine Hepburn. You can tell from her accent that she's not a native New Yorker. But she does maintain a residence in Manhattan. No wonder, then, that we New Yorkers claim her as our own. She is magnificent.

In 1988 I decided it would be appropriate for the City of New York to honor her distinguished career in film by bestowing upon her the Handel Medallion, the highest award for artistic achievement given by the city. Other medallion winners have included Isaac Bashevis Singer,

Robert Joffrey, Leontyne Price, Andrés Segovia, Lena Horne, and John Lennon. The distinguished Miss Hepburn surely belongs in their distinguished company.

I'd asked a friend of mine, Robert Whitehead, to inquire informally of Miss Hepburn if she would accept the medallion. She declined. Naturally, I was disappointed. I hoped a more formal and direct approach might get her to change her mind:

*I was told that you have declined the Handel Medallion, having been approached by Robert Whitehead at my request. I don't take your decision personally, since I am told that you turned down an invitation to have lunch with the Queen of England on two occasions.*

*While I can certainly understand your distaste for awards and ceremonies, I am disappointed. Through your many activities in theater, film, and on social issues, you have contributed to this nation and our City in ways that are unique and unsurpassed. I would very much like the City to recognize you and your work; and while you may prefer that we do so posthumously, that is a circumstance which I, for one, refuse to contemplate!*

*Let me renew my request. Would you consider accepting the Handel Medallion at a small luncheon at Gracie Mansion without any ceremony or fanfare? The luncheon guests would be those of your choosing. Do please let me know.*

*All the best.*

Regrettably, I failed and Miss Hepburn again declined. Her letter of reply was among the most eloquent, elegant, and lovely I have ever received.

"Let me present my case to you," she wrote. "When you have been around as long as I have, you are approached to receive honors of the most delicious sort. Honors because you are so fascinating, thrilling, and brilliant. But the fact of the matter is that you—yourself—have to appear. This to me is a terrible burden. Appearing and trying to be as fascinating, thrilling, and brilliant as I'm supposed to be.

"My effort is to try to enjoy whatever years are left to me," she concluded. "I hope you understand and at the same time understand that I'm delighted to be asked but perhaps even more delighted to refuse.

"Thank you—dear Mayor Koch."

To a letter as charming and wonderful as that, what could I say? "I understand," I wrote back. "You are terrific. All the best."

The only two people I know of, in fact, who have the strength to resist the honors the public wishes to confer upon them are Katharine Hepburn and Greta Garbo. Oh, yes, there was one more, a man, who also refused the Handel Medallion. His name was Irving Berlin.

# Mother Teresa

Over the years, I've had the good fortune to enjoy good health. All the credit for that goes to the good genes of my mother and father.

Like anyone else who lives in a four-season climate, I get my share of sniffles and sneezes. But I'd never missed a day at City Hall due to illness until August 6, 1987. As I wrote in the *Staten Island Advance*, this is what happened:

Thursday, August 6, was an important day in my life.

As usual, I awoke at 5:30 A.M. Instead of going to the gym as I normally do, I went directly to City Hall to study my notes for a forum on AIDS I was to attend at 9. I read over the material until 7:45, at which time my first meeting was to begin. That ended at 8:15 and I then headed for the forum.

It went very well. Press reports indicated that Dr. Steve Joseph, my Health Commissioner, and I had effectively laid out the city's case.

Regrettably, what followed drew press attention away from more extended coverage of the debate at the forum.

It ended at 10:10. After a short press conference, I left for my next appointment, a visit to a Human Resources Administration income maintenance center in Harlem.

I headed uptown with HRA Administrator Bill Grinker and my press secretary George Arzt.

As Bill began to answer my questions about Senator Moynihan's welfare reform bill, I began to feel ill.

I could hear Bill, but I wasn't really listening. In fact, I was totally disinterested. That's just not like me. I could also tell that my speech was somewhat slurred. My mouth felt strange, the way it feels from the after-effects of novocaine.

"I'm having a stroke," I thought. "Well, I'll go to Harlem and worry about it later." Then I recalled what happened to Dr. Arthur Sackler, a good friend of mine. While in Boston, he had a heart attack and apparently knew he had it. Rather than going to a Boston hospital, he took a plane back to New York. He died on the plane.

I knew I couldn't and shouldn't wait. "I'm not feeling well," I said, tapping Detective Eddie Martinez's shoulder. "Let's go to the hospital. Take me to Lenox Hill or Bellevue"—Lenox because we were so near, Bellevue because it's the best, or at least equal to the best, hospital in the city.

It took only a minute to get to Lenox Hill. It seemed much longer. I got out of the car by myself and Eddie helped me to the emergency room. I was put on an examining table and asked how I felt. A doctor gave me a neurological exam, the first of many, many more I'd take over the next four days.

Preliminary neurological testing consists of simply raising your hands and closing your eyes. A hand which wanders to the left or right may indicate weakness from a neurological dysfunction. My left hand wandered. Left-side weakness means a dysfunction on the right side of the brain.

Pressure was then applied to my arms, shoulders and legs. My left side didn't resist as strongly as my right. Then I took the Babinski test—you close your eyes and the doctor runs an object with a rough surface along the soles of your feet. If your toes point the wrong way or you're slow in telling the doctor which way they're pointing, you have a major dysfunction. Mine pointed the wrong way.

"You're not going to need your trousers for a while," a doctor said. Off they came. I knew then I wasn't leaving for a couple of days.

Before I go further, a medical cast of characters is in order. At Lenox Hill, my principal doctors were Dr. Anthony Mustalish and Dr. Roger Bonomo. At the Neurological Institute at Columbia-Presbyterian Hospital, I received care from Dr. J. P. Mohr, Dr. Sadek Hilal, and Dr. Robert Barrett. I also asked that my personal physicians—Dr. Phil Brickner and Dr. Tony Lechich—be consulted as well as Dr. Bruce Barron, a close friend.

I recovered so quickly because of the doctors and nurses who attended me. Not only will I follow their advice, but I'll always be grateful for their help and support.

Back to the story. As the day progressed, my speech cleared up. I felt I was on the way to complete recovery. At about 9 the symptoms returned. The doctors were worried. To tell you the truth, so was I.

Again I underwent a battery of exams, including the Babinski test. My oral responses regarding the movements of my left big toe were much slower than my responses to the right toe. At 10, I was examined again. The doctors gave me an aspirin and let me go to sleep.

But consultations continued into the night. At midnight, the doctors decided to transfer me to the Neurological Institute for a nuclear magnetic resonant imaging test, or NMR. Only three hospitals in New York—the Institute, New York Hospital, and University Hospital—have the technology to do the test.

It's a very sophisticated, $7 million machine which takes magnetic pictures of the brain. The pictures are even more detailed than those taken in a CAT-scan procedure, and the test avoids the needles, pain, and potential side effects of a spinal tap.

The next morning, Dr. Barron came to my room. "I believe you should go to the Institute." I said I didn't want to offend anyone's feelings because all of the people at Lenox Hill had taken such good care of me. He assured me no one would be offended. "Okay," I said. "Let's do it."

At the Institute, I met Dr. Mohr. From that moment, he was in charge. His cherubic face, lovely manner, and compelling voice exude intelligence, experience, knowledge, and comfort. He explained that what I'd undergone was either a TIA or a stroke.

A TIA—transient ischemic attack—passes relatively quickly and is caused by a temporary spasm in a brain artery, an artery closed due to side-wall cholesterol or a thrombosis. A thrombosis occurs if a small fleck of a blood clot elsewhere in the body breaks away and gets caught in a brain artery. A TIA is a transient blockage; a stroke is a permanent one.

If there's a stroke, the question arises as to permanent consequences. The answer depends on where the stroke took place in the brain and what functions that particular part of the brain controls. We hoped the NMR test would give us the answer.

Dr. Sadek Hilal conducted the test. "Eddie, don't worry," he said, "you'll be okay." It was nice to have him talk familiarly with me. Until then, everyone had called me "Mayor" or "Mr. Mayor" out of respect or courtesy. But it seemed so impersonal. I really wanted to be hugged and shielded from harm at that particular moment. Dr. Hilal figuratively hugged me.

The NMR machine looked like a torpedo. I was to be put inside, head first. "It takes about half an hour for each test," Dr. Hilal said. "Some people are claustrophobic and we once had to let someone out. But there's nothing to worry about."

"When I come out," I asked, "do I get a lollipop?"

In I went. It was very dark and noisy. All I could think of was the "ping-ping-pong" of the German U-boat's sonar in the movie *Das Boot*.

I closed my eyes, trying to wile away the time as I do when I'm on the treadmill at the gym. "What do you think?" Dr. Hilal asked when the test was over. "I'll tell you how to improve it," I answered. "Either play music inside the machine or a cassette with a short story that fills the time you're in there and diverts attention."

"That's a good idea," he said. "We'll try it."

Then we looked at the pictures of my brain. "You have a very young brain," he said. "That's nice," I thought. He and Dr. Mohr said I'd suffered an injury in a small artery the width of one hair on my head. It was blocked but was located in a part of the brain that exercised no motor control. I was, they explained, very fortunate.

I was taken back to my hospital room. Just prior to the press conference on Friday morning, Dr. Mohr explained he could medically describe my condition as either a TIA or a trivial stroke. Obviously, he was concerned that use of the term "stroke" might disturb me or unduly alarm the public. I told him to describe my condition without reservation.

That's what he did at the press conference that followed, which I watched from my bed. He described what happened to me as a "trivial stroke." He said they'd examined 1,800 people in the last two years who'd suffered from similar incidents. Only two had worsened. All other arteries in my brain were clear and in great shape. From a statistical point of view and based on the examination of my brain, he said, I was in very good shape and better shape than many people in the forty-to-sixty-five age group.

Doctors and nurses weren't the only busy ones while I was in the hospital. Cards, calls, flowers, and visitors poured in. I'll write personally to each person who took the time to wish me well. They were wonderful to do so.

One of my first visitors was John Cardinal O'Connor. "I'm not going to stay long," he said. "I just wanted to come and say hello to my friend. You're in my thoughts and prayers. I'll even say Jewish prayers for you if you want me to."

"Your Eminence," I said, "I've taken care of those. You just pray for me in Latin." In fact, later that day, my own rabbi, Arthur Schneier, visited and said a special benediction in Hebrew. "Heal me and I shall be healed," I repeated in English. "Save me and I shall be saved."

On Friday, Governor and Mrs. Cuomo flew down from Albany to visit. She brought cookies and he brought a book on the splendors of Albany.

"Is there anything that I can do for you?" he asked as he left. "Yes," I replied. "There's this pension bill," a reference to a bill passed by the legislature that, if not vetoed by the Governor, would have forced us to cut essential city services. "Wait, wait," the Governor said, "I'm getting out of here. I can't afford it." A few days later he showed great courage and vetoed the bill.

U.S. Attorney Rudolph Giuliani and Police Commissioner Ben Ward also visited. So did members of my City Hall staff, including deputy mayors Alair Townsend, Bob Esnard, and Stan Brezenoff. All three did a marvelous job of keeping me posted and the city running. And, of course, throughout my stay members of my family visited regularly.

Sunday was a beautiful day. The doctors said I could go home. Fifty reporters waited for me as I left the hospital. So did a picket line across the street protesting a homeless shelter in the neighborhood. "I feel right at home," I told the reporters.

"I'm delivering these extemporaneous comments to prove I'm not slurring," I said. "I'm feeling very, very good. What you see before you is a twenty-eight-year-old brain in a sixty-two-year-old body. And it's my intention to bring that body of sixty-two years down to the age of the brain. I know that I could have had a huge problem because I came in with a medical condition that could have worsened. But that didn't happen. I'm walking out of here. I'm going back to work."

Then I thanked my doctors and gave a kiss on the cheek to Dr. Hilal and to my nurse, Joy Skinner. I also thanked everyone who visited me and who sent me their wishes for a speedy recovery and my staff for working so hard. "I have a wonderful job as mayor," I said. "I intend to keep it for a long time."

Then I raised my thumbs in the air, smiled, and asked the reporters and photographers, "How'm I doing?"

When we got to Gracie Mansion, I was applauded as I got out of the car. More television reporters were waiting for me. I wasn't going to hold another press conference, so I simply said, "Look, the monster talks and the monster walks."

Naturally, I'm more conscious of food now. On Saturday, Dr. Mohr came to see me. "You are very lucky," he said. "Your stroke was not in an area of the brain that controls motor functions. But if it had crossed over a little more, we would worry." I knew that he was saying I was very fortunate—that had this crossed over I would not be speaking and my left side would be paralyzed. "The likelihood of that happening now is very remote," he said, "but you do have to take care of yourself. You have to watch your diet—less salt and less fats. And you have to lose weight." I've already begun to diet.

Monday night a friend called me at Griace Mansion. "How are you?" he asked. "I'm fine, Charlie." Then he said, "It's amazing what happened on Thursday and over the weekend. The entire town shuddered because of what happened to you. They suddenly realized what it would be like if you were not here. You should be very moved by that." I said, "I am."

I will always remember the outpouring of affection and concern New Yorkers showed me that summer. Amid all of the controversy and contentiousness, the sound and fury, that come with being Mayor, the response was pure sweetness and light.

I am eternally thankful to God for keeping me well, and grateful to all of my friends—thousands upon thousands of them, it turned out—whose thoughts and prayers kept me strong. New Yorkers really are wonderfully caring people.

Two years later, by the way, my "trivial stroke" weighed on my mind as I began to run for election for a fourth term as Mayor. I was worried, irrationally I'm sure, that I would be stricken again, a fear that I confided to only one person, David Garth.

But it wasn't a stroke that ultimately did me in in Campaign '89. It was David Dinkins. And he did it fairly, squarely, and hugely. May he be well and enjoy good health for many years to come.

After I left the hospital, my doctors advised me to take a week off from work. So I decided to spend the week at Gracie Mansion, dedicating part of each day to meetings with my City Hall staff and part of it to rest and relaxation. With so wide a porch, so spacious a lawn, and so beautiful a view, Gracie Mansion was just what the doctor ordered.

On the Sunday afternoon I returned from the hospital, I was sitting on the porch at the mansion. The phone rang. A police officer at the front gate was calling.

"Mr. Mayor," he said in a shocked voice, "a car just pulled up and there are four nuns in it. One of them says that she is Mother Teresa. What should I do?"

"It's unlikely that she's here," I told the officer. "But I know what she looks like. I'll come right over to check it out."

I walked over to the car, looked inside, and, sure enough, there was Mother Teresa.

"Mother," I said, "what are you doing here?"

She got out of the car. "I knew that you were ill, Ed, and I came to see how you are doing. You were in my prayers."

"Well, they worked," I said. "I'm O.K., thank you. Stay awhile and let's chat."

I then took her by the hand and we went up the path and onto the porch, the three nuns who were with her following behind. The Gracie Mansion chef came out with a pitcher of lemonade and some freshly baked chocolate-chip cookies. It was a very hot day and I drank my lemonade immediately. But Mother Teresa and the three sisters didn't even lift their glasses.

I said, "Mother, why don't you drink your lemonade? Aren't you thirsty?"

"I work with poor people around the world, but especially in India," she explained. "If I and my sisters were to accept comparable hospitality from a poor family in India, it would cost them a week's wages. So I have a rule. We never drink or eat in the homes that we visit, whether of the rich and mighty or of the poor. They know our rule, so that no one is ever offended or insulted when we decline their hospitality."

"But Mother," I protested, "at least have a chocolate-chip cookie. They're the best cookies in the world."

She paused, looked at the sisters, looked at me, then looked at the cookies.

"Well," she said, "then wrap 'em up!"

Now, that is a saint with common sense.

Mother Teresa recently suffered a heart attack and was hospitalized in Calcutta, India. Of course I wrote to her:

*I know that thousands of letters are pouring in from people around the world to tell you how much you are loved. Many of those people have never met you. I feel honored not only to have met you, but to have had you pray for me when I was in the hospital. Undoubtedly your prayers because of all that you have done in God's name were heard more quickly than others, and they certainly benefited me. I want you to know that my prayers are with you, and I am sure that God will listen to my voice and the thousands of voices praying for you at this moment.*

*You will be pleased to know, if you have not already been told, that I was able to turn over two buildings to the missionary sisters which your order is rehabilitating to house homeless individuals. You and the missionary sisters have helped us so much with your AIDS hospice and other facilities that you are operating for the poor and those most in need. We in the City of New York are very grateful to you for all that you have done, and we are always aware of your presence even when you are in a country as far away as India.*

*All the best.*

Mother Teresa is believed by many, myself included, to be a living saint. My religion does not allow for saints. So what? I am convinced that Mother Teresa is one and that I personally benefited from her saintliness.

# Bishop Paul Moore

It is no secret that the Reverend Paul Moore, Jr., until recently the Episcopal Bishop of New York, and I often do not see eye to eye.

Simply put, I believe he is more a Pontius Pilate than a humble worker at the feet of the poor. He believes service to the poor is really government's obligation, not the church's. Whatever happened to the principle of charity?

During the holiday season in 1982, for example, I suggested that the city's churches and synagogues should play a greater role in providing temporary shelter to homeless men and women. The City of New York was rapidly expanding its shelter system, but I believed that religious institutions might be able to bring their expertise to bear in ministering to the needs of the hard-to-reach homeless. It seemed perfectly consistent with the role of churches and synagogues here on earth.

Not so, said Bishop Moore and a group of the city's religious leaders. "Last week, Christian and Jewish leaders joined at a press conference convened by Episcopal Bishop Paul Moore, Jr.," reported Rabbi Marc Tanenbaum of the American Jewish Committee the day after Christmas. "The religious leaders committed themselves to help provide temporary food and shelter. But they insisted that the problem is so great that only the government has the resources to provide permanent low-cost housing and jobs. Mayors, governors, and the President," he said, speaking for Bishop Moore and the group of religious leaders, "cannot be allowed to shift the buck primarily to churches and synagogues."

I wasn't trying to "shift the buck." I was only trying to get them to help out. At the same press conference, the Reverend William Sloane Coffin of Riverside Church said that he hated for "churches, synagogues, and mosques to become havens in a heartless world, and by caring for victims of that world, increase its heartlessness." It was an unbelievable statement, to the best of my knowledge said without objection from Bishop Moore or Rabbi Tanenbaum.

For if religious institutions are not havens, what are they? If there is not room at their inn, where is there room for the hungry and the homeless? I replied as follows to Rabbi Tanenbaum, the Reverend Coffin, and other religious leaders who had attended Bishop Moore's press conference:

*In a recent WINS religious commentary, Rabbi Marc Tanenbaum stated, and I quote, "The time is past due for Mayor Koch and the religious leaders of the City to bury their polemical hatchets over the agonizing issue of the homeless." Unquote.*

*Unfortunately, Rabbi Tanenbaum failed to take his own advice. The rest of his commentary was marked not only by polemical hatchetwork, but by serious errors in fact. Let me be specific.*

*Rabbi Tanenbaum says that I have harangued churches and synagogues for failing to be "prime movers" in caring for the homeless. This is false. The City of New York has been, and will continue to be, the prime mover in sheltering the homeless. We have asked our religious institutions to help in that job by providing shelter to homeless people who, for one reason or another, will not come to City shelters.*

*Rabbi Tanenbaum says that churches and synagogues are not equipped to provide long-term permanent housing and jobs for the homeless. This is true, but who asked them to? Not I. Not the City of New York. We have asked only for help in providing temporary shelter on an emergency basis.*

*Rabbi Tanenbaum rebukes me for being critical of synagogues in this matter, but neglects to mention that I was invited to a synagogue to speak on the question of what the Jewish community could be doing*

*to help the City. I pointed out that sixteen churches, and no syna-
gogues, were helping to shelter the homeless. It was a simple statement
of fact.*

*Finally, Rabbi Tanenbaum says that I should have known that the
Federation of Jewish Philanthropies has been operating four major
shelters for the homeless. Unfortunately, Rabbi Tanenbaum is playing
fast and loose with the facts. According to a Federation spokesperson,
three residence facilities for the elderly and for mental patients are
being planned, and only a fourth facility offering shelter to homeless
young people is actually in operation today. It's not in a synagogue, but
it's there, and it's helping, and the Federation—a wonderful organization—deserves credit.*

*A year ago, I asked religious organizations to help in sheltering the
homeless. Today, both synagogues and churches are cooperating with
the City. It is indeed time to bury the hatchet. But, Rabbi Tanenbaum,
the place to bury a hatchet is not in someone else's neck.*

It was not the last time Bishop Moore and I would disagree. In 1983
I went with then–Health and Human Services Secretary Margaret
Heckler to visit AIDS patients. Bishop Moore sent me a note saying
he was "most impressed" by my visit. I sent him a thank-you note
which also included my views on an objectionable comment he had
made at his own press conference on the subject of AIDS, which I
viewed to be an attack on Judaism. And I am a Jew in love with my
faith and its traditions.

*Thank you for your nice note of August 17 commenting on my visit
to an AIDS patient with Secretary Margaret Heckler.*

*I read with interest your statement of June 23, which you enclosed
with your note. I was, to say the least, deeply pained and startled by
your statement, "The God whom Jews and Christians worship is a
loving merciful God who does not punish his children like a wrathful
father. Such concepts of the nature of God are found only in the
primitive barbaric passages of the Old Testament."*

*I have never heard what you call the Old Testament and what the
Jewish people throughout the generations have revered as a Jewish
Bible or any section of it described with adjectives such as primitive or
barbaric, particularly by a distinguished member of the clergy who has
on so many occasions displayed such sensitivity and concern for the
beliefs and practices of other traditions and persecuted minorities. I
personally revere the Jewish Bible and know that Christians revere the*

*Jewish and Christian Testaments as the word of God, divinely revealed or inspired. While your language was undoubtedly not intended to be insulting, let me tell you that it has had that effect. Various Christian traditions in the past in describing Jews and their beliefs unthinkingly have included such words as* perfidious. *It is a tribute to so many contemporary Christian and Jewish leaders, including yourself, who have worked so tirelessly to create a climate of mutual reverence, that words like* perfidious *have been deleted from their sacred liturgies.*

*I mention all of this to you because I am sure that you will have other occasions to make further comments on this matter. I simply wanted to alert you to Jewish sensibilities when simplistic distinctions are drawn or implied by reference to the Jewish God of vengeance as opposed to the Christian God of love. I believe that the God referred to is the same God for both the Judeo and Christian traditions.*

"You missed my meaning. Both Christians and Jews accept the Old Testament as containing the Word of God," Bishop Moore replied. "The earliest understandings were primitive and barbaric." He closed with a handwritten postscript saying, "I certainly meant no offense."

In an act of Jewish charity, I accepted his statement that he had meant no offense, no matter how offensive his words had been:

*I received your letter of September 8, for which I thank you. I never thought you meant offense, but it is comforting to have you reiterate that as you did in your letter.*

*I must disagree with your view that "almost any rabbi" would use the words* primitive *and* barbaric *in discussing any paragraph of the Torah.*

*I'm glad that we had an opportunity to fully discuss and voice our feelings on a very fundamental matter and go on to other challenges that confront us each and every day.*

*All the best.*

And then consider the case of a building known as the Seamen's Institute in lower Manhattan, which had long served as a safe harbor for wayfaring sailors coming through the port of New York. With the rise of container cargo ships during the seventies and eighties, there were fewer sailors in need of its temporary lodgings.

As a result, by 1985 the institute's board, on which Bishop Moore served as honorary chairman, wanted to sell the building and the land upon which it stood. Located just a few blocks from Wall Street and the stock exchanges, the institute most surely would have been demolished and an office building erected in its place.

But there was a problem. At my request, the City Council had been moving forward with a bill to impose an eighteen-month moratorium on the conversion of single-room-occupancy buildings such as the institute to other purposes. The city's SRO stock had shrunk significantly in the prior decade, and the law was a means of preventing a further loss of housing units of critical importance to low-income individuals.

On April 4, 1985, I received a call from Bishop Moore. He expressed his support for the moratorium bill, but also said he believed that the institute should not be covered by its provisions. Frankly, I was surprised. After all, I'd also had a call from John Cardinal O'Connor, who also supported the bill and had no objection to the fact that a nearby building owned by the Archdiocese might be subject to its provisions. Bishop Moore's position did not seem to be much of a model of Christian charity.

I wrote to him:

*I was interested in your telephone call to me of yesterday asking that I keep abreast of the SRO legislation now pending in the City Council with its eighteen-month moratorium, which might affect the pending sale of the Seamen's Church Institute.*

*It is your position that the building which is now vacant should not be considered subject to the SRO moratorium so that you could demolish it. You indicated that you would use the funds for other worthwhile purposes, and, of course, we know that the worthwhile purpose in the case of a church should be to administer primarily to the needs of the poor. At the end of our conversation you said, "I am for the SRO moratorium."*

*I thought about that comment, and it is the kind of comment that many developers would make after objecting to the SRO moratorium being applied to their particular buildings. I suspect that even those who sought to tear down the SROs on West 44th Street in the dead of night without legal permits, if given an opportunity, would say that they too favor the continuation of SROs elsewhere but their buildings should be treated as special cases and not be subject to the moratorium. Indeed, almost every time an SRO is the subject of demolition, the developers will insist that the City will receive much more income to apply to its expense budget to aid the poor as a result of increased real estate taxes which would come from the new building to be constructed on the site.*

*As you know, the City of New York now spends more than $170 million annually on the homeless, and that figure rises every year. In 1978 we were spending only $14 million. So you can see that we do need more revenue. And yet we also believe that the current SROs should be the subject of an eighteen-month moratorium in order to determine what is in the best interest of all of the people who live in this City without reducing the number of units available as SROs during that period of time.*

*Wouldn't it make sense for you to consider continuing to maintain the building rather than keeping it closed as it currently is? And perhaps you could not only take in seamen who are in need of shelter but other individuals who would be grateful to have a room at the Seamen's Institute, particularly because the atmosphere in a facility operated by the clergy is normally much better than the shelter we can provide in our dormitories for upwards of 7,400 men and women. One of our most pressing problems at this time relates to shelter for women and the Seamen's Institute might be an ideal place for that purpose. What do you think?*

*All the best, particularly during this Easter season.*

Four years later, I happened to tell the story of Bishop Moore and the Seamen's Institute on a very-late-night television show. "The synagogue and the church are supposed to help people in desperate need of help," I said, but the incident demonstrated that "Bishop Moore is more interested in the sale of air rights over churches than he is in those individuals who need help."

As I drove home from the studio, I began to regret what I had said, realizing I'd probably been unduly harsh. So I wrote the following letter to Bishop Moore the next morning:

*I have been thinking about our relationship, which has been estranged over the years, although when we first met I thought we had established a good rapport. I believe that even though we agree and disagree on a number of issues, ultimately, we have the same goals of a better life for all of the people of the City of New York. At times, I have felt that your criticisms of me were unfair, and I am certain that you believe that my comments about you at times were unfair, as well.*

*I propose that we start afresh. When you resigned your pastorate at*

73

*St. John's and I was asked for a comment, I said that you would be around for a long time. I think that is good for the City, even if it means that you and I will be, on occasion, marching to different drummers. I would like to put aside the past and that includes critical comments I recently made regarding our differences while being interviewed for a television program which, undoubtedly, you will hear about.*

*I want to make it crystal clear that this letter is not intended to solicit your support for my reelection. I am certain that another candidate will receive that support. Nevertheless, I know that I could benefit from your suggestions and advice on issues that are of concern to this City. I want you to feel free to call me at any time to discuss any matter of interest or to arrange a meeting with me at the office if you conclude that it would be helpful to the City.*

*To start this relationship off, best foot forward, let's have lunch as we did when we first met!*

*All the best.*

Bishop Moore replied. My comments were apparently the last straw. He said my statement about the institute "was a blatant distortion of the facts." Given that, he said, "it is not appropriate for me to just have lunch without an apology and your setting the record straight publicly. For it is not just myself you have deeply offended, but my office, my people, and my fellow clergy."

I replied:

*I have received your letter of May 3. After reviewing it and the issues it raises, I am sorry to realize that we just can't agree.*

*All the best.*

God had spared me from what would have been a very unpleasant lunch for both of us. And who says, "God Almighty does not hear the prayer of a Jew"? Not Bishop Paul Moore, of course, but Dr. Bailey Smith, former president of the Southern Baptist Convention.

In early 1989 Bishop Moore retired. The Reverend Richard F. Grein was selected as his successor. "I don't want you to be misled," I said in a friendly way when I first met him. "I did not like your predecessor. I do believe you and I will get along."

"Oh, I know very well of your relationship with Bishop Moore," he said. "You did not like him. He did not like you.

"Let me tell you what he said when we first discussed you," the new Bishop continued. "He took me outside the Cathedral of St. John the

Divine and pointed to a large pothole in the street. 'You see that pothole?' he said. 'Mayor Koch, because he does not like me, has refused to allow that pothole to be fixed for seven years.' He was very upset."

"If that isn't paranoia," I replied, "what is?" Bishop Grein laughed.

After this, I wrote to Ross Sandler, Commissioner of Transportation, relating the substance of my conversation with Bishop Grein and concluding: "In any event, now that I am aware of the potholes, I wanted to bring them to your attention. Please do make every effort to have them filled as quickly as possible. Thanks."

"Immediately upon learning about this," Commissioner Sandler informed Bishop Grein in response to my request, "we dispatched a crew to fix potholes and failed utility cuts that our inspectors tell us are the predominant problem at that location. . . . We are also aware that there is major construction work in progress on the water system underneath the street at that location." And, he said, "we understand that the entire street will be resurfaced when the construction work is complete, which will provide a much smoother roadway."

Some "pothole," Bishop Moore.

# PART
# 4

# A PROUD JEW

---

## To Joseph V. Reed, Under Secretary-General of the United Nations

I once called the United Nations a "cesspool." Indeed, it is probably one of the best-remembered and most controversial comments I made during my twelve years as Mayor of the City of New York.

No, I wasn't suggesting that the U.N. pack its diplomatic bags and move elsewhere. I'm glad the U.N. is in New York City and I hope it stays here. It's one more proof of New York's status as the premier international city.

Nor do I think the U.N. is merely a debating society whose proceedings are irrelevant to the real world. Its peacekeeping forces have often been crucial in bringing hostilities to an end in various parts of the world. Its relief efforts have often meant the difference between life and death for hundreds of millions of poor and hungry people in countries ravaged by floods, torn by war, or beset by locusts. And it continues doing its remarkable, though sometimes thankless, work even after the television news crews have left and the front-page stories are no longer being filed about that particular human tragedy.

But sometimes the U.N. is foolish. And sometimes it is dangerous and grossly discriminatory, especially when Third World, Warsaw Pact, and Arab countries join together to condemn the United States or the U.N.'s regular victim, Israel. Fortunately, we've had some outstanding representatives to the U.N.—people like Pat Moynihan, Jeane Kirkpatrick, and General Vernon Walters—who have been willing to stand up and talk tough when unfair attacks from these quarters begin.

But sometimes we've not been so lucky. As a permanent member of the U.N. Security Council, the United States retains the prerogative to make various high-level appointments to the U.N. Secretariat, its operational arm. One of these was a gentleman named Joseph Verner Reed, Under Secretary for Political and General Assembly Affairs and the highest-ranking American in the Secretariat.

I had met him on prior occasions and had always thought him rather unctuous and silly.

In November 1988, the General Assembly invited Yasir Arafat, Chairman of the Palestine Liberation Organization, to speak in New York. To their credit, President Reagan and Secretary of State George Shultz declined to issue Arafat the visa necessary to enter the United States. While I believe that the PLO should be allowed to maintain offices in New York as long as the U.N. grants it official observer status, I was very pleased that Arafat would not be granted a visa.

Federal law prohibits terrorists from entering the United States. And there was no doubt in Secretary of State Shultz's mind that Arafat is a terrorist. Just ask the widow of Leon Klinghoffer, an American citizen and New York City businessman. In 1985 he and his wife had the bad fortune to book passage aboard the *Achille Lauro* for a Mediterranean cruise. It was not smooth sailing. Under the leadership of Arafat's personal friend and terrorist ally Abu Abas, PLO brigands hijacked the *Achille Lauro* in order to demonstrate how easily they could disrupt our world if their demands were not met. To make sure no one missed their message, the PLO terrorists seized Mr. Klinghoffer, who was elderly and confined to a wheelchair, shot him through the head as his wife watched, and then, without ceremony or regret, threw his body overboard.

Arafat and Abas, his major lieutenant, were both implicated in this cold-blooded murder of an American citizen. And now the U.N. wanted Arafat to come to New York City. It was appalling.

But it did not stop there. Shortly after the invitation was extended and the visa denied, I read in the newspapers that Under Secretary-General Reed had sent and publicly released what he called a "missive" to Reagan in which he objected to the President's decision. It was more a missile than a missive.

"I write you this evening with a heavy heart," his letter to the President said. "The bottom line, Mr. President, is that the action taken to deny the opportunity for an invited guest of the United Nations [to appear before it] has done incalculable damage to United States credibility in the world arena."

Though I disagreed with his position, I believed that Mr. Reed had the right to share his advice and counsel with the President. That is what he is appointed to do. But, in my view, it was absolutely unacceptable for him to have gone a giant step further and shared his critical view of the President with the rest of the world by publicly releasing his letter. He's not appointed to do that.

And it's just not the way it's done in diplomatic circles. Indeed, on the day Mikhail and Raisa Gorbachev visited New York there was a small reception at the U.N. to welcome them. I attended, along with such luminaries as Henry Kissinger and David Rockefeller. So did Mr. Reed.

"Isn't it incredible," I asked the President of the General Assembly, Dante Caputo of Argentina, "that Mr. Reed, an appointee of President Reagan and Secretary Shultz, would attack them publicly?"

"We were all shocked here that it occurred," he replied.

"Has any other U.N. employee ever publicly attacked his own country?" I asked. "Not to my knowledge," he answered.

In my mind, what Mr. Reed had done clearly deserved a reprimand in the strongest possible and certainly public terms. Since no one else had done it, I sent him the following letter:

*I have read the appalling letter that you sent to President Reagan concerning the Administration's refusal to issue a visa to Yasir Arafat.*
*You are the highest-ranking American in the United Nations Secre-*

79

tariat. *Understandably, since your allegiance in your current capacity is to the U.N., you might want to convey to the Secretary of State your opinion that his actions are harmful to the U.S. or to the U.N. However, do you think you have the right to engage in the kind of criticism that your letter displayed?*

*I have discussed your actions with other high-level officials at the U.N., including foreigners, and they were shocked by what occurred. I also asked them if any other international servant had ever engaged in a similar denunciation of his/her country or Secretary of State. I was told no, never in the history of the U.N., and that you stand alone in your action.*

*In your letter you complain that Secretary Shultz's decision was "baffling and contradictory." I suspect that if you were asked directly, do you believe Secretary George Shultz is a man of great personal honor and intellect, you would have to say yes. And, if you were asked, has he consistently and articulately rejected terrorism and those who practice it, you would have to say yes.*

*Are you aware of the federal law which expressly prohibits terrorists from entering this country? That law was cited by Secretary of State Shultz as warranting his action in denying Arafat's entry. Surely you are aware that Abu Abas, the person who was found guilty in Italy of killing an American citizen, Leon Klinghoffer, was lionized at the Algiers/PLO conference by his colleagues in attendance, including Yasir Arafat. Surely you are aware that it was Secretary George Shultz who himself was the target of a Fatah bomb after the PLO's last renunciation of terrorism.*

*Rather than having decried and denounced the policy of Secretary Shultz, you should either have given the Secretary your private opinion—without denunciation—on the political consequences of his highly moral act, or you should have said nothing. But for you, the top U.S. national at the U.N., to add your critical opinion to those issued by others at the General Assembly, criticizing your government and the people that you used to serve at the State Department, is unacceptable.*

*Perhaps you will suggest that the views you related to the President were personal and not for general consumption. Were that true, would your letter have been so widely distributed? You clearly intended for all those in and around the U.N. to know of your criticisms of the Secretary of State and of President Reagan, the people who put you where you currently are. Sometimes people forget who they are and how they got where they are. They also forget the obligations of being a simple citizen of the U.S. as well as an international leader with obligations to the U.S. In my judgment, you have failed those obligations.*

A few days later, Mr. Reed replied. "As an international civil servant," he wrote, "I am obliged to support the Organization I am privileged to serve. As an American, I am unflinchingly committed to defending the principle of free speech."

I sent a second letter to Mr. Reed:

*I would like to acknowledge your letter of December 13, 1988.*

*Without seeking to continue our correspondence on the issue, since we are clearly not in accord, I feel compelled to say that apparently at the United Nations you stand alone in your deed. I consider your comments to be unpardonable and defamatory actions against your country, President, and Secretary of State. Your response could have been written by the character in the novel,* The Man Without a Country.

*All the best.*

Mr. Reed and I crossed paths one more time. In April 1989 I was alerted to the fact that he had been nominated by President Bush to the post of Ambassador-at-Large. An article which appeared at the time in *The Washington Post* reported that in 1982, after visiting with Mr. Reed in Morocco, where he was the American ambassador, then-Senator Thomas Eagleton advised Secretary Shultz that Reed was "a fourteen-carat nitwit." Truer words were never spoken.

I immediately sent a letter to each member of the U.S. Senate's Foreign Relations Committee urging them to reject the nomination. Regrettably, both the committee and the full Senate ultimately approved the appointment.

Too bad. Joseph Verner Reed isn't a diplomat. He's a dope.


# To King Fahd of Saudi Arabia


In 1985, Dr. Maarouf Al Dawalibi, Counselor to the Royal Court of the Kingdom of Saudi Arabia and its ambassador to the United Nations, gave a speech to the U.N.'s Center for Human Rights. His comments easily could have been delivered in the thirteenth century and contained, in fact, what is normally referred to as the blood libel against Jews.

"The Talmud," he told the audience, says that "if a Jew does not drink every year the blood of a non-Jewish man, then he will be damned for eternity." He then went on to say that these "are documented facts on which 150 years ago sixteen French books were written and which I, myself, have seen."

It is, of course, an outrageous fabrication, one that normally should bring smiles to the lips of those who hear it, denunciation of the person who utters it. So far as I know, there was no public denunciation of Dr. Al Dawalibi's remarks at the United Nations, that tower of virtue. So I decided I would pursue the matter by writing to His Royal Highness King Fahd of Saudi Arabia:

*I read with great distress the translation of the speech delivered by Dr. Maarouf Al Dawalibi, who represents you and the Kingdom of Saudi Arabia at the United Nations. This letter is not intended to engage in a discussion with you on the subject of Israel since you have a point of view which is different from mine, and that issue is one on which we will probably never concur.*

*However, it must disturb you to have your representative to the United Nations seek to attack Jews as guilty of engaging in the murder of non-Jews for ritual purposes. Surely, in this day and age for a representative of the Saudi Arabian government to quote as factual a statement which appeared in his address, to wit, "The Talmud says that: 'If a Jew does not drink every year the blood of a non-Jewish man, then he will be damned for eternity,' " must shock intelligent human beings and disgust them as well. That statement, among others, engaging in a blood libel against Jews appears in the remarks made by Dr. Al Dawalibi on December 5, 1985. I am enclosing a copy of the full text in English of his remarks.*

*I represent in the City of New York the most diversified population in the world of nearly 7.5 million people, amongst whom are Arabs and Muslims from every country in the world. I have great respect for their tradition. I am their mayor as well as the mayor of Jews, Christians, and non-believers. I am quite certain that the statement of Ambassador Al Dawalibi must disgust Muslim citizens of the City of New York as well as myself. I would urge you to take the Ambassador to task and, indeed, if . . . possible, to have him apologize for these grotesque, false state-*

*ments, which can do nothing other than frustrate efforts to achieve
peace in the Middle East.*

*I would love to hear from you.*
*All the best.*

I never did hear from King Fahd. So I sent a copy of my letter to
Prince Bandar Bin Sultan, Saudi Arabian ambassador to the United
States. I never received an answer to or even an acknowledgment of
my letter.

The State Department did respond to my letter. It said it had been
forwarded by diplomatic pouch to Saudi Arabia. The State Department
expressed to the U.N. as well as to the government of Saudi Arabia
through our embassy in Riyadh "the unacceptability and the harmful-
ness of such statements especially in an international forum intended
to promote religious tolerance."

An interesting side note occurred when I was invited to a reception
to honor Soviet President Mikhail Gorbachev at the U.N. While I was
waiting in a small reception hall with about a dozen others, a tall,
impressive, handsome middle-aged man came over to me.

"Mayor," he said, "I am a great admirer of yours. I think you do a
terrific job."

"Thank you," I said. "May I ask your name?"

"I'm Prince Bandar, the Saudi ambassador to the United States," he
answered.

I asked if he'd like to come to Gracie Mansion for dinner some
evening. He said he'd love to come, but he never accepted the several
invitations that I extended.

## To Prime Minister Yitzhak Shamir

Tight elections can result in fundamental changes. In 1988 Israeli
voters went to the polls to elect a new Knesset, that nation's parliamentary body. When the votes were counted, neither of Israel's traditionally dominant parties—the Likud Party or the Labor Party—had won
enough seats to control the parliament. As a result, both scrambled to
forge coalitions with smaller parties that would give one or the other
the majority needed to control the Knesset and run the country.

The electoral crisis gave Israel's smaller religious parties the political upper hand. Traditionally, these parties have represented the Orthodox wing of Judaism. They tend to believe that Israeli society has moved far away from the religious tenets upon which the state was founded. High on their parliamentary agenda, then, is passage of laws to require stricter observance of the Sabbath and other customs.

Given the electoral turmoil, in 1988 the Orthodox parties expressed interest in forming a coalition with either Likud or Labor. But for a price. Specifically, they wanted stripped from Conservative and Reform rabbis the authority to administer conversion rites for non-Jews. Under the Law of Return, a Jew by birth or conversion who does not have a criminal record has an unconditional right to enter Israel at any time.

The question of who is and who is not a Jew has long divided Jews. Under traditional Jewish law, only someone born of a Jewish mother is by birth a Jew. There is no patriarchal line of descent, since if the mother is not a Jew there's no 100 percent guarantee that the child born of that mother was conceived in union with a Jewish father.

Alexander Schindler, a leading Reform rabbi, tried to change all that. He believed that any child born of a Jewish mother or a Jewish father ought to be considered a Jew. Ending the matriarchal line of descent, of course, was anathema to the millions of Orthodox Jews whose adherence to Talmudic law and custom is far more rigorous. And Rabbi Schindler's proposal was certainly ill considered in a time when consensus and closed ranks are required because of attacks on Israel by other countries.

But you can also go too far in the other direction. In order to form a new government, both Yitzhak Shamir of the Likud and Shimon Peres of Labor seemed ready, even eager, to give in to the Orthodox parties and strip Conservative and Reform rabbis of their authority. It seemed possible, even likely, that Orthodox sects, though forming a relatively small proportion of all Jews in or out of Israel, would nonetheless emerge as the ascendant and dominant power in Israel, both politically and religiously. Reform and Conservative Jews throughout the world waited, watched, and, in many cases, worried about what alliances the new government would form, what changes would be forthcoming.

In some sense, the issue was a tempest in a teapot. Each year, after all, only a few converts—maybe fifty—invoke the Law of Return and enter Israel. But the symbolic consequences of a change were tremendous. Stripping Conservative or Reform rabbis of their authority to perform conversions would have sent a troubling signal to millions of Jews, particularly in the United States, where so many live and worship. And that might even shake their faith in and support for the State of Israel.

I am a Conservative Jew. I was born of Jewish parents, both mother and father. So the proposed change did not directly affect me. Nonetheless, I was troubled. I thought it important for my voice to be heard on the issue, so I wrote to Prime Minister Shamir:

*As a son of Abraham and a proud Jew, I am sure you know I am committed to the security and well-being of the State of Israel. I know the American Jewish community is providing you with daily advice in opposition to your forming a coalition with the religious parties that seek major changes in the fundamental law of the State of Israel. Even if you don't take that advice, I want you to know that I will still be a supporter of Israel. The reason is very simple.*

*Israel is the one country that will take every Jew in need of sanctuary. Regrettably, every day somewhere in the world, Jews are persecuted by countries in which they reside. They are not permitted to practice their religion and are in need of a place to which they can flee and renew their lives. Had Israel existed in the 1930s, millions of Jews who were the victims of the Final Solution because no country was willing to accept them would be alive today. While I will have problems in my own mind should you go forward with your announced goal, my support will still be with you.*

*I don't think that is necessarily true of millions of Jews in this country who are offended by the thought that the Orthodox Rabbinate will now be the sole arbiter of who is a Jew. I myself belong to the Conservative tradition. There are millions of Jews who identify with this branch of Judaism or the Reform tradition. We all consider ourselves to be Jews in good standing, the congregations we attend to be as good as any, and the rabbis who officiate to be equal to the best.*

*The proposed change in the Law of Return deciding who is a Jew will change all of that. It will place Jews like me in what can best be described as a lesser position in comparison with Orthodox Jews. That is not acceptable to us.*

*And it does not serve Israel. Surely Israel was not created as a* theocracy. Most Jews around the world, and there are close to 14 million of us, think of Israel as a democracy. All people, including Jews, have a right to observe their faith as they wish.

It is quite clear that the actual impact on non-Jews who seek conversion will be minimal. After all, not many people desire to assume the obligations that we impose on ourselves as Jews and the burdens that others want to impose on us. But even if we are not talking about many people, it is more than that. It's a matter of principle.

In the United States, we removed restrictions on Sabbath activities years ago. Israel should not impose similar laws on its own citizens against their wishes. They want to decide for themselves whether or not they will use a car on the Sabbath, swim in a pool with men and women, or go to a movie on a Friday night. Imposing those restrictions would move Israel closer to the fundamentalists of the world, including Iran and Saudi Arabia.

I believe that you are risking support for Israel in the United States among those who fight each year to provide Israel with the military and economic aid that it so desperately needs. To reduce the energy, drive, and support of your supporters in these crucial times would be a gross error.

As others have, I urge you to reinstitute the grand coalition between Likud and Labor and then change Israel's electoral system to create parliamentary electoral districts, as Ben-Gurion desired at the time of the state's founding. If you should choose to retain party lists, I suggest the law require a minimum of 5 to 10 percent of the vote before a party wins seats.

If you enact changes in the Law of Return, I fear the gain will not be worth the price, and you will eventually regret having ceded the rights of the vast majority of Jews to a small group of fundamentalists. I urge you to avoid taking steps that damage our common cause.

As I've said, it was an essentially symbolic change affecting only a handful of people. But small as it was, it sent tremors throughout the world. Fortunately, there was an outpouring of letters and editorials critical of the proposed change. And even better, ultimately Shamir and Peres agreed, in the interest of the security of Israel, to again renew the grand coalition between the nation's two largest parties. The fundamentalist fervor which has swept through Mecca, Tehran, and other capitals of the Moslem world, I am pleased to say, has yet to take hold of Jerusalem.

# About Minister Louis Farrakhan

Minister Louis Farrakhan of the Nation of Islam is a charismatic figure and a superb speaker. So was Adolf Hitler.

And like Hitler, Farrakhan is a hate-monger. He has called Judaism a "gutter religion," later correcting himself to say he had meant to call it a "dirty religion." Some correction. He has said that "the presence of the State of Israel is an outlaw act" and has accepted a $5 million, interest-free loan from Libyan strongman Muammar Khadafy. "I wanted black people to know you don't have to hide the fact that you have a friend America does not like."

"No black woman," he also believes, "should send her son to the United States armed forces." When a "black man in office . . . betrays the best interests of those of us who put him there," he says, "we will tar and feather them, we will hang them from the highest limb." He has even said he believes Hitler was "a very great man."

In October 1985, Farrakhan and his message of hate came to Madison Square Garden in New York. A predominantly black audience of 25,000 cheered his every word. It was frightening. Many people had called for picket lines outside the Garden to protest against and even try to prevent his speech. The former would have only elevated interest in the rally. The latter, of course, would have been a violation of his First Amendment right, a right extended even to those who preach hate. So I discouraged both actions.

But I did not hesitate to speak out against him. "When Farrakhan preaches, truth is abandoned. He buttresses his bigoted precepts with whatever lies, hatred, or false promises are required to manipulate his listeners," I said in the *New York Post.* "Some black leaders in particular fear that if they forcefully repudiate Farrakhan, there may be a backlash from their own black constituents who support the concept of self-help. They also worry that Farrakhan will individually target them for speaking out.

"Whatever their reasons," I continued, "all community leaders— whether they be black, white, Hispanic or Asian, Muslim, Christian, Jew or other believer or non-believer—share a responsibility to protect the truth. When truth is attacked, it makes no difference who is doing the attacking."

Some argued that the only reason I opposed Farrakhan was because I am a Jew. He is a good friend of Khadafy and, thus, an enemy of Israel. Of course, as a Jew, I feel special about Israel, just as Irishmen feel special about Northern Ireland and hostile to Great Britain. But I have always spoken out against bigotry practiced against blacks, Hispanics, and gays, and, exactly on target, I spoke out in 1989 in defense of Arab merchants in Brooklyn who were victimized by anti-Arab hostilities in the aftermath of the murder of Marine Colonel William Higgins, who had been kidnapped by pro-Iranian terrorists.

In 1988, Farrakhan visited New York again, this time at the invitation of a group of students at Manhattan Community College. He was going to be paid $10,000. I thought it was wrong. And even though my comments about Jesse Jackson during the New York primary the month before had drawn strong criticisms, I was not inhibited and I spoke out again. I called the invitation deplorable and wondered why a student organization would issue an invitation to a hate-monger. As I wrote in the *New York Post:*

I asked myself if I was once again getting into areas of racial polarization. Students at a public college have invited Farrakhan to speak, knowing this invitation will be perceived as an anti-Semitic act. They are paying Farrakhan with money from a student fund to which all students—including Jews—are required to contribute.

What would be the reaction of black students if Nobel Prize–winner William Shockley or Rabbi Meir Kahane were invited to speak at Manhattan Community College and paid $10,000? I think it's safe to say the students—white and black—would not give either of those individuals his First Amendment right to speak.

Is there a difference between Shockley, Farrakhan, and Kahane? I don't think so. Yet there was no outpouring of opinion denouncing Farrakhan. Everyone is afraid.

I saw only one news report on Farrakhan's speech at Terrace on the Park. According to the New York Post reporter, the Reverend Calvin Butts, assistant pastor of the Abyssinian Baptist Church was there. It was reported that Reverend Butts said, "I salute you, Brother Minister Farrakhan and I stand with you."

The complete text of Minister Farrakhan's comments is not available at this time because, according to the report, there was a "body search;

tape recorders were confiscated . . . and ID's surrendered." Farrakhan apparently referred to "Jewish enemies." He called the Christian cross "the sign of white supremacy." He went on to say, "the Jews cannot defeat me. I will grind them and crush them into little bits."

The deadly virus of bigotry and racial hatred is gaining strength. We pay a price for speaking out against it. Shall I hold back my outrage for fear of being called divisive? Or shall I speak out?

I chose, of course, to speak out. If I wanted to live with my conscience, frankly, there was no other choice I could make.

The Reverend Leon H. Sullivan, Pastor Emeritus of the Zion Baptist Church in Philadelphia, has consistently provided a moral point of reference for Americans opposed, as I am, to the apartheid government of South Africa.

A set of principles that he first articulated—rightfully known as the Sullivan Principles—has offered Americans a way to determine whether or not a company doing business in South Africa helps maintain that racist system or, by offering equal and full employment opportunities to black and "colored" South Africans, is helping to bring it down.

In 1988, however, I learned that he had permitted Minister Louis Farrakhan—a man, he had told Murray Friedman of the American Jewish Congress, for whom he had "very high regards"—to speak at his church. As I wrote to the Reverend Sullivan, I was stunned, for it seemed so out of character:

*We have met on a number of occasions. I have supported and continue to support your position on South Africa and apartheid. Because of the admiration and respect I have for your views, I was shocked when I read your explanation for inviting Reverend Louis Farrakhan to your church.*

*You say you have "very high regards" for Mr. Farrakhan. Reverend Sullivan, I appeal to your sense of fairness. If someone referred to the Baptist faith as a "gutter religion"—a term Mr. Farrakhan used to describe Judaism—and that person was invited by a nationally respected religious leader to speak in church, wouldn't you be distressed by that leader's decision? Wouldn't you be even more distressed if the invitee had described Adolf Hitler—the very incarnation of racist evil—as "a great man"?*

*What makes the situation even worse is that Mr. Farrakhan puts out surreptitiously anti-Semitic material, including the tape recordings of*

*Mr. Cokely in Chicago, who alleged that Jewish doctors injected the AIDS virus into black children. I fail to understand how you, who have worked so hard to build a coalition against racism and bigotry, can have a high regard for Mr. Farrakhan, who deliberately seeks to encourage fear and suspicion among different groups of Americans.*

*It is not enough to say that you're sorry we don't agree on this particular matter. You would not accept such an explanation from a leader who supported Prime Minister Botha or the evil of apartheid, which uses fear and suspicion to separate different groups of South Africans. I assume you would, quite correctly, think such a person should be rebuked.*

*I hope to hear from you.*

The Reverend Sullivan replied. "Please remember, Mr. Mayor, that my community is in a most, most distressed condition," he wrote. "We need so very, very much, any help we can get to help strengthen our people, to help build self-pride, and to help us towards greater self-sufficiency and greater unity within our families." While he did "not support any racial or religious condemnations" and had not invited Farrakhan to speak, he said, "I believe Mr. Farrakhan's thoughts on self-pride and self-sufficiency are needed in our community at this time."

I appreciated the fact that the Reverend Sullivan responded to my letter. But I could not accept his explanation:

*I appreciate your history of working so hard through the years "to build a coalition against racism and bigotry." I also appreciate the fact that you are concerned with the "poverty and continuing racial discrimination [which] have increased the social, economic, and psychological deterioration among [your] people." Indeed, helping to build self-pride and self-sufficiency is a necessity. However, should it be done with someone who is particularly famous in white and Jewish communities for his anti-white and anti-Semitic comments?*

*Assume for a moment that a southern minister invites the leader of the Ku Klux Klan to speak from the pulpit. Let us also assume that the minister invited this man because the Ku Klux Klan has taken a strong hand in favor of law and order, something the minister feels should be impressed on his parishioners. Wouldn't you agree that though the message has some value, the source from which it comes is polluted by bigotry and outrageous racism? Should such a person be given the authority of a pulpit, or should he be shunned?*

*You say you consented to his appearance at your church because your "Church historically has been open to different points of view." Would you suggest that the point of view of the Ku Klux Klan or a Professor Shockley be given opportunity for discussion at the churches and synagogues of this country? I doubt it.*

*When you say "we are reaching for strengths in our community," I can only conclude that it is erroneous to perceive Minister Louis Farrakhan as such a strength. He is to the black community what Adolf Hitler was to the German community, no less, except less effective—thank God.*

*I do "remember our march together in Washington against apartheid in South Africa," and I want to march again in opposition to apartheid and in opposition to religious bigotry. Your supporting Minister Farrakhan's appearances at your church creates huge obstacles for me in joining with you—shoulder to shoulder—to achieve our common goals of fairness and justice for all.*

*All the best.*

Surely there is no need to cite other illustrations of the double standard employed by so many whites and blacks in demanding so much of others, but so little from themselves.

# On the West Bank

I am one of those liberals who believe that outrages committed by the left ought to be condemned as strongly and as loudly as outrages committed by the right. My view is not shared by many other liberals. There is no question that what Prime Minister Botha did in South Africa or General Pinochet did in Chile to violate human rights is reprehensible and ought to be condemned. But so too is what Castro has done in Cuba or Ortega in Nicaragua.

And Pinochet, at least, allowed the Chilean people to decide whether he should stay in power. They said no. So he agreed to leave office and kept his word, according to all reports. Ortega promises that, come 1990, he'll allow the Nicaraguan people to decide in free elections whether the Sandinistas should stay in power. Only time will tell, but I do hope he keeps his promise.

The unexpected and unprecedented changes in Eastern Europe, where Communist governments are now permitting some democratic measures and some forms of capitalism, of course, ought to be applauded. Tearing down the Berlin Wall is an important symbol. But does it lay a real foundation for political and economic freedom? Only time will tell.

Regrettably, liberals too often remain strangely silent about the excesses of leftist governments. I think that is because leftist governments clothe themselves in such lofty language that their good intentions are taken as an article of faith, no matter how brutal or barbaric their actions may be.

If there is one nation which suffers most from the double standards liberals apply, it is the State of Israel. For this reason in 1988 I wrote the following letter to the United Nations Security Council:

*Historically, members of the Security Council demonstrated little hesitation in casting votes criticizing and/or sanctioning Israel for engaging in what the members believe to be repressive action against Arab residents on the West Bank and Gaza. Israel's defense is that it must guarantee security for all inhabitants in the occupied territories and that these peacekeeping measures in violent situations, of necessity, may include physical harm to those individuals confronting the peacekeepers.*

*Since the most recent violence began eleven months ago on the West Bank, 294 Palestinians and 6 Israelis have died, and Israeli security forces have again been vilified for defending themselves with real bullets, plastic bullets, rubber bullets, clubs, and the threat of expulsion. It appears to me that whatever Israel does is subject to criticism at the United Nations and at the Security Council.*

*As you know, I am a strong supporter of the State of Israel and believe that the Israeli security measures are warranted. While reasonable people can differ on the characterization and extent of those security measures, I am distressed as, I believe, are other fair-minded people by the different standards that the members apparently use when measuring Israeli security responses as opposed to other nations' responses.*

*To be specific, in Burundi, in 1972, the Tutsi-controlled government slaughtered at least 100,000 Hutus. More recently, The New York Times reported that at least 5,000 and as many as 20,000 people were slaughtered and an estimated 40,000 became homeless as refugees fled*

*their own country to enter neighboring Rwanda. In the war between
Iran and Iraq, reports indicate both sides engaged in violations of the
Geneva Convention by bombing undefended cities and intentionally
killing civilians and using poison gas against both troops and civilians.
More recently, Iraq used poison gas against its own Kurdish citizens,
slaughtering hundreds, injuring several thousand men, women, and
children, and causing at least 70,000 more to become refugees and take
sanctuary in Turkey. The latest incident involves Algeria's slaughtering
of civilians by the military. The Wall Street Journal of October 13th
quotes unofficial reports that "as many as 500 people were killed in the
week of unrest. About 3,000 demonstrators remained in police detention." These are civilians who in the last few days were engaged in
protest marches against rising food prices in that country.*

*Has the Security Council raised any of these issues—not merely for
discussion, but in the context of sanctions? If not, I must ask—is a
double standard being applied?*

*I believe the world recognizes Israel's predicament in confronting
internal violence prompted by states dedicated to reinforcing violence
in the occupied territories—and, tragically, recognize the people of
those territories responding affirmatively to the calls for violence.*

*Surely, the Security Council does not intend to condemn Israeli
efforts to maintain internal peace while other nations commit atrocities. For these nations, it appears that no matter what violence is
perpetrated, there is only silence.*

*In this era when the award of the Nobel Prize for Peace recognizes
the unselfish commitment of the U.N. to maintaining peace, cannot
the Security Council develop and maintain a posture on a beleaguered
nation's security consistent with that applied to other nations?*

*Is my criticism unfair or my judgment clouded?*

*All the best.*

# On the Sentencing of Three JDL Members

Terrorists are the scum of the earth. And the causes for which they
fight, no matter how worthy or noble, do not excuse their barbarity or
the bloodshed they leave in their wake.

Some might think that, as a Jew, I might be a bit more inclined to look the other way when the terrorist act is committed by the Jewish Defense League. Not at all. Like the PLO, the FALN, the IRA, the BLA, or any other terrorist organization, the JDL is a group of murderers or would-be murderers. Their religious faith earns them no special dispensation.

This opinion doesn't sit well, of course, with the approximately 25 percent of Jews who support the Jewish Defense League, particularly when the Jewish community believes itself to be the victim of rising anti-Semitism and increasing hostility to the State of Israel.

I find Meir Kahane, former head of the JDL, to be especially reprehensible. It has always distressed me that after being convicted of manufacturing explosives, Kahane was let out of jail and allowed to emigrate to Israel.

Kahane ran for and won a seat in the Knesset, Israel's parliament. Israeli law forbids a member of the Knesset from advocating terrorism or from practicing the kind of racism against Arabs for which Kahane is infamous. Indeed Israel's Central Election Commission prohibited his party from seeking election to the Knesset for that very reason. The Israeli Supreme Court upheld that decision in 1988.

The JDL continued under new leadership after Kahane left the United States. From 1984 to 1986, some JDL members engaged in firebombings in New York City. A firebomb was set off at the stagedoor entrance to Avery Fisher Hall on the night of a performance by the Moscow State Symphony. A tear gas grenade was thrown into an audience at the Metropolitan Opera House during a performance of the Moiseyev Dance Company. Fortunately, no one was injured. But it was still terrorism, pure and simple.

The JDL terrorists were apprehended and charged, and pleaded guilty. When they were scheduled to appear before Federal District Court Judge I. Leo Glasser, I felt it was important for my voice to be heard:

*Having learned that the above defendants yesterday pleaded guilty before you in connection with three bombings attributed to the Jewish Defense League, I take this opportunity to urge that they receive sentences of incarceration proportionate to the severe potential for loss of human life wrought by their actions.*

*It is my understanding that each defendant pleaded guilty in connection with three bombings in the City of New York: the firebombing of a Soviet residence in Bronx County on February 23, 1984; the* bombing of the stage entrance to Avery Fisher Hall at Lincoln Center on October 20, 1986; and the bombing of a loading dock of the Pan Am terminal at Kennedy Airport on April 28, 1986. I also understand that the maximum sentence for the count involving those bombings is twenty years.

As Mayor, it is my duty to speak out about acts which threaten the safety of the citizens of the City of New York as well as the many millions of people from all over the world who work in or visit our City. In my view, there is no more heinous act than a terrorist bombing of the sort involved in this case. In pursuit of their aims, these terrorists have threatened the lives of the targets of their bombings and have destroyed valuable property. Even more important, they have irresponsibly and indiscriminately placed in jeopardy the lives of countless innocent people who merely cross their path.

These actions are an outrage in a civilized society and must not be tolerated. Neither this nor any other "cause" entitles a group or individual to indulge in this vile and despicable behavior.

I believe that it is the responsibility of our courts to punish severely those who commit terrorist acts and to do everything possible to deter others from acts of deadly cowardice such as these bombings. The only certain deterrent is swift, sure, and severe punishment.

While I appreciate that your sentencing decision will be based on all of the facts before you, I believe it appropriate—even required—that I urge you to seize this opportunity to send exactly that signal to these defendants and to others of their ilk. I believe that a sentence that is not commensurate with the devastating potential for mayhem which these bombings represent would be worse than no sentence at all.

Accordingly, I respectfully submit that the crimes to which these defendants pleaded guilty cry out for sentences of lengthy incarceration. Perhaps more than most other cases found in our courts, this case illustrates the potential for disaster to life and property on a grand scale.

On behalf of the citizens of the City of New York, I thank you for this opportunity to submit this letter in aid of sentence.

All the best.

Judge Glasser, I am pleased to report, did dispense severe punishments. Describing one defendant as "a danger to this community," the judge sentenced Victor Vancier to ten years in federal prison. A second defendant, Murray Young, received a five-year sentence. A third defendant, Sharon Katz, received six months of house arrest and a suspended three-year prison sentence for her part in the Lincoln Center tear gas episode. Although she had pleaded guilty, the judge apparently felt that since she had only carried the tear gas into the auditorium and had not actually thrown it, she warranted a lighter sentence. Obviously, there is a certain amount of sexism in our courts. Sometimes women are not punished as heavily as men. And that is wrong.

# To Susan Sontag and Arthur Miller

Throughout my public life, I have been an unabashed, unashamed partisan and defender of the State of Israel. Indeed, I have been told by members of the Israeli government that I am the one American public official with an international forum available to him who has consistently defended Israel from attacks, whether they come from the White House, the Congress, the United Nations, or television networks and columnists. I believe when I took my positions I was right on the facts and conclusions, and I was not afraid to defend Israel when it lost its popularity and was no longer perceived as a "David" in world affairs.

As an American, obviously, American interests are first and foremost in my mind. But Israel has been our closest and often our only ally in the Middle East. When its interests are at risk, so, usually, are those of the United States.

Regrettably, world opinion about Israel has changed noticeably since 1973, the year of the war that it won against its three Arab neighbors. So overwhelming has been the anti-Israel tirade that few columnists or networks remain supportive of or even sympathetic to Israel. In fact, they are more often opponents, even going so far as to suggest that the government of Israel and the terrorists of the Palestine Liberation Organization enjoy some equivalency in the moral scheme of things.

Even worse, a growing number of what I call Herodian, or assimilationist, Jews seem to have become more concerned about how they are perceived by their non-Jewish colleagues and friends than they are about the security of the State of Israel. Updating the shtetl mentality to the modern era, they are often as quick to berate Israel's motives as they are to defend them.

The changed attitudes toward Israel have been most evident during the Arab uprising on the West Bank. If an American city is racked by a night or two of rioting and looting, virtually no one second-guesses a decision to call out the National Guard to protect people and property. It's considered a prudent and necessary step.

Not so with the Israelis. For three years they've had troops on the West Bank in an attempt to maintain order in the face of a sustained and violent uprising which has led to the death of scores of Arab and Jewish residents. And for those three years its decision to use troops to put down the uprising has been condemned repeatedly. The United Nations has even considered imposing sanctions.

Had the U.N. considered imposing sanctions against the United States for calling in the National Guard after the Liberty City riots in Miami, Americans would have been outraged. But when it considers sanctions against Israel, few people speak out.

But I do. Here is my op-ed piece "Stop Picking on Israel," which appeared in *New York Newsday:*

The weekend before last, I took the time to go through the Sunday papers from cover to cover. As I read the stories concerning the troubles in Israel, it struck me that the Israelis have every right to believe they are being subjected to a double standard by the world press.

They see their actions in the occupied territories of Gaza and the West Bank—those that are totally defensible and those that are not—portrayed unfairly on television screens and on the front pages of newspapers. The coverage seems intended to harass and intimidate them, to get them to change tactics and comport themselves in a manner consistent with the world view of columnists and editorial writers, who maintain a relentless drumbeat of criticism against Israel.

In the same news columns were many stories from other countries where brutality is the order of the day. The articles were small, nonjudgmental, not even critical of the brutal events in those countries. They simply presented the facts.

Do we see television reports on the bloody clashes in Soviet Armenia or Azerbaijan? The Soviets say dozens of people were killed and injured. We can't be sure of the actual death toll because that government has permitted no independent press coverage or television coverage from the scene.

Also from the Sunday papers: "In Sri Lanka a Tamil rebel mine killed nineteen Sri Lankans and wounded seventeen today in the Trincomalee district, military officials said." That same article states that the Tamils "shot to death fourteen Sri Lankans and a Tamil last Wednesday."

Does anyone believe that the Sri Lankan government reported all of the killings taking place on that island? Do we know what the Indian army—which is not exactly known for its benign attention to human rights—is doing in response? Has any of this violence been reported on television? I don't recall seeing it.

Have we seen reports on what the People's Republic of China is doing to the Tibetans? A Sunday news article did mention that rioting broke out in Lhasa on March 5. The article went on to say: "The outbreak of violence is apparently the first anti-Chinese disturbance since three violent protests in October, in which at least a dozen people were killed, some by Chinese policemen who fired automatic weapons into crowds of Tibetans."

I don't remember seeing that on television. Do you?

What we *are* seeing on television—day in and day out—is anti-Israel street violence in Gaza and the West Bank. And the violence is getting worse. It is reported that three Arabs—allegedly Palestinians and part of the Arafat wing of the PLO—seized a busload of Israeli civilians who were on their way to work. This attack was met by an assault by the Israeli army. Three Israeli civilians were killed, as were three Arab terrorists. Did the deaths of those Israeli civilians receive the same attention on television as the beatings of Arabs who, with their stones, slingshots, and Molotov cocktails, also like to kill Israeli civilians or soldiers? I doubt it.

I believe the remarks Henry Kissinger reportedly made to a group of prominent American Jews last month make sense, though it was later denied that he said them. He reportedly said he believed Israel should bar TV cameras from occupied territories and should use whatever force is necessary to end Palestinian protests there. It also was reported that Kissinger said, in effect, that Israel should "accept the short-term criticism of the world press and put down the insurrection as quickly as possible."

Maybe other nations throughout the world are experiencing troubles similar to those now taking place in Israel. Should Israel be the only nation to allow full television coverage of these troubles? This creates a false impression in the minds of television viewers that such events are happening only in Israel. The more television and the print media subject Israel to unreasonable criticism, the more Israel will lose faith in the power of reason.

The consequences of this unfair media treatment can only be to discourage Israel from accepting Secretary of State George Shultz's admirable peace proposal and from risking the return of some of the occupied territories in exchange for peace. That, ironically, is an outcome Israel's fiercest American critics would not welcome.

Ultimately, the Israeli government did ban television coverage of the uprisings, while allowing nontelevision coverage to continue. I believed then that it was a singularly excellent idea. And I still do.

I held more than 130 town hall meetings and hundreds of other public meetings during my twelve years as Mayor. All of them were open to television cameras. Beneath the glare of television lights, otherwise normal human beings suddenly went bonkers. The most demagogic were the most likely to be the only ones on that evening's television news.

What happened when cameras showed up at some of my town hall meetings has also happened on the West Bank and in Gaza. Your cause is far more likely to be heard and seen around the world when you're tossing rocks at armed soldiers and Jewish civilians, injuring many and killing some, than when you're sitting quietly, but productively, at a negotiating session.

My comments defending Israel's decision to ban television coverage drew immediate and harsh criticism. After publication of my first two books—*Mayor* and *Politics*—I was nominated by the authors Gay Talese and Lucinda Frank Morgenthau and elected as a member of International PEN, a distinguished group of writers concerned with protecting the rights of authors to write without retaliation by the governments they may criticize. Little did I know that if a PEN member doesn't toe the ideological line of those in leadership positions at PEN, there's a good chance that member will face retaliation.

After making the comments, I received a letter from the novelist and essayist Susan Sontag and the playwright Arthur Miller, president and vice president, respectively, of the PEN American Center. "We urge you to remember that as a member of PEN you have pledged to uphold the International PEN Charter, which affirms the 'principle of unhampered transmission of thought within each nation and between all nations.'" It was my obligation as a PEN member, they argued, to oppose the Israeli government's ban.

Their position was ludicrous. This was my reply:

*I have received your letter of April 26, in which you cite my member-ship in PEN as a reason why I should not support the banning of television news cameras from the West Bank during a period of strife and bloodshed.*

*I value my PEN membership and have always defended the right to a full and free expression of ideas by people everywhere. However, I wasn't aware that PEN subjects its members to scrutiny by the thought police. How do your comments square with my First Amendment rights?*

*May I also ask if you have sent a similar letter to Mrs. [Daniel] Ortega about actions within her own country? She is a member of PEN. Censorship has existed in Nicaragua since the Sandinistas took power. Also, have you reprimanded British writers who supported press censorship during the Falklands war? Are American members subject to censure for supporting the news blackout during the Grenada opera-tion?*

*In times of war, there are occasions when—regrettably—press cen-sorship must be temporarily imposed to save lives. Think back to World War II in this country. Israel has been at war, in one form or another, since 1948. Instead of singling out Israel, wouldn't it be more fair and accurate to discuss the vital issue of censorship in a true international context?*

*The broader point is this: while reasonable people might differ (and do differ) about the wisdom of banning television coverage of violence on the West Bank, there should be no difference among Americans that all of us should remain free to speak out vigorously and candidly. We should never be subjected to censure for having had the effrontery to do so.*

Were Sontag and Miller applying a standard to me different from that applied to another PEN member, Mrs. Ortega? I guess we'll never know. More than a year later, you see, they still haven't replied to my letter. If they're going to raise an issue, why are they so unwilling to fully discuss it?

# PART
# 5

# CALLING THEM AS I SEE THEM

## Having Fun

During my years as the Mayor of the City of New York, my administration and I accomplished a lot of important things. We brought the city back from the edge of bankruptcy. We balanced ten straight budgets according to the strictest accounting standards. We regained investment-grade bond ratings from Moody's and Standard & Poor's. We embarked on a ten-year, $57 billion program to rebuild the city's bridges and roads, parks and playgrounds, hospitals and schools.

We cut class sizes in the early grades and dropout rates in the upper ones. We launched a program to produce 252,000 units of low- and moderate-income housing, enough apartments to house the residents of any city in the United States except the ten largest. We made steady progress in rebuilding our police departments to their pre-fiscal-crisis levels—two of the three have already exceeded their 1975 head counts—while putting officers back on the beat in all seventy-five precincts. Our streets are cleaner, our subways are better, and our municipal work force is far more productive than twelve years ago.

As a hands-on mayor, I'm pleased to say that I was directly involved in the policy decisions and budgetary choices which made these improvements possible. And many more, for I've given you only a short list of all we achieved.

But if there's one achievement of which I am most proud it's that I helped the city and its citizens regain our spirit and pride as New Yorkers. When I took office, the city was a down-in-the-dumps kind of place. Our books were $1 billion out of balance. People and businesses were fleeing to the suburbs. And a lot of people were ashamed to admit they hailed from the Big Apple. "We live on Long Island," they said when asked.

Basically, I'm a shy person. But I knew when I became Mayor that I would have to be more outgoing, more of a cheerleader. Now, columnists use "cheerleader" as a term of derision. "All style, no substance" is exactly the way they like the public officials who are the targets of their barbs to be perceived.

Their problem with me has always been that I've clearly shown I'm a Mayor of substance. And if "cheerleading" means cutting a ribbon on a new building that will bring new jobs and new tax revenues to the city, or putting on a top hat and tails to welcome 500 homeless kids to an opening-night performance of the Ringling Bros., Barnum & Bailey Circus, or, even, going out to the foot of the Brooklyn Bridge every morning for eleven days during the subway strike to shout encouragement to the thousands of commuters turned pedestrians who'd been inconvenienced by a transit union that wanted to bring the city to its knees with an illegal strike, then I plead guilty. I'm a "cheerleader."

But not everyone appreciates what I'm up to. In late 1984 a city worker named Lynne Kanner wrote to *Newsday* to complain that while thousands of municipal workers rallied outside City Hall to demand overdue contracts on November 7, I was having "fun" at the Brooklyn Academy of Music and, later, at a party in honor of WNBC-TV reporter Gabe Pressman.

"Mr. Mayor," she wrote, "how about setting aside a few hours from your busy schedule to meet with those of us who work our tails off for the people of this great city, while you develop your 'show-biz' style?"

I answered:

*I read with interest the letter of Lynne Kanner which appeared in the November 27 edition of* Newsday. *Since it is totally erroneous, I thought I should reply.*

*Ms. Kanner is distressed that I as Mayor have not capitulated to the municipal union's exorbitant demands for salary increases. The City of New York is willing to provide fair increases, but we do not perceive the municipal employees as partners to share in the tax revenues of the city simply because the revenues are available. For every 1 percent increase that we provide city employees there is a cost to the city in the first year of the contract of $71 million and in the second year of $89 million.*

*Let me tell you what $89 million would provide if spent on essential services: 1,000 new cops; 500 workers and materials for street repair; a 50 percent increase in repair and maintenance of school buildings; job training for 1,000 youths; 200 park maintenance workers; a reduction in second-grade size from an average of more than 29 students per class to an average of 25; and a 10 percent increase in funds for school books.*

*Because Ms. Kanner does not approve of my refusal to cave in to unreasonable union demands, she unfairly attacks my daily schedule. She is distressed that I attended a Brooklyn Academy of Music event at 7 P.M. for a half-hour on November 7. Why was I there? That event was held to raise money for one of Brooklyn's great cultural institutions. Should I have stayed away? I doubt it.*

*Ms. Kanner then states that I attended a party celebrating Gabe Pressman's thirtieth anniversary in television. Regrettably, I was not able to attend the party; but apparently Ms. Kanner looked through the window and saw someone else, thinking it was me. But assume that I had attended. Would it have been so terrible to celebrate the anniversary date of the senior television reporter in New York City? I doubt it.*

*She then attacks me for having appeared on the* Saturday Night Live *show. I do indeed appear on television programs and occasionally in a movie, because I think it is helpful to New York City to encourage such programs to be made locally. The monies that I receive are given to charitable organizations and not accepted by me personally, e.g., for a*

Saturday Night Live *show I recently received $230.52 and that money was sent to the New York Foundling Hospital. Should I stop doing that? I doubt it.*

*I don't think even my most vociferous critics would deny the fact that I work very hard for the City of New York. My day begins at 5:45 A.M. and it does not end on most evenings until midnight. And the events I attend are generally in my capacity as Mayor. Being Mayor is a great honor and privilege. Being attacked unfairly requires a response. This is it.*

The contract about which Ms. Kanner complained was ultimately settled, and she and hundreds of thousands of other city workers received a reasonable, responsible wage increase. Retroactive, by the way, to the date the earlier contract had expired, as required by law, something not ordinarily the case in the private sector after a strike.

But as we moved from 1984 into 1985, a mayoral election year, I could sense that the question of whether a mayor was allowed to have fun was almost certain to be raised against me by my opponents. I decided to launch an editorial first strike, in a column in the *Staten Island Advance,* entitled "A Time to Be Serious, A Time to Have Fun," making the point that while of course government is serious business and a business that I take seriously,

I've also come to realize that not every issue or problem is best addressed by glum expressions, somber tones, and predictions of doom. If people think you think a problem is impossible to solve, they'll not want to waste their time trying to help. Will they?

On the other hand, if people have a little fun, relax a bit, and notice that you think a problem you've presented to them can be solved, they'll be much more ready to help. Enthusiasm, as my mother and probably your mother used to say, is contagious.

Above all else, that's what New York City needs. People enthusiastically helping people to help people. As a city, we've had good times and bad times, solved big problems and small ones. When all is said and done, however, in getting the job done we haven't been averse to having fun.

That's what makes New York exciting and what makes New York hum.

Is a mayor of the City of New York allowed to have a sense of humor and enjoy the job?

Some of my critics think I shouldn't. They worked in 1981 against my reelection and failed. So they want to try again next year. That's okay. In fact. I hope—and think—they'll fail again.

What's not okay, though, is that they want me to be a plastic, humorless mayor appearing and acting only when there may be reason for New York to despair, but not when there are occasions to celebrate. Never.

I'll confess to the sin of which they've accused me. I've had my photograph taken with Michael Jackson.

And, yes, I've welcomed the comic book superhero Spiderman to a press conference at City Hall, made a television commercial with Mr. T, answered questions and posed for photographs with *Sesame Street*'s Big Bird at my side, and danced across a stage—not so elegantly, I'll admit—with Twiggy and Tommy Tune while wearing a toy pigeon atop my hat. I've even been honorary drum major for a day with the Grambling State University Marching Band. . . .

. . . Government is a serious business. We put out fires, educate the young, care for the sick in hospitals, patrol the streets and subways, pick up the garbage, provide hot meals to the hungry, offer financial and technical assistance to businesspeople, give shelter to the homeless, pave the streets, and provide public assistance to almost one million New Yorkers.

The list of what government does goes on and on. Those are the issues that concern me every single day, from 6 in the morning to 11 P.M. or midnight, seven days a week. As Mayor I'm always on call, and since becoming Mayor, I've always answered the call. I take government seriously.

Apparently my editorial first strike in defense of a mayor's right to have fun was persuasive, even to my opponents. Rather than trying to beat me on the issue, they joined me during the 1985 mayoral campaign.

At 2:30 one morning, then–City Council President Carol Bellamy, who was running against me, journeyed to Queens to meet the Ringling Brothers circus train. She was scheduled to climb atop an elephant and ride it through the Midtown Tunnel, into Manhattan, and over to Madison Square Garden, where the circus would perform later in the day.

Admittedly, a politician riding an elephant is almost certain to be a great visual event. The problem was that even pachyderms don't crack a smile that early in the morning and only one television crew was up and about at 2:30 that morning. So her ride went virtually unnoticed by the press.

I felt sorry enough for the elephants having to be up so early in the morning. But I felt even sorrier for Carol. There are limits to what a person should be expected to do for a picture, no matter how far behind in the polls you are, no matter how much "fun" it is.

# The Homeless

Norman Siegel is the executive director of the New York Civil Liberties Union. I have utter contempt for him and mixed emotions about the organization. When it or the American Civil Liberties Union defends the right of someone to advocate an unpopular cause, I support that. But when they actually advocate a cause, I part company with the NYCLU and ACLU.

Norman Siegel doesn't see it that way. He not only defends the right of others to espouse controversial positions, as head of the NYCLU he advocates positions himself. And that means he was often on television, attacking me for positions I had taken. Apparently, Norman's interpretation of the right to free speech doesn't extend to mayors.

Siegel is also a master at making headlines by issuing threats he'll never keep, making charges he'll never be able to prove. He's even had the gall to make untrue statements about me or my administration in my presence. That happened in 1985 when he and I made a joint appearance on *The MacNeil/Lehrer Newshour* to discuss homelessness. His infuriating comments provoked the following letter:

*During our joint appearance on* The MacNeil/Lehrer Newshour *last night you made two serious charges which, I believe, warrant further investigation. I would appreciate any assistance you or your staff might be able to provide in this regard.*

*Your first charge was that "very often there's not enough transportation for people to go to the shelters. I have on two occasions seen at Grand Central Station a woman there wanting to go to a shelter and there's only a bus for men. There was no transportation for the woman."*

As you may know, Human Resources Administration vans or buses stop each night at Grand Central, the Port Authority, Penn Station, and Bellevue, Harlem, and Metropolitan hospitals in order to offer transportation to city shelters to homeless individuals who desire it. Our policy is that these vans and buses simultaneously transport both men and women to their respective shelter facilities. On those occasions when I have visited sites where HRA vans and buses offer transportation, the policy has been followed.

However, your charge suggests that our policy may not be adhered to in every case. I would therefore like to request that you provide me with any details such as time, date, van or bus number, and driver's name that would allow the Commissioner of the Human Resources Administration to substantiate your charges and take action if appropriate. I expect this policy to be followed by all HRA employees, and your cooperation can help to ensure that it is.

Your second charge was that "I've had homeless people who have told me that cops have come by and said if you don't get in the vans, we're going to break your legs." If the charge is substantiated, it is clearly in violation of Police Department policy and, moreover, is repugnant to all decent New Yorkers. Thus, I would appreciate any information you can provide to me as to the time, date, place, officer's name and/or badge number, or the names of the homeless people who have told you of this that would allow the Police Commissioner to investigate fully this very serious charge and to take appropriate disciplinary action if it is substantiated. Our "cold weather emergency" policy does not and should not condone any police officer or other city employee who is rude or makes threats against the people it is intended to serve. Your cooperation would help to ensure that no one is rude or threatening to them.

One further request. Like you, I visit the city's shelters in order to determine the adequacy of the facilities and programs we provide to the homeless and tour the city's streets to talk with the homeless and encourage them to come to our shelters. On these occasions I often am made aware of problems that need to be corrected and services that can be improved. Judging from the comments you made last evening, you reach similar conclusions after each visit you make.

In the future, then, I would very much appreciate hearing from you if you become aware of problems of the sort you raised during last night's program. I believe both of us are committed to ensuring that *homeless New Yorkers do have adequate and decent temporary shelter. Both your comments and your criticisms can greatly aid the city in its continuing efforts to meet that commitment.*

*I'll look forward to hearing from you on these two specific charges and on more general observations you may have made. Thank you in advance for any cooperation you might provide.*

*All the best.*

But again, Siegel is predictable. Despite his bravado, I never did hear from him with information which might substantiate the charges he'd made. It really calls into question his sincerity as an advocate. He says the people he represents are being denied service and are even at risk of physical danger. But when I asked him for details that might allow us to identify and to prosecute those guilty of this breach of city policy, Siegel was nowhere to be found.

He must have had another television interview to get to.

Advocates play an important role in New York City. They help keep government's feet to the fire. As someone who sought to make sure my administration was as efficient as possible and met the standards I had set for it, I often found their outside pressure to be very helpful. When they play a constructive role, advocates are a welcome part of politics in our town.

Regrettably, some advocates play a destructive role, resorting to near slander and libel at every opportunity to malign the intentions and the accomplishments of those who work for city government. Crucial to their technique is never, ever saying anything nice about government programs or government officials.

Nor can the advocate ever acknowledge that the city is obligated to deliver a whole host of services, not just the one in which the advocate is interested. That would be giving up the spotlight. Instead, their service and their cause, they argue, must be at the top of the heap of city priorities, if not the only city priority. All other services and all other constituents will just have to wait.

One of New York's best-known advocates is Bob Hayes of the Coalition for the Homeless. He's done much good work, but he also exemplifies in part the kind of advocacy I'm talking about. For example, four years ago I appeared on a nationally televised news program to talk about the problems of homelessness. During the discussion, I said that a major issue in serving homeless individuals was the finding by a number of studies that many homeless singles are substance abusers or alcoholics or have a history of mental illness. "One third of those who are homeless in the City of New York," I said, "are those who have psychiatric problems . . . one third are alcoholics or reformed alcoholics. . . . And one quarter are drug addicts. That's 90 percent." The answer to their problems isn't merely, as Bob would say, "housing, housing, and more housing."

When Bob heard my comments he erupted, sending me an angry letter the next day at City Hall attacking the accuracy of what he termed my "uninformed comments" about homeless individuals. "This inaccurate portrait plays into an apparent strategy of yours," he wrote, "which is to isolate the homeless as people so very different from everyone else. It's a false portrait, and you should acknowledge it as such."

"Not a single study undertaken by your agencies or by anyone else," Bob claimed, "supports such nonsense." So I went back and checked my facts. Contrary to Bob's charge, as I explained the next day to the press, which had received copies of Bob's letter (in many cases even before I did), "the numbers I used" in the interview "were supplied to me by the Human Resources Administration, and are accurate."

However, I did point out and apologize for having made the mistake of adding the "numbers together, when in fact there is overlay among them." But I also pointed out that while the figure I gave on television was "too high, my point was valid: the percentage of shelter clients with serious problems is much higher than President Reagan seems to believe." HRA, in fact, had two reports: one says that two thirds of the homeless, the other that 80 percent, cannot function on their own.

So I wasn't the one playing with numbers. It turns out, however, that Bob apparently was fudging the facts and pulling the wool over a lot of people's eyes. Indeed, for four years, *The New York Times* reported in 1989, Bob, along with other advocates for the homeless, "shied away from discussing the problem of addiction . . . in part because they feared the public would lose its sympathy for the homeless."

But not anymore. In fact, Bob was quoted as saying that drug and alcohol problems among the homeless were "horrendous." The "bottom line," he told the *Times* in 1989, "is that we have to tell the truth." Better late than never, I suppose.

The problem, however, is that apparently Bob Hayes has "shied away" on other issues too. The truth hasn't always been his bottom line. In late 1987 I launched a new program known as Project HELP to provide outreach and treatment, including involuntary hospital admissions, to the most hapless of the mentally ill homeless—those who, if they went without help, would be at substantial risk of harming themselves or others in the reasonably foreseeable future.

Bob and the New York Civil Liberties Union attacked me as soon as my program was announced. No surprise. Norman Siegel of the NYCLU said that it posed "broader threats to individual liberty" and that there was "enormous potential for abuse." Bob called the program a "roundup."

I responded with the following letter to Bob Hayes:

*Thank you for your letter of September 1st. I am surprised you were surprised that I described as "reprehensible" your comment that our efforts to expand upon our Project HELP model and to apply a broader, but still legal standard of when we may act to help gravely disabled homeless individuals is a "publicity stunt." After all, wouldn't you consider it reprehensible if I suggested that a legal action filed by the Coalition is just a "publicity stunt"? When it comes to helping the homeless, Bob, neither of us is in it for the publicity. I'm trying to help people. I believe you are too.*

*It is both unfortunate and offensive that you describe this program as a "roundup"—unfortunate because it is untrue and offensive because you know that it is untrue. Since 1982, our Project HELP has acted on a case-by-case basis to help a targeted group of seriously disabled homeless New Yorkers. No one, even you, has ever described its work as a "roundup." Although a broader definition will be applied so that we may intervene earlier, our new program will use the same case-by-case method and [be] directed at the same target population. If it wasn't a "roundup" under the old program, what makes it a "roundup" now?*

*In your letter, however, you did ask a question that is critical to the success of our efforts to help this group of homeless New Yorkers— "Where're the beds?" Regrettably, you asked it of the wrong component within the mental health care continuum. As I am sure you know but failed to acknowledge in your letter to me or your release to the press, presently the City's municipal hospital system has 1,122 acute care psychiatric beds. 402 of those beds, by the way, have been added since 1978 and 197 added in the last eighteen months. Another 162 beds are currently in the works. The 28-bed unit we are designating at Bellevue Hospital Center for this population was created so that we could be sure they don't have to compete for limited resources with other needy mentally ill patients. We will try to limit the numbers of people we bring into this unit, but if we identify more people who are seriously disturbed than the unit can handle, we will identify other beds either within Bellevue or at another HHC facility.*

*But the fact is that unless patients can be moved out of acute care beds into state intermediate- and long-term care beds, the system will continue to back up in the municipal hospitals and emergency rooms. Most of the patients coming into the emergency room wouldn't need to be there if there were adequate long-term care facilities, either inpatient or community residences.*

*Acute care beds will never substitute for the required expansion of long-term, intermediate care and community-based facilities for the mentally ill—all responsibilities of the state. I'm sure you've heard these numbers before, but since you seem to ignore them, I thought they would be worth mentioning. Since 1960, the number of state psychiatric beds in the City has dropped from 15,800 to a current low of 4,173. Stan Brezenoff back in 1985 asked you to raise your concerns about psychiatric overcrowding with the state—did you? I ask you to do the same again.*

*This is not to say that the state hasn't made efforts to increase its beds in communities, and it has created a substantial number. But the need is enormous and the numbers created in the community are a drop in the bucket compared with the dramatic declines on the institutional side. The state is also supporting the City's four-year facilities plan designed to move certain populations—primarily the mentally ill, elderly, and youth—out of shelters and into more appropriate long-term settings. A total of nearly 4,400 beds will be produced over four years as part of the initial plan. The City is in the process of expanding the plan to nearly 5,900 beds, and we will be submitting this to the state shortly for their review.*

*I have no intention of letting the state off the hook in this area or of abrogating my moral responsibility to make sure these people are not left on the streets when they require care. I wouldn't want anyone in my family treated that way, and I believe we as a city government and human family have a special responsibility to care for those who can't take care of themselves.*

*Finally, I am not distressed by the data you have on our cold weather alert policy, which shows that the police did not transport large numbers of people involuntarily last year. In fact, the policy was meant to have an indirect effect by encouraging people in need of shelter to seek it out when the weather gets cold. I am pleased that we did not have to resort to using the police for such transportation too often, in only five cases, and that in most instances, in 326 cases, the police were able to convince the person to go voluntarily to a shelter.*

*Thank you for your thoughts. I hope that you will communicate them to the state so that appropriate resources—hospital as well as community-based—can be made available for this population.*

*All the best.*

What's the latest on Project HELP, the program Bob was so quick to condemn? Well, from the beginning of the program, in October 1987, through April 1989, it made some 1,400 evaluations of the mentally ill homeless on the street. Of these, 460 were transported to the hospital for further evaluation, and 443 of these were ultimately admitted.

Of the 221 court hearings held to determine the appropriateness of admission or treatment for people brought in by Project HELP, the courts upheld the recommendations of city doctors in all but 21 of the cases.

Not quite the "roundup" Bob Hayes promised the world it would be or the infringement on constitutional rights Norman Siegel claimed it would be, right? Well, the *Times* says Bob now believes even advocates have "to tell the truth." Better late than never, I suppose.

# Gay Rights

Throughout my public life I have tried to ensure that homosexual men and women are able to exercise the same rights and enjoy the same protections against discrimination as heterosexual men and women.

As an unsuccessful candidate for State Assembly in 1962, I was considered in the political avant-garde because my three campaign planks called for establishing the right of women to have abortions, allowing for divorces on grounds other than just adultery, and repealing criminal laws against consensual sodomy between adults. When I ran for Mayor in 1977, I said I would support and sign a gay rights bill, which I did when, ultimately, one was enacted by the City Council in 1986.

Pending passage of such legislation, I said I would issue an executive order prohibiting discrimination by city agencies on the basis of sexual orientation in the areas of housing and employment. It was the first substantive order—Executive Order No. 4—that I issued upon taking office. On April 25, 1980, I went an important step further and issued Executive Order No. 50, extending the prohibition to cover not-for-profit agencies and private firms which received city contracts to perform services or provide goods.

For four years Executive Order No. 50 generated very little controversy. But then John O'Connor became Roman Catholic Archbishop of New York. He didn't believe I had the authority as Mayor to issue such an order, especially since there was no federal, state, or local law authorizing me to do so.

He also believed that requiring Catholic Charities—the Archdiocese's social services arm—to comply with such an order would violate the First Amendment by interfering with the Church's religious teaching on homosexuality. As a result, the Archdiocese joined a lawsuit filed by the Salvation Army and Agudath Isreal—two other religious organizations which provided social services under city contracts—to overturn my order.

Despite the fact that the city and the Archdiocese were in litigation over Executive Order No. 50, Cardinal O'Connor and I became and have remained good friends. "Only in New York," His Eminence has said, "could two people who sue each other so much still be friends."

On Christmas Eve he would invite me to attend Midnight Mass at St. Patrick's Cathedral. It bothered some gays that I went. "It has taken a lot of courage for you to speak as openly and forcefully as you have in favor of equal rights for same-sex oriented citizens," Jim Cooper wrote in *The New York Native* in April 1985. But he was "shocked" that I had "honored" Archbishop O'Connor by attending Mass. It's "like you are saying to him—'I'm challenging your homophobic disregard for equal treatment of all persons, but don't take me seriously about it.' " It was, he said, like "fraternizing with the enemy."

I wrote to Cooper in reply:

*I read your December 27 letter, which appeared in the January 28 edition of* The New York Native. *I am distressed with your apparent dismay, disappointment, and disillusionment with me, which comes, as you say, from the fact that I accepted Archbishop O'Connor's invitation to celebrate Christmas Eve at St. Patrick's. Your feeling is that*

113

*somehow that diminishes my support of those actions I have taken to prohibit discrimination based on sexual orientation.*

*If I adopted your position that I should have no friendships—personal, social, or professional—with people with whom I have a disagreement, I suspect there are very few people with whom I could ever meet. Isn't it possible for people to disagree on a major issue, such as the death penalty, racial quotas, discrimination based on sexual orientation, discrimination based on sex, opposition to the State of Israel, and a whole host of other issues and still maintain mutual respect and friendship for one another?*

*Why not look at it another way. Here am I who take the position which the Archbishop disagrees with and he invites me to attend the service. Should I be less open-hearted than he? Would that help your cause and the cause of a whole host of other people on a whole host of other matters? I doubt it.*

*Think about it.*

*All the best.*

When you've prevailed on the merits in a public policy debate, sometimes your critics will decide to shift the terms of the debate by questioning your motives and attacking your character. And the attacks can be of the most personal, most private sort.

Regrettably, that happened during the controversy over Executive Order No. 50. "For all we know Koch may be the quintessence of macho heterosexuality," wrote Rabbi Choneh Sarner in the *New York City Tribune*, "but there are those who may not choose to bet on that."

I replied:

*I was amazed but not offended by the letter of Rabbi Choneh Sarner which appeared in the April 25 edition of the* Tribune.

*Many of us engaged in the civil rights demonstrations of the sixties. And in my case, I participated as a lawyer representing black and white defendants in Mississippi who were falsely charged with assault because they had engaged in a voter registration drive. Should I have worried that someone might have whispered that perhaps I was black?*

*The rabbi also writes, "It is also an undeniable fact that Mayor Koch has become the target of frequent ridicule and jokes dealing with his ardent preoccupation with the homosexual cause. Now for all we know, Koch may be the very quintessence of macho heterosexuality, but there are those who may not choose to bet on that." Should that statement deter me from doing what is right?*

*I believe that we are all the children of God. Indeed, the rabbi should know that whenever I mention God I upset some people who apparently believe no public official should ever refer to the Supreme Deity. Nevertheless, I have and will continue to do so. And because I believe we are all the children of God and that the private sexual acts of consenting adults are just that—private—and not to be the subject of governmental supervision, the government must not discriminate against individuals based on their homosexuality or heterosexuality.*

*As I read the rabbi's letter, I thought to myself, what did he think of the King of Denmark and the Christians of Denmark when in order to save the Jews from the Nazis many of them, the King included, put on the Yellow Star of David? The rabbi should know that when the Nazis took to the concentration camps those they believed did not deserve to live, included in that group were the Jews, gypsies, homosexuals, Communists, and others whom they saw as less than human. And when these people were shoved into the incinerators, in some cases to be burned alive, or into the showers of poison, to have their lives snuffed out, do you think as God received them that he asked whether they were Jews, Christians, gypsies, homosexuals, or Communists? Or did he simply say, "Come to me." I think he said the latter. Apparently the rabbi does not.*

Regrettably, the kind of homophobic hysteria which surrounds gay issues and AIDS issues is as strong as ever. How do I know? Well, the most glaring illustration is the fact that the State Senate refuses to pass a bill that would increase the penalties against persons found guilty of bias crimes simply because the definition of such crimes in the proposed bill includes crimes against individuals because they're homosexual. The Senate says it's not a real problem. But it most certainly is.

Every time there's a reported bias incident involving assaults against people because of their race, ethnicity, or sexual orientation, I invite the victims to City Hall to explain what happened. If the victims are in accord, after we've talked privately I'll call in reporters to hear the story. The more publicity is given to such outrageous acts and the more those perpetrating these crimes are held up to public scorn, the more likely it is that others will not copy them and engage in the same kind of hateful activity.

Newspapers generally give a lot of attention to such incidents when they occur. But they seem to give far more coverage to incidents motivated by racism than to those motivated by homophobia. In the summer of 1988, two gay men—David Frank and Barry Finnegan— were set upon by a group of young thugs on Manhattan's Upper West Side. Mr. Frank's arm was broken in two places by a baseball bat and Mr. Finnegan was stabbed repeatedly.

The police determined that the attack had occurred because the thugs didn't like David and Barry's sexual orientation, and initially the incident received press coverage. But the story died quickly. Too quickly, in my view.

I invited the two men to my office to meet with the press. As far as I can recall, no newspaper, wire service, or radio station ran a story about our meeting. The lack of coverage disturbed me because Mr. Frank had used the occasion to report that, in a television interview shortly after the attack, his landlord had threatened to evict a friend of his because of his sexual orientation. In New York City, that's against the law.

The next Saturday morning, in my weekly radio commentary on WINS, I spoke about my meeting with David and Barry and expressed my surprise that there'd been so little press coverage, especially since a bill was then pending in the State Legislature in Albany to impose stiff penalties against those who assault people because of their race, religion, ethnic origin, sex, and, yes, sexual orientation.

"Every other time I've met with victims of racist, sexist, religious, or ethnic violence, stories have appeared in the papers the next day. But not in this case of homophobic violence," I observed in my broadcast, "not even in a time when the Senate is debating what to do, indeed whether to do anything, to prevent such crimes. . . . Why, then, was there an apparent newspaper blackout on my meetings with Mr. Frank or with gay leaders? If outrageous violence or invidious discrimination isn't news, what is?"

Usually, WINS would invite someone on the other side of the issue I was addressing in my weekly commentary to do a rebuttal. On this particular occasion and this particular issue, WINS invited the editors of three of the city's largest newspapers to reply. Frankly, I didn't think their comments made much sense. So I drafted a letter to send to them. One was to go to Jane Amsterdam, then the editor of the *New York Post:*

*I wanted to thank you for taking time to respond to my WINS commentary of Saturday, September 3, concerning continuing press coverage of homophobic violence of the sort recently directed against*

David Frank and Barry Finnegan on the Upper West Side of Manhattan.

As you know, I believe that the more press attention that is focused on such outrageous incidents, the more likely it is that our legislators in Albany will pass the legislation necessary to protect its victims and, I hope, prevent further increases in such attacks. In this regard, I do want to express my appreciation to the New York Post for its coverage of the incident involving Mr. Frank and Mr. Finnegan.

At the same time, I do believe that you have missed the point of my commentary. As you suggested, "a journalist's role is not to lobby" for a particular position, "but to cover the facts." The reason I was so surprised that there were no press reports to my meeting with Mr. Frank was that he reported new facts—to wit, that a landlord threatened on television to evict a friend of his because of his sexual orientation. To me, those facts should have been presented to the public.

After all, if a victim of a bias incident had reported in the days following the attack that a friend of his was being evicted because of his race or ethnic origin, wouldn't the Post have seen it as a fact worth reporting and, indeed, a problem worth calling to the attention of its readers? I believe so. Then why not report the new facts concerning discrimination [against] someone because of his sexual orientation? It's just as newsworthy, just as big a problem.

I agree with you that, except on editorial pages, reporters shouldn't lobby for one position or another. But for readers and legislators and, even, editorial writers to know what's happening in the world—for example, that there is housing discrimination against homosexuals— they often depend on newspapers. Not until newspapers help make them aware of a problem can they go to work trying to craft a solution. Obviously, the kind of discrimination which Mr. Frank, Mr. Finnegan, and others suffer is in need of just such a solution.

All the best.

The letters to the editors of these three papers were never sent. After drafting a letter, I usually ask Dan Wolf, a longtime friend and my special advisor, to edit it. "It's a thin-gruel lecture to the editors," Dan said of the draft. "Worse than that, it sounds like special pleading to get your name in the papers. . . . Are you suggesting that the papers give coverage to everyone who feels that he or a friend has been subjected to bigotry?"

I took Dan's advice. In hindsight, however, I probably should have sent the letters. After all, maybe the only way to persuade people who are tempted to engage in such discrimination and violence, whether motivated by racism, sexism, or homophobia, that such acts are simply unacceptable in our city is to hold up those who commit such acts to public scorn. The surest, fastest way to do that is to put such criminals on the front page.

I don't believe the response to AIDS of any other city in the country matches New York's—quantitatively or qualitatively. Ever since the disease was first reported by the federal Centers for Disease Control in the summer of 1981, the City of New York has been at the forefront in providing services to people with AIDS and in trying to prevent the spread of the HIV virus.

To the best of my knowledge, for example, the City of New York was the first city to enter into an AIDS surveillance agreement with the CDC, the first to include people with AIDS as members of a protected class under my administration's anti-discrimination orders, the first to engage in widespread distribution of condoms to reduce AIDS transmission, the first to close bathhouses and other facilities which permit high-risk sexual activity, the first to provide rental assistance to people with AIDS so that they can maintain their current residences, the first to establish an enriched foster care system for children with AIDS, the first to provide a local subsidy to assist with the development of a nursing home for people with AIDS, and the first to go to court to assert the right of a child with AIDS to attend public schools.

And that's not all. To the best of my knowledge, we were also the first city to fund extensive AIDS outreach and education campaigns in the intravenous-drug-using community; the first city to fund anonymous counseling and testing centers; the first to establish pediatric day-care programs for infants with AIDS; to provide local tax dollars to build housing for people with AIDS; to sponsor the development of multimedia AIDS education campaigns targeted to particular risk groups; to move forward on a needle exchange program to prevent AIDS transmission among intravenous drug users; to establish an AIDS anti-discrimination unit; to provide local subsidies for the development of an AIDS research laboratory; to expand services to include not just those with full-blown AIDS or who are HIV-ill, but also to those with depressed immune systems; and the first city to provide AZT, bactrim, and aerosolized pentamadine therapies without regard to a person's ability to pay and despite the lack of federal reimbursement.

Yet, despite all that we have done, the critics give us very little credit. They want us to do even more, regardless of whether we have the resources to do it and regardless of the consequences for other essential city services. And even when they do give us credit, reporters don't pay any attention. Stories about a city doing things right, after all, don't sell newspapers.

# The Needle Exchange Program

One of the most controversial actions taken by my administration began as a result of a 1985 memorandum sent to me by then–New York City Health Commissioner Dr. David Sencer. In it he proposed that we seek a change in state law to eliminate the requirement that sterile hypodermic needles be purchased only with a doctor's prescription.

His reasoning was simple but sound. Even then it was clear that the fastest-growing group of people with the human immune deficiency virus which causes AIDS were intravenous drug users. Indeed, it's since been determined that, thanks in large part to outreach and education programs funded by not-for-profit organizations and the city, the rate of AIDS seropositivity among homosexual men is now practically zero.

But in the IV community, where it is apparently a custom for one addict to share his or her needle with others, the HIV virus is spreading quickly. Already, in fact, some 60 percent of the city's heroin addicts carry the virus, which, absent an AIDS cure or vaccine, means certain death. If that 60 percent shares their dirty needles with the other 40 percent, they'll soon also be under sentence of death.

By eliminating the prescription requirement, Dr. Sencer hoped to eliminate the practice of needle sharing and, as a result, reduce the prospect of the HIV virus being transmitted from one addict to others. On the surface, it's not so radical an idea. After all, currently thirty-nine states allow hypodermic needles to be bought without a prescription. In New York, which probably has the largest concentration of intravenous drug users and certainly has the largest number of reported AIDS cases in the country, it makes medical sense to follow the example of these thirty-nine other states, make sterile hypodermic needles more easily available, and thereby cut the spread of AIDS.

But what makes medical sense doesn't always make political sense.

Knowing that Dr. Sencer's proposal was sure to spark controversy, particularly in the black and Hispanic communities, which have considerable numbers of heroin addicts and where easier access to needles could be portrayed as encouraging the use of drugs, I wrote to every district attorney and U.S. attorney in the city asking for their views on this subject. I knew that without the support of the law enforcement community, no bill to change the law would pass.

Their reaction was fast, their opposition unanimous. The proposal, they generally argued, could be seen as putting the government's imprimatur on the use of heroin, and, further, sharing needles was a part of addict culture that government would be unable to change. The risks, they felt, outweighed any potential gain.

Frankly, I shared their skepticism. I publicly said that I did not believe that providing easier access to or distributing sterile needles would have the result Dr. Sencer expected. I knew that as a layperson I was not qualified to decide the matter adequately. As a purely medical decision, it seemed to me to be best left in the hands of Dr. Sencer and other health experts.

But the responses from the law enforcement community clearly indicated that it was not a purely medical matter. By the time Dr. Sencer, a first-rate public health official and a friend, left the Health Department to take a job in Boston, it appeared as though his proposal was dead.

His successor, Dr. Stephen Joseph, soon raised the idea in a different form. Rather than moving forward with a wholesale, statewide change in the law, he proposed a limited study to determine whether or not a city-sponsored needle exchange program would reduce AIDS transmission. One hundred addicts would receive free needles from the Health Department, and their rate of HIV infection would be compared with that of a hundred addicts in a control group who did not receive sterile needles. It was, by the way, the kind of limited research approach that had been recommended by the National Academy of Sciences in its report on AIDS.

Even Dr. Joseph's scaled-back proposal generated controversy. Submitted for approval by the state's Commissioner of Health, Dr. David Axelrod, it was not authorized for almost two years. Throughout this period, in fact, Dr. Axelrod sought to distance himself from direct involvement with the proposal, and generally his comments on the proposal were made through a spokesperson. He was doing his job, but without much enthusiasm.

Dr. Joseph was extraordinary in his support for the proposal, despite all the criticism he received. So was I, for that matter, since I took a lot of the flak as Mayor. An attack which particularly rankled Dr. Joseph was made by his friend Dr. Benny Prim, a black doctor who runs one of the largest methadone maintenance clinics in the city. When methadone first came on the scene as a "blocker" for heroin, providers like Dr. Prim were attacked for engaging in a form of genocide against the black and Hispanic communities by keeping them on drugs, albeit methadone. Ironically, Dr. Prim used the same kind of language against Dr. Joseph, his friend, in attacking the needle exchange program. Amazing.

One of the strongest criticisms of the program came from members of the City Council's Black and Hispanic Caucus, which is chaired by Enoch Williams, one of the most distinguished and able members of the Council. "As you must know," he wrote to me on behalf of the caucus in October 1988, "many medical professionals and others at the forefront of fighting drug abuse and counseling drug addicts oppose this program. . . . It is beyond all human reason and common sense for the city to hand out needles to drug addicts at a time when our police officers and our citizens have become casualties in the drug war."

Obviously, he and his caucus colleagues were very distressed. I sent them a letter, hoping to address and allay some of their concerns:

*I have your recent letter on behalf of the members of the Black and Hispanic Caucus, and I must disagree in the strongest terms with your characterization of the needle exchange study and its role in the protection of the health of New Yorkers.*

*We are at only the beginning of the worst epidemic in memory. AIDS is already the number-one killer of New York City men aged 25 to 44 and women aged 25 to 39. Almost 100 infants infected with the AIDS virus are born each month in this City. The AIDS virus has already infected half of the City's 200,000 intravenous drug users. It is spreading, virtually unabated, to the other half, and to their sex partners and their unborn children. If we do not slow its spread, it will ravage the City's poorest, drug-ridden communities and strike down not just IV drug users but whole families on an almost unimaginable scale.*

*I must face squarely what lies ahead. The decision to allow an investigation of needle exchange as a supportive bridge to drug treatment and AIDS prevention is not one that I take lightly or come to* easily. Certainly, it is not the measure of highest urgency; the rapid expansion of drug treatment program capacity is, and I have urged the state, where responsibility for drug treatment is lodged, for over a year to provide the authorization and resources for a rapid expansion of drug treatment in this City.

But I must face facts. Without enough treatment slots to give every addict treatment on demand, tens of thousands, currently hundreds of thousands, of IV drug addicts will remain outside of treatment.

Needle exchange may help. Your letter claims that "this needle exchange program would do nothing to alleviate the spread of AIDS." The best available public health evidence suggests the contrary. Needle exchange has been tried elsewhere, with some success. No one knows if it would work here; it merits a trial in this time of crisis. I have said before that I don't believe it will work, but it is my obligation to do everything in my power to discover its possible worth to protect the health of the public, particularly the increasing numbers of minority women and children who are being infected through exposure to drug use.

The study has been extensively debated, approved by State Health Commissioner Axelrod, and widely adjudged to be scientifically sound. Those who have either supported this needle exchange trial here or endorsed it in principle include the Surgeon General of the United States, the National Academy of Sciences Institute of Medicine Task Force on AIDS, the American Public Health Association, the New York County Medical Society, the Committee on Medicine and Law of the New York City Bar Association, the World Health Organization, and a number of the nation's leading drug treatment and public health experts.

No less an expert than the Surgeon General has said, "If a needle and/or syringe program could contain in any way the spread of HIV, who could possibly be against it?"

I regret that as leaders of communities that are being devastated by the AIDS epidemic, you have chosen to align yourselves, not with this attempt to find another weapon to slow the spread of AIDS, but with those whose misplaced concern or mistaken reasoning have allowed this issue to become bitterly divisive.

What will the people who do not want this study in their neighborhoods—this trial, which involves only 200 people, less than one-half of one percent of the City's IV drug users—do in the years ahead when they are faced with the incalculably greater tragedy of thousands of

*AIDS deaths tearing apart their entire communities? Will they not then turn to you and demand, with justifiable anger, "Why didn't we try everything possible to stop this disease when we had the chance?"*

*I must allow every available reasonable measure to arrest the rampaging AIDS virus. Based on a review of the evidence before me, I believe this study reasonable.*

*All the best.*

Another criticism—justifiable in my view—had to do with the fact that the proposed sites for the two needle exchange clinics were very close to schools. Since I have supported legislation, which has since become law, to impose double penalties against people who sell drugs within 1,000 feet of a school, it made no sense to me or to others to locate needle exchange clinics which would serve drug users within 1,000 feet of a school.

So I directed Dr. Joseph to relocate the facilities, and today the needle exchange program operates out of only one site, Health Department headquarters at 125 Worth Street in lower Manhattan. Addicts from all over town have to come to that one site to participate in the program, and, not surprisingly, it took a very long time for addicts to participate in the numbers planned. I wonder if that has anything to do with the fact that the Health Department headquarters is in an area surrounded by state and federal courts and just a couple of blocks from 1 Police Plaza, home of "New York's Finest."

Thanks to the hard work of Dr. Joseph and his staff, the number of addicts in the experiment is finally approaching two hundred. Had it enjoyed broader public support that would have permitted it to go forward without controversy, I believe the needle exchange experiment might have demonstrated its efficacy at reducing AIDS transmission. But because of the controversy and the resulting changes in the program, ultimately I don't think it will yield valid scientific results. On the other hand, it has encouraged scores of addicts to seek help for their habits and to go into drug treatment programs. It may not have been the intended result of the experiment, but it is still a good result.

# The Helms Amendment

AIDS is not a political cause or a religious crusade. It is a disease. Regrettably, some AIDS advocates seem to care more about the political change they can effect than about the victims of the disease. On the other side of the issue, there are those who see AIDS as God's revenge on gay men. Both sides do a great disservice to AIDS victims and to society.

Jesse Helms, the senior United States Senator from North Carolina, is one of the anti-government types who consolidated his political fame and fortune during the so-called Reagan Revolution. For him, gay rights is anathema. And in 1987 Senator Helms took the lead in fanning the flames of homophobic hysteria. He was able to attach a rider to a routine appropriations bill that would deny federal funding to any programs that "promote, encourage, or condone homosexual activities." His target was the Gay Men's Health Crisis, an organization which has been at the forefront of caring for people with AIDS and of educating others on how to avoid transmission.

The people served by GMHC, said the Senator, are "perverts" and are not worthy of federal help. It was an unbelievable statement. Even more unbelievable, though, was the fact that only forty-nine members of the U.S. Senate and the House of Representatives stood up against Helms and tried to vote down his outrageous amendment.

I was shocked. Hence the following op-ed piece in *The New York Times:*

> "We have to call a spade a spade," said Senator Jesse Helms in offering an amendment to the fiscal 1988 appropriations bill for the Departments of Labor, Health and Human Services, and Education, "and a perverted human being a perverted human being." Ironic comments, indeed, given the profound perversity of the policy his amendment advances.
>
> It prohibits the Federal Centers for Disease Control from funding AIDS programs that "promote, encourage, or condone homosexual activities." The Senate passed it, 96 to 2. Only 47 House members had

the good sense and common decency to resist homophobic hysteria and oppose the amendment.

Mr. Helms introduced it because he's upset with the New York Gay Men's Health Crisis. The organization has established a brilliant reputation in caring for and counseling those with AIDS and in educating others on how to prevent the spread of AIDS.

It serves gay men—Mr. Helms's "perverts"—because they're a primary AIDS risk group. Gays comprise about 10 percent of the United States' adult population, or 20 million people. If only half are male, 10 million men are at risk and in need of education and counseling on how to cut the risk. That's why the Gay Men's Health Crisis and organizations like it around the country exist.

The amendment, protests Senator Edward M. Kennedy, is "toothless" and a "foolish exercise." Then why did he vote to make it the law of the land, particularly since it ignores the proven effectiveness of AIDS education efforts and severely impedes our ability to expand them?

To date, New York has had 11,513 AIDS cases reported; of these, 6,605 have died. Of the total cases, 55 percent are homosexual and bisexual men. Among these, the Gay Men's Health Crisis and city educational efforts have helped contribute to a decline in the seroconversion rate to 1 percent annually. In nonscientific terms, this means that if you took blood samples from homosexual or bisexual men one year and found them not infected with the AIDS virus, there's only a 1 percent chance that samples from the same men would be infected the next year.

Among intravenous drug users there's an 8 percent seroconversion rate. Obviously, education changes behavior among those whose faculties aren't impaired and enslaved by needles and drugs.

Gay Men's Health Crisis materials, complains Senator Helms, use blunt words and sexually graphic illustrations that "perpetuate the AIDS problem." But those the materials reach aren't innocents who'll be shocked by such literature. They already practice sex; they want to know how to practice it more safely. The organization tells them and thereby helps save lives.

If we're shy with one risk group, we'll probably make the same mistake with others. Today, AIDS is found principally among men who engage in homosexual or bisexual practices or intravenous drug abuse. By 1991, some 40,000 people in New York and 270,000 nationally may have AIDS. Some will be heterosexuals who've had intercourse with a bisexual man or a drug user. If they don't know how to protect themselves, how will they? Cutting off federal funds to organizations like the Gay Men's Health Crisis may only help spread the disease, causing the deaths of not only homosexuals but heterosexuals of both sexes and, most tragic of all, innocent infants.

Senator Helms may not like homosexuals. But he and those who voted for the amendment should remember that homosexuals—and intravenous drug users—are the sons and daughters of families who love them. They too deserve protection against the gravest public health threat our nation faces.

Regrettably, lousy politics overwhelmed good public health policy. Apparently fearing an adverse reaction that a homophobic demagogue might inflame in their home states or districts, members of Congress gave in to homophobic hysteria. Only a few had the courage to vote against this foolish amendment. I commend Senators Daniel Patrick Moynihan and Lowell Weicker and members of New York's House delegation who joined the honor roll: Gary L. Ackerman, Bill Green, Major R. Owens, James H. Scheuer, and Ted Weiss. They hold the moral high ground.

The amendment is a fait accompli. The blot on the Congress can't be erased. But what can't be undone can be uncovered. That alone may insure that future Congressional action on AIDS ignores the homophobes by supporting programs and policies that have proved so effective in fighting this tragic disease.

Senator Helms tried to have the last word. A few weeks later a letter appeared in the *Times* taking me to task for my "mean-spirited" piece. "The Mayor," he wrote, "appears willing to play Russian roulette" by allowing gay men to get counseling on safer sex techniques. "I am convinced that it would be far better to remove the bullet and discard the gun." Ignorance is bliss, right, Senator Helms?

Fortunately, the Helms amendment was killed later in conference committee. But that still doesn't explain why it was allowed to get that far in the first place. Of the 535 members who constitute the House and Senate, fewer than 1 in 10 voted against the Helms amendment.

Where, I wondered when I read the roll call, were all the liberals? Ted Kennedy, who voted for the amendment, called it a "foolish exercise." But had it become the law of the land, it would have been a frightening and terrible signal that homophobes were in control of the Congress and homosexuals and others at risk of AIDS had better be on the run.

Thanks to the acquiescence at the beginning of the process of illiberal liberals like Ted Kennedy, with the Helms amendment the homophobic hysteria almost overwhelmed the U.S. Senate. The Senate is supposed to be immune from the mob. Why on this occasion did it so cravenly cater to it? It's a question Senator Kennedy and others have not answered. Until they do, it's a blot that cannot be erased, a vote that cannot be forgiven.

# "Ax" and "Ask"

In September 1985, I sent a memo to then–Schools Chancellor Nathan Quinones. I wasn't aware then how controversial it would soon become:

*I want to pursue our conversation of last week, which tracks the conversation I had with Frank Macchiarola early on in this administration. What concerned me then and still concerns me is our failure to do more to bring our students—and teachers—to the point of speaking English correctly.*

*I was appalled when I visited one of our high schools several years ago to discover that there were teachers who pronounced "asked" as "axed." It appears that this linguistic violation is extremely common. Of course, there are many other egregious examples. I know there must be programs which seek to address these failures, but they are obviously inadequate. I facetiously suggested to Macchiarola that he embark upon a new program and call it "The rain in Spain stays mainly in the plain" program, but to no avail. Maybe that isn't a bad title for a new program.*

To me it seemed like a good idea. To Chancellor Quinones it seemed like a good idea. But then we heard the thunderous editorial voice of *The New York Times.*

"Anyone would be annoyed to hear a teacher 'ax' a question," it commented shortly after I sent my memo. "It's understandable that Mr. Koch, who pronounces his own words with e-lab-o-rate care, would be especially bothered. The problem here is not pronunciation but priorities. In New York City, four school-age children out of every ten drop out of school before graduation. . . . Everyone would be glad if

New York City schoolchildren were better spoken. But if Mr. Koch were truly nonpermissive, he'd focus his educational energies on not permitting so many children to drop out of school altogether. His 'ax' memo is a dis-trac-tion."

To say the least, I was surprised at the *Times*'s attitude. Its editorial writers are committed to educational excellence, and though staid in reputation, usually the paper keeps an open mind on innovative proposals. So I thought I might be able to change its view with a humorous but substantive letter to the editor. Was I wrong:

*Your October 2, 1985, editorial criticizes my request that Schools Chancellor Nathan Quinones establish a program to raise the consciousness of students and teachers on the importance of speaking English well . . . and concludes my concern "is a dis-trac-tion" from the real issues affecting our schools. I disagree.*

*Permit me an historical example. It is a cold, blustery January 20, 1961, as we stand at the steps of our nation's Capitol. A new President has just taken the oath of office and is delivering his first inaugural address. It is a stirring speech, a great speech, outlining the challenges of the age and exhorting the American people to respond.*

*We are in the palms of his rhetorical hands. One last flourish and 200 million countrymen will be ready to follow his lead. He is knocking at the threshold of oratorical greatness. "Ax not what your country can do for you," he thunders, "ax what you can do for your country."*

*Ka-boom! The door slams and a murmur runs through the crowd. "What did he say? Who does he think he is, the President of Cuber? Throw the jerk out of office!" There but for the proper verb would have gone the oratorical reputation of John Kennedy and, maybe, the political aspirations of an entire generation. Had he flubbed instead of flourished, would we still recall his stirring phrase? I don thinx so (sic).*

*If we are what we eat, we certainly are what we say and how we say it. Indeed, you acknowledge that when you quote one of my favorite words—ridiculous—with due deference to my syllabic preferences. If it is of consequence to you that I, a grown man, place the emphasis on the second syllable rather than the first, third, or fourth, isn't it also of consequence that a young child puts "ks" where "sk" belongs and, worse, that the child does so following a teacher's example?*

*Of course it is. That's why I have requested that Chancellor Quinones examine steps that might improve the speaking of English by our* *schoolchildren and our teachers and why I am pleased he will allocate $1.5 million for such a program.*

*It is ri-dí-cu-lous for you to suggest that this $1.5 million program is inappropriate because it does not address what all of us agree is a priority—to wit, cutting the number of drop-outs. In fact, this year we're spending $32 million in new state and city funds to address the drop-out problem and have announced that any ninth grader who completes high school is guaranteed admission to the City University of New York.*

*Your assumption is that we can address only one problem at a time. It's like arguing that the Police Commissioner shouldn't attack the drug traffic until the homicide rate is zero or that the Transit Authority shouldn't fight subway graffiti until every train runs on time. It's a foolish argument.*

*That should have been obvious, even to the* Times. *So let me ax the* Times *sumpin—wud u hyer reportas hoo belief in reporting all the nus that fits to print?*

The letter to the *Times* didn't appear for four years. Shortly after I sent it, I received a call from an editor asking that I cut it back significantly and omit what he considered to be comments potentially offensive to those readers of the *Times*—particularly minority readers—who might occasionally commit the grammatical errors with which I was concerned.

My own view was that the *Times* was being overly and unnecessarily cautious in the matter. The simple fact is that too many of New York City's students and too many of their teachers—white, Hispanic, Asian, and African-American—commit too many errors of these sorts. Every New Yorker knows it. So why was the *Times* so afraid to allow a free discussion of the problem and a potential solution? After all, nothing I had written was intended to be derogatory to anyone.

The *Times* wouldn't relent. "You don't cut," they said, "we don't print." I'm not the kind of person or writer who likes editorial ultimatums. So I refused the editor's request. And the letter went unpublished. When the issue arose again in 1989, however, I'm pleased to report that Sam Roberts, a columnist for the *Times*, printed most of my letter on the front page of its Metro section.

Yes, passages deemed "offensive" by a *Times* editor in 1985 were published in 1989. I still can't understand what cooled the censor's heels. Maybe it was just that distinguished paper's way of admitting that, as they say, I was a man ahead of my *Times.*

Mixed editorial signals and unresolved mysteries notwithstanding, our pilot program worked marvelously well. In February 1989, in fact, then-Chancellor Richard Green sent me a memo outlining both his short- and long-term plans to establish a system-wide "Putting Your Best Speech Forward" program. As soon as I'd read it, I sent a reply:

*I have your memo of February 22 regarding improving oral communication skills. Your memo is superb. Both the short-term and long-term programs that you are now committed to fulfill my maximum expectations, and I am grateful.*

*I am going to release our correspondence because I think that all of those concerned about education will, after reading your memo, sing "Hosanna to the Highest!"*

A final comment is in order. As a born-and-bred New Yorker, I'm guilty of committing some grammatical errors myself. When a reporter asks me a question, I'm not reluctant to give an answer which includes sentences long enough for most people to consider paragraphs. When you look back on those sentences—millions over the course of twelve years—you'll almost always find a subject and a verb and you'll notice I don't mix up my syntax.

But I do have an annoying habit—too many "ums" and "ahs" punctuate my spoken words. In the middle of the controversy over speaking English well, a woman from Liberty, New York, took me to task for condemning the mistakes of others but not confessing my own. I wrote back:

*Thank you for your letter on my speaking style. I may be an author, but I am not an orator. Nevertheless, I've gotten this far with a lot of "ums" and "ahs," so I guess I'm stuck with the habit. But I do appreciate your concern.*
*All the best.*

If it's true that you can't teach an old dog new tricks, maybe the "ums" and "ahs" for which I am known will continue to come trippingly off my lips. But even if I'm a lost cause, we shouldn't consider our schoolchildren lost too. If they're the future of New York City, let's make sure they're prepared for it, by helping them learn how to read, to write, to do math, and, yes, to speak English well.

# A Fish Story—New York–Style

I'm not a fisherman. But I do have a fish story. A major issue in the 1977 mayor's race was whether the city should build a proposed 4.2 mile highway along the Hudson River on Manhattan's lower West Side. As a candidate, I opposed the project known as Westway.

On becoming Mayor, however, I took a second look and realized that the traffic congestion Westway would relieve, the jobs it would create through development, and the taxes it would generate for a financially strapped city made it a project worth supporting. It was, my opponents later charged, a flip-flop. But what's wrong with changing your mind on the merits?

Building Westway called for landfill in that part of the Hudson that laps up against the southwestern tip of Manhattan Island. Do that, the environmentalists warned, and you'll destroy a good chunk of the breeding grounds of the striped bass. Millions of dollars were spent, hundreds of engineers put to work to find a way for the striped bass to continue to cavort and the city to have a much-needed highway. In early 1985 it appeared as though we'd answered all of the environmentalists' challenges, satisfied the courts, gotten the necessary permits from the Army Corps of Engineers, and were ready to break ground on Westway.

Not so fast, said members of the New Jersey Congressional delegation, who as economic competitors were seeking to do us in. Both of that state's Senators and eleven of its fourteen Congressmen introduced legislation to block federal funding for Westway. As a result of the time limitations imposed by the Congress on our right to draw down the Westway highway funds, ultimately, the Governor and I had to throw in the towel and abandon Westway for fear of losing over a billion dollars in federal highway funds.

Coincidentally, in late 1985 *The National Lampoon* asked me to write a piece for its "Mad as Hell" issue on what was making me really angry. It was like dangling red meat in front of a hungry shark. Plenty was on my mind. I could have complained about the devastating effects President Reagan and his particular brand of economics were having on cities like New York. Complained about the fact that every good idea I had to improve the schools, to help people get off welfare and into the job market, or to expand the city's supply of affordable housing seemed to take forever and a day to get done. Even complained about a New Jersey Congressional delegation so shortsighted as to kill a project which would have greatly benefited both their state and mine. Instead, I wrote the following for *The Lampoon:*

I have something of a reputation for speaking out on controversial topics, for telling both individuals and groups exactly what I think of them, with no holds barred. Nevertheless, close friends and advisers were alarmed to learn that I planned to lash out at a special group that, until now, has pretty much had its way in New York City.

"They have powerful contacts in Washington," I was warned. "One word against them and you'll be pilloried on every front page in the nation."

Maybe so. But there comes a time when a man has to stand up and say what's on his mind. So damn the denunciations, clear the decks, and pass the ammunition! Ed Koch is going toe-to-toe with the striped bass.

Yeah, you heard me. Striped bass. The "Mr. Big" of the fish mob. Piscine tyrants who loiter in the Hudson River, aching for a chance to mug a highway.

You've probably heard the story by now. How the state and the city of New York have been trying to build a highway called Westway along the West Side of Manhattan. You're probably just as outraged as I am that this important link in the interstate highway system has been delayed for years because the striped bass lobby convinced a judge their fishy friends would have no place to mate if we put a little landfill in the Hudson.

I tried to be nice about it. I explained that some of my best friends are snail darters. I even offered to build the bass a motel in Poughkeepsie. "No dice," the fishfaces replied. "Our delicate bass prefer the underwater charm of rotting piers and the organic ambience of sewer outlets."

It seems hard to believe that such a Stygian species could sink any lower. But lower they have sunk. The bass now have friends in New Jersey.

Well, t.s. for the stripers. Their dirty little secret is out. Their interiors are toxic. They are contaminated by chemicals with dangerous initials. New York State health authorities have banned the sale of striped bass caught in western Long Island Sound, but I have it on good authority that some of these aquatic chemistry sets are swimming east to get themselves hooked and netted.

Don't let them get away with it. Fight back now, or one day soon a judge may forbid us to clean up our rivers and streams. On what grounds? It's obvious. If they can't snack on toxic waste and sewage, striped bass just can't be themselves.

The tide began to turn when the striped bass around New York City was found to be toxic. State Commissioner of Environmental Protection Henry G. Williams reported in March 1985 that the level of polychlorinated biphenyls—PCBs—"in striped bass taken from marine waters in New York in 1984 have consistently and significantly exceeded 2 parts per million." *The New York Times* said the commissioner believed that such striped bass should not be consumed, "in the interests of public health." The *Times* also suggested that the state was "concerned about the impact on the commercial fisheries" in the event of a ban on consuming striped bass.

I immediately wrote to Dr. David Sencer, the city's Health Commissioner. "In a strange way," I said, the quandary raised by Commissioner Williams reminded me of Henrik Ibsen's 1882 play, *An Enemy of the People*. In that play, I said, "the town administration did not want to make public the fact that the water used at the town's celebrated spa was contaminated and dangerous. And when a doctor made it public, he was branded 'an enemy of the people.' In truth, he became a martyr for the people.

"Fortunately," I added, "there is no need for you or me to become a martyr in this matter." Instead, I asked Dr. Sencer to determine what the facts were. He reported back that shipments of striped bass arriving each morning at Fulton Fish Market were showing dangerously high levels of polychlorinated biphenyls. PCBs had been found to cause cancer in laboratory rats.

Revenge was sweet. "I'm asking people to think not twice but four times before you order striped bass," I warned New York City's restaurant-going citizenry upon receiving Dr. Sencer's advisory. "I can tell you of a wonderful alternative. Try Norwegian salmon," I urged, "sautéed with a little garlic." Norwegian salmon sautéed in garlic as an alternative to striped bass à la PCB? Now that made sense to me. But not to *The New York Times*.

"The Mayor of New York," it wrote in an editorial note, "is a man who knows his onions. And his scallions. And his shallots. Not to mention his Peking duck, his lasagna bolognese, and his steak *aux pommes frites.*" But salmon and garlic, it argued, are "a culinary misalliance. Marry the first's cool diffidence to the second's saucy intrusiveness and the result is one long argument. The garlic shouts, the salmon whimpers . . . ah, no, it doesn't bear thinking about."

So I invited my skeptical friends at the *Times* to a sit-down at the Bridge Café, where they might sample Norwegian salmon sautéed with a little garlic. I, of course, loved the fare. The salmon was just perfect, the garlic just right.

I eagerly awaited a verdict from the *Times*'s taste buds. "The Mayor, who surely wanted us to eat our words, promptly invited several interested parties to a salmon-and-garlic tasting," Mary Cantwell wrote the next day in collaboration with Max Frankel, both of whom had attended the lunch. "Our conclusion is this: what you get when you marry one to the other is not so much a war as a retreat. The garlic conquered . . . and the salmon just swam away."

I wrote the following letter to Max Frankel at the *Times* the day the note appeared:

*Lunch yesterday was perfect. The Norwegian salmon salted with garlic may or may not please every palate, but it certainly provided the basis for a good discussion. We started with salmon and ended with Gross, with lots in between.*

*Your colleague Mary has an extraordinary wit and she writes superbly, and that includes today's editorial note.*

*Garlic aside, sometimes I wonder if my travail will ever end. Garlicky salmon will clearly never replace the invidious striped bass. That I must come up with a replacement is clear from the attached memo sent to me by Commissioner David Sencer.*

*All the best.*

"The shipments of striped bass to the Fulton Fish Market," Dr. Sencer's note to me reported, "have decreased from 10,000 pounds per day to 300. Never underestimate the power of your advice."

Generally people do take my culinary advice. Indeed, as Mayor I often gave out-of-towners a list of the best restaurants for Chinese and Italian cuisines, my two favorites. "Just tell them you want what the Mayor eats," I would advise. There are, in fact, dozens of restaurants I've visited in Chinatown and Little Italy with my picture in the window.

But take a tip from me. If I'm asked to pose with the chef or the owner, I never refuse, whether I've enjoyed the meal or not. If I liked the meal, I smile. Let the picture be your guide.

# The Talent Bank Under Fire

Reform of campaign financing and government ethics were important issues during my third term on both the city and state level.

A State Commission on Government Integrity, headed by Michael Sovern, the president of Columbia University, issued a series of reports in 1986 and 1987 recommending, among other things, public financing of elections for state executive and legislative offices and a substantial tightening of conflict-of-interest rules pertaining to state officials and employees. Unfortunately, the State Legislature refused to enact a public financing law and managed to pass an ethics law that made only marginal improvements.

In New York City we acted more boldly in spearheading an effort to achieve public financing for all elected city positions, and the City Council passed this law in 1987. New York City thus became one of the first cities in the United States to have public financing of local elections. In addition, the Charter Revision Commission, then headed by Dick Ravitch, proposed amendments to the City Charter to strengthen the rules pertaining to conflicts of interest. These amendments were approved by the electorate in 1988.

Both Governor Cuomo and I felt that more needed to be done on these issues. Although the Sovern Commission had produced a fine set of reports and recommendations, it had failed to generate the public support necessary to move the Legislature. We thought it would be desirable to create a second Commission on Government Integrity which would have subpoena power and would hold public hearings to dramatize the existing problems and the need for reform. The Governor appointed John Feerick, dean of Fordham Law School, to head the commission.

I believe that, on balance, the Feerick Commission has been a disappointment. Although it too has issued a series of lengthy reports, it has been ineffective in generating the public and political support necessary for meaningful reform. And I believe that in connection with its investigation of patronage, it acted in a manner that was highly selective, partisan, and unfair.

In May 1988, the commission leaked to the press reports that the Mayor's Talent Bank had been diverted from its affirmative action mission and had become "a patronage mill." In addition, according to the leaks, Joseph DeVincenzo, one of my special assistants, had ordered the destruction of documents demonstrating the preference given to job applicants referred by political sources. DeVincenzo vehemently and publicly denied these charges.

These leaks were obviously quite damaging to me politically—intentionally so, I believe. Members of the press reported to my staff that the source of these leaks was Richard Emery, a commission member. Emery is a friend of Jack Newfield, who is a political operative in the guise of a reporter, and is clearly antagonistic to me.

In January 1989, the Feerick Commission held two days of public hearings at which it aired the evidence collected up to that point concerning the Talent Bank. I responded with the following letter to Dean Feerick:

*I have been reading with great distress the allegations relating to the "Talent Bank" that have been made at your hearings this week.*

*I believe that I must determine what actions, if any, are appropriate for me to take in response to these allegations. In order for me to make a reasoned determination, it is very important that all of the relevant information be examined, including the information gathered during the lengthy investigation which preceded your public hearings. I would very much appreciate it if the commission staff could supply us with the information.*

*I am sure you can appreciate the importance of this request; it would be impossible for us in any reasonable period of time—nor would we wish—to recreate the extensive investigation you have already done.*

Dean Feerick replied that the commission would not provide copies of the private hearing transcripts but assured me that the commission intended to conclude the investigation expeditiously. However, several months would pass before I was given an opportunity to respond to the serious charges made at the January public hearings.

Then, in March 1989, I was informed that the Feerick Commission wished to take my deposition in private. This was the first time in the course of its investigation that the commission had sought the private testimony of an elected official. I thought this procedure was unfair both to me and to the public. So I wrote again to Dean Feerick:

*The day before yesterday, I received your letter dated March 2, 1989. I have great respect for you and your commission, and I believe in the work you are doing. As you know, I, together with the Governor, called for the creation of the commission. However, I must respectfully disagree with your assessment that it is appropriate for Stan Brezenoff and me to testify in private.*

*The commission has been investigating the Mayor's Talent Bank for almost a year. In the middle of January, you held public hearings during which an accusation was made that the Talent Bank was a sham, i.e., that it was a patronage mill masquerading as an affirmative action program. It was only fair to assume that such a serious accusation, which served to tarnish the reputation of my administration, would not have been made unless the commission had completed its investigation. It now appears that the public hearings at which this accusation was made preceded rather than followed the gathering of all the information. I was surprised to learn that the commission's staff has only recently—after the public hearings—requested the city to turn over many documents relevant to the performance of the Talent Bank and, more generally, to the city's hiring practices. Since the charge was made in public, it seems fair that our testimony should now also be given in public.*

*Public testimony would also eliminate the possibility of selective leaks. I know that you share my concern that such leaks do damage both to the reputation of the leak's victim and to the reputation of the commission for fairness. Public testimony would thus be preferable for everyone. I want the public to hear all of our testimony, and I am sure that the commission would like to avoid selective leaks.*

*Moreover, the public has a right not only to hear our testimony in its entirety, but also to observe the manner in which the commission conducts its inquiry, including the types of questions the commission asks of all public officials. Indeed, in my opinion, high public officials, when questioned about the performance of their public duties by a commission like yours, should give testimony only in public unless there is a compelling reason to proceed in secret. I am not aware of any such reason here. To the best of my knowledge, the commission's previous practice has not been to request private testimony from any other high public officials.*

*Finally, the procedure you suggest necessarily contemplates further delay. According to* The New York Times, *some people have questioned whether the timing of the public hearings was calculated to affect the upcoming municipal elections. I do not believe that, but I also think it is important not to give unfortunate credence to that idea by delaying any further. It is already two months since public accusations have been made. If the commission intends to hear from Stan and me, I believe that should be done immediately in public.*

Eventually, I agreed to a compromise procedure whereby I was interviewed on the record by the Feerick Commission staff prior to the public testimony.

Before I had a chance to testify, however, Dean Feerick and Richard Emery appeared on WNBC-TV's *News Forum.* In response to Emery's performance on that program, I drafted a letter to Dean Feerick which my staff convinced me I should not send. While not sending it may have been the diplomatic thing to do, I believe the letter, which follows, told the truth:

*Sunday, March 19, on a WNBC-TV news program, Richard Emery used his position as a member of your commission to make inappropriate statements which were not only unfair but also threaten to damage the reputation of the commission and therefore undermine the important work it was created to do.*

*Before all the evidence had been presented, Mr. Emery repeated the accusation made at the commission's public hearings in January that the Talent Bank was a patronage operation in the "guise" of an affirmative action program. He referred to a comment I was alleged to have made to the press as "damage control." He said that everything I was now doing was "political." He said that in his view the Talent Bank was not like the corruption scandals because, with respect to the Talent Bank, the Mayor could not say that "some people were off in a corner, conspiring against the public interest of the City and conspiring against him."*

*He talked about the City's bridges, which he said are "falling," our schools, which he said are "in a wreck," and our streets, which he said are a "mess." He linked these supposed conditions to public employees who are "demoralized by patronage" or, as he also said, "a city of demoralized people, because political patronage has demoralized them."*

*These are partisan political statements both in tone and in sub-*

*stance. They arouse the unfortunate suspicion that the commission's investigation is not designed to gather facts but rather to justify public accusations prematurely made. How can the public expect that the commission will gather and analyze the evidence impartially and issue a balanced report when, at the public hearings in January and again yesterday, one of the commissioners has so strongly and publicly committed himself to a conclusion before hearing all the evidence?*

*If a judge or arbitrator publicly announced his findings before the completion of hearings, I am sure that Mr. Emery would not hesitate to criticize such conduct as improper. The same standard of conduct should apply to him. I believe that the commission must take some corrective action. Otherwise, it may appear, by its acquiescence, that the commission approves of Mr. Emery's conduct.*

Throughout the course of the commission's investigation into the Talent Bank, Dean Feerick had insisted that neither his fellow commissioners nor his staff had ever leaked information to the press. I believe that Dean Feerick is a good and decent man. He is known by his former law partners as "John the Good" or "John the Fair."

But I also believe he was never able to control his own commission. The final proof of that was that excerpts of the commission's report on the Talent Bank were leaked to the press four days before the final report itself was issued. I believe these leaks, like the earlier ones, demonstrated that some members or staff of the commission were motivated not by a search for the truth but rather by a desire to hurt me and to advance the political candidacies of my opponents.

In fact, read in its entirety, the report contained little that was new or significant. It concluded that patronage is not illegal and found no violation of the law in connection with the operation of the Talent Bank. Moreover, in its press release, the commission acknowledged that "it did not find that the Mayor knew or approved of the questionable practices revealed by its investigation."

Furthermore, the fact of the matter is that during the period 1983–86—the period which is the subject of the commission's report—there were fewer than 400 unskilled laborers hired through the Talent Bank, slightly more than 1 percent of the 30,204 discretionary jobs that were filled in that period.

Some patronage mill! If I had wanted to have a massive patronage program, I could have, within the law, used those 30,000 jobs to create one. But I did not want to have—nor did I have—a patronage operation. This is evident from the way in which I have excluded political considerations from the filling of such traditional sources of patronage as summer youth jobs, the choice of city marshals, the hiring of lawyers at the Law Department, and the selection of judges. Indeed, my administration's record of hiring on the basis of merit, rather than connections, is clearly better than that of prior city administrations or other governments in this state.

In response to the commission's report, I issued a press release, which concluded as follows:

> Finally, the report stated that I must bear "ultimate responsibility" for the Talent Bank. I agree. I have always said that as Mayor I must take final responsibility for all that occurs during my administration— both the good and the bad.
>
> Is the commission willing to do the same? Leaking excerpts of its report is a violation of state law. Is the commission going to investigate those leaks? Is it going to place its own commissioners and staff under oath? Alternatively, will the commission refer the leaks to the District Attorney for investigation?
>
> Or will the commission sit idly by and ignore a breach of government integrity that, unlike anything dealt with in its report, involves a criminal act? If the commission demands integrity from others, the commission ought to demand the same of itself.

Not surprisingly, the commission refused to accept my challenge and never undertook any investigation of those leaks. The moral of the story is sad but true: investigators are willing to investigate everyone but themselves.

# The Death Penalty

Whenever a horrendous crime is committed, social scientists are sure to trot out and suggest that it is not the perpetrator's fault but society's that the crime took place. "How can you punish someone for something society made him do? Until you change society and give that person a chance to get ahead without resort to criminal activity," goes the argument, "he's simply not to be blamed, not to be punished."

Ridiculous! Usually the explanation given for criminal activity is social deprivation and poverty: "They had no choice, no other way out of poverty." But check the records. You'll find that the overwhelming majority of poor people, just like middle-class or well-to-do people, don't commit crimes. They go to work, raise their families, and obey the law.

In any city, crime is generally the work of a relatively small handful of people: those who need money to feed a drug habit, those who have made a conscious decision that the fastest way to make a fast buck is through crime. Society didn't make them rob banks, burglarize homes, or steal cars. They chose to do it. It's not something social scientists and social engineers like to hear. But it happens to be true.

For as long as I have been a public official, I have been a proponent of the death penalty. I supported it as a member of the City Council, then as a member of the U.S. Congress, and, for the last twelve years, as Mayor.

That bothers my critics. They believe it is wrong for me to use my mayoral pulpit to speak out on an issue over which I do not have direct control. "The death penalty's not a local issue," they argue. "Only a judge can issue a stay of execution, only a governor can grant a petition for clemency, and only a state legislature can enact a death penalty. A mayor ought to keep his mouth shut on the issue."

But think about the logic of my critics' argument. If my purview extended only to issues over which I have direct control as Mayor, I would not have spoken out in support of the Equal Rights Amendment. I would not have spoken out against the federal failure to condemn apartheid in South Africa adequately. And I would not have spoken out against the Reagan administration's efforts to provide federal funds to institutions of higher learning which discriminate against people on the basis of their race or its efforts to cut the cost-of-living adjustment received by senior citizens on Social Security. None of these are under mayoral control. But all of them, I believed, required mayoral positions. Would my critics have preferred that I remain silent on these issues? Since they are issues so near and dear to their hearts, I think not.

Go a step further. None of my critics will ever take issue with a mayoral candidate who opposes the death penalty. In fact, it'll be one more reason for my critics to support and applaud that candidate. If it's O.K. by them that my opponents speak out against the death penalty, why is it not O.K. for me to speak out in support? If I'm labeled demagogic for supporting it, why aren't they labeled demagogic for opposing it?

No one in his or her right mind would argue that crime in the streets of a city is not a local issue. According to opinion polls, it's the most local, most pressing issue of all. And when the crime rate goes up, a local official's job approval rating is sure to head down. Just ask my critics. They usually lead the charge.

But if the death penalty is, as I believe, an effective deterrent against the most violent of those crimes, doesn't a mayor, a city council member, or a local police chief have the right, even the obligation, to importune the state legislature to make maximum use of that deterrent and enact a death penalty? I believe he does. And I do. Year after year after year, as in the following column, which appeared in the *Staten Island Advance* in February 1985:

A bill has been introduced in Albany to restore the death penalty for the murder of a police or correction officer, for murder by a person previously convicted of such a crime, for murdering a witness to a crime in order to ensure silence, for murder committed in the course of another crime such as kidnapping, burglary, or rape, for murder committed to terrorize or mutilate the victim, and for murder committed in conspiracy with and in the expectation of payment from another.

It's the ninth straight year such a bill has been introduced in the State Legislature. Unfortunately, it also appears it will be the ninth year in a row the bill does not become law.

Central to the debate that occurs will be the question of whether the death penalty is a deterrent to crime. Does its harsh and final judgment discourage criminals from murder and mayhem they might otherwise commit?

The Supreme Court thinks so. In the 1976 case of *Gregg v. Georgia*, it said capital punishment is "undoubtedly a significant deterrence." Others are less sure. Professor Charles Black of Yale and Professor James Q. Wilson of Harvard argue that the deterrent effect of the death penalty can be neither proved nor disproved.

Maybe it's best to ask the person it's intended to deter—the murderer. Ask Luis Vera. Not too long ago Vera decided to burglarize the Brooklyn apartment of Rose Velez, who was at home at the time. He not only got away with the goods, but left Rose Velez dead on the floor. "Yeah, I shot her," Vera said later. "I knew I wouldn't go to the chair." If the fear of death had been in the heart of Luis Vera, Rose Velez might be alive today.

Also central to the debate is the fear that reinstituting the death penalty may result in the death of an innocent New Yorker. It's a legitimate concern and is why I believe no execution should be permitted until the accused has had a full opportunity to exhaust every legal remedy. Those who are fearful, though, ought to be aware of a review by Adam Bedau, a foe of capital punishment, of 7,000 executions in the United States from 1893 to 1971. He didn't find a single instance of a person being executed for a crime he or she did not commit. In fact, he concluded it was only "an abstract possibility." As the families of the 1,622 city residents who were homicide victims last year know, murder isn't an abstract, but a real possibility.

Others argue that the death penalty has been discriminatory in its application with more blacks than whites being executed. Earlier in this century there appears to have been a dual standard in imposing and carrying out the death penalty.

In recent years, however, the dual standard has been eliminated through reforms in our criminal justice system. If such discriminatory application still exists, however, it argues for more, not less use of the penalty so as to include those who escaped the penalty because of such discrimination. Moreover, it's a tragic fact of modern-day life and death that disproportionate numbers of homicides occur in minority communities. Does a penalty that deters some of those murders serve or disserve that community?

In the debate over the death penalty bill, however, the most appropriate question is: What's the alternative? Consider the case of Lemuel Smith.

Mr. Smith was an inmate of Greenhaven Prison. One day he lured correction officer Donna Payant into the office of a prison chaplain. There he strangled Officer Payant, mutilated her body, then dismembered it. Her remains were found days later in four plastic bags dumped at a nearby landfill.

It wasn't the first time Mr. Smith had hurt one of his fellow citizens. He'd been convicted of kidnapping and rape in Schenectady. He'd been convicted of two murders in Albany. And he'd confessed to others. By the time he ran into and, ultimately, ran over Officer Payant, he was already serving three twenty-five-year-to-life sentences for three earlier heinous offenses.

After the jury tried and found Mr. Smith guilty, what was his sentence? A fourth twenty-five-year-to-life sentence. It may seem a harsh punishment. In fact, it's ridiculous.

When you take a car thief off the streets it results in fewer stolen cars.

When you put a rapist in jail, you expect fewer rapes. But when you put a murderer on murderers' row for life, is there any guarantee he or she won't murder again?

In Lemuel Smith's case there wasn't. Officer Payant paid the price for the lesson we all should have learned. Mr. Smith was a man—a murderer—undeterred by the harshest penalty that could be inflicted by his fellow citizens, life imprisonment. He just kept on murdering.

Mr. Smith's case isn't unique. In 1976 and 1977, eighty-five of those arrested for homicide in New York City had prior arrests for murder. Six of them had two prior arrests and one had been arrested for murder on four prior occasions. Similarly, once every three days an inmate of one of America's prisons is murdered. About half are committed by inmates already doing time for murder. Just because killers are taken off the streets and locked away in a cell doesn't mean they won't kill again.

Sometimes murder is an act of passion, a tragic mistake. Then there may be explanations sufficient to excuse the convicted from the maximum penalty under law. Human beings are fallible and society must be prepared to forgive their mistakes.

Other times murder isn't a mistake. Then it's a premeditated act of violence against an individual. Someone convicted of a second, third, or fourth premeditated murder has run out of excuses and has no reasonable explanations. They're not seeking forgiveness but forbearance.

Murderers shouldn't get away with murder. Human beings form societies for protection, not just against acts of God or nature but against the acts of their fellow humans. For it to fulfill its promise and protect those who accept and abide by its rules, society needs tools to punish those who don't. Otherwise, rules are mere rhetoric and society is only as safe as its most treacherous link.

If that's all the security society offers, we're probably better off hiding in caves.

We must have the right to decide when enough is enough, when there are certain crimes we cannot tolerate and cannot live with. When we find that someone has sold secrets to an enemy, we reserve the right to execute the traitor. A convicted traitor shouldn't enjoy the liberties and blessings of a nation he or she was so ready to betray. A society where traitors run free is bent on self-destruction. So too is one where murderers run free of the expectation that they shall pay for their crimes.

When someone repeatedly takes human life, he or she is stepping outside of society and saying its standards don't apply. To the murderer, a victim's life has no value. We shouldn't apply a standard to murderers that murderers don't apply to their victims.

When society turns the other cheek too often, the only result is a bloody face. The fundamental question is whether society has a right to deliver final, irrevocable judgment on those who live outside of its rules.

Human society can't save human souls. It can and must, however, keep its members safe and secure. If those who knowingly, repeatedly, and barbarically take the lives of others want mercy, let them pray for it in the life to come. Their actions warrant no mercy from us.

The bill before the Legislature won't punish those who in a moment of passion step outside the rules. It would reserve the right to juries and judges to punish appropriately only those upon whom society has no hold. If we want to preserve society, let's not preserve those who so deal in death that a jury and a judge believe they should be condemned to death. Donna Payant and Rose Velez need not have died. I hope the Legislature will act this year and help achieve the goal that other innocents will not follow their path to the grave.

More than four years have passed since I wrote this column. Though the State Legislature has come closer than ever to enacting a death penalty, it still hasn't done so. And the murder toll continues to rise.

I am not against developing effective alternatives to the death penalty. My own position is that life imprisonment without parole is acceptable without capital punishment. My critics, by the way, do not attack me for publicly advocating life without parole. Since it fits their ideology, they feel it's perfectly appropriate for me to speak out. Otherwise, they want me to keep my mayoral mouth shut.

I do believe we ought to do away with the "not guilty by reason of insanity" defense. I favor a "guilty but insane" plea. Under the first an individual is held in a hospital until he regains his sanity. He never serves time in jail. Under the second, an individual is sent to a hospital to regain sanity but, having done so, is then sent to jail to serve the remainder of his sentence. Who knows when and if someone who's been insane and committed a crime actually regains sanity? Too often, regrettably, those declared sane return to society and commit more crimes. Doesn't society have a right to be protected against that? I believe it does.

In May 1989, I received a letter from the Most Reverend Francis

J. Mugavero, the Roman Catholic Bishop of Brooklyn. He is a longtime friend and someone I greatly admire. We first met when I ran for Mayor in 1977, when I went to visit him at his chancery in Brooklyn.

"Mario Cuomo has the potential to be a good mayor of New York City," he told me at the time. "But you have the potential to be a great mayor." He's told that story publicly, so I'm not violating a confidence. But now you know why I like him as much as I do. Even if he'd not uttered those magic words, I would have liked and respected him because of his compassion and activism on behalf of the poor and his recognition of and support for the city's people of all colors and stations in life. His heart truly is open to all New Yorkers.

At age seventy-five, in the spring of 1989, Bishop Mugavero was scheduled to retire. Always the battler, though, he decided to enter the fray then raging in the State Legislature in Albany over the death penalty bill. His view was expressed in a beautifully written pastoral letter, which he shared with me. Though we may disagree on particular issues, the Bishop has always had the common decency and courtesy to believe that those on the other side of the issues are not eternally damned or disgraced because they disagree with him. In an age of contentiousness, it is a refreshing and rare quality.

"Capital punishment is a violent solution," he wrote in his pastoral letter. "To reinstate capital punishment in New York State will only make us all partners in the continuing downward spiral of the dehumanization of all life."

I responded immediately to Bishop Mugavero:

*I would like to acknowledge your letter of May 26, 1989.*

*It pains me not to be able to oblige you, but I disagree with your position on the restoration of the death penalty. I understand why you conclude that it should not be restored. However, I have concluded that its restoration would save many innocent lives, particularly the lives of police officers who are being gunned down with regularity by those who know they will not suffer the loss of their [own] lives.*

*You officiate at many funerals, and I certainly know how much you value human life. The only funerals that I attend are those of my family members, close friends, and every police officer killed in the line of duty. I truly believe that I would be attending fewer police officers' funerals if the criminals knew they would pay the ultimate price for engaging in the ultimate crime. I hope you will forgive me for disagree-*

*ing with you on this matter since we are in accord on so many other issues.*

*Although you may be leaving your current position, I look forward to working with you in the future on various projects. I know that you will never retire. Your energy, intelligence, courage, and sense of service will not permit that.*

*All the best.*

Though he certainly does not agree with me, I believe that Bishop Mugavero has a mind and a heart large enough to understand the anger that I and the vast majority of New Yorkers feel. I only wish others would be so understanding. For what is so distressing in the debate over the death penalty is that many of those who oppose it portray its supporters as immoral and themselves as holders of the Holy Grail.

As the Supreme Court of the United States has found, the death penalty is not only a deterrent to crime but also an appropriate and constitutional way for our society to punish those who would egregiously take another person's life.

There is no question that a moral person can hold the moral position that an individual's rights are more important than the rights of society. But there is also no question that an equally moral person can hold the view that society's rights are paramount. The debate over the death penalty should be waged on a high moral plane. I never attack the decency and bona fides of my opponents on this issue; I resent it when they attack mine.

# Cop-Killing

When I became Mayor in 1978 I was perceived by police officers as a liberal "flake" from Greenwich Village. I was a reform Democrat who supported John Lindsay's independent civilian complaint review board. When the referendum, backed by the Patrolmen's Benevolent Association, was put on the ballot to repeal the board and remove civilians who did not work in the department from the board, I opposed it.

The PBA's referendum won big—80 percent for, 20 percent against—with a majority of voters, and a slim majority at that, in only one borough, Manhattan, supporting the Lindsay board. It was one of the most contentious, divisive proposals to appear on a city ballot in the years I have been in politics.

That's the way matters stood until 1986, when, at my request, the City Council passed a bill originally sponsored by the late Councilman Fred Samuel of Harlem to create a board with six civilians from outside the NYPD, to be named by the Mayor and confirmed by the City Council. Six civilians from inside the department, to be named by the Police Commissioner, would also serve on the board.

When Fred had introduced a similar bill earlier, I had not supported it. But I finally concluded the bill would be supported by the people and not opposed with another referendum by the PBA. I persuaded the City Council to support it. It is fair to say that, without my support, the bill would never have become law.

Given my previous support for the Lindsay board, when I took office in 1978 I knew it was essential for me as Mayor to let cops know how much I and all law-abiding New Yorkers value their work and admire their courage. I decided that no matter what the time of day or night, whenever a police officer was wounded in the line of duty and taken to an emergency room, I would drop whatever I was doing to visit him or her in the hospital.

And when a police officer was killed, I always attended the officer's funeral. As Mayor, unfortunately, I attended more than forty funerals of police officers. It is a duty which, as Mayor, it pained me to have to perform. The loss of a man or woman in the prime of their life is sad enough. But the tears in the eyes of the widows, children, and parents left behind always bring tears to mine.

Some columnists argued that my appearance at hospitals or at funerals was simply a political act. It was not. I go to many funerals, but I have been overwhelmed and wept only at those of my immediate family and those of fallen police officers. In some strange way I, like many other New Yorkers, feel I am part of a police officer's extended family.

When a cop is charged with racism or brutality in the aftermath of an incident, invariably militants and columnists are quick to act as judge and jury and call for the cop to be suspended and prosecuted. The presumption of innocence accorded anyone else goes out the window when a police officer is charged with brutality by advocates or the press.

I don't rush to judgment in such matters. Fighting crime isn't child's play. When a cop is reported to have used force in an incident, I believe the assumption should be that he or she acted professionally. If facts to the contrary are so overwhelming and compelling that it's clear that brutality was involved, of course, I will not hesitate to call for a cop's suspension. Except in those rare cases, however, cops have always received my full support unless or until a hearing has established their culpability. If they didn't, why should or would they ever extend themselves or do anything other than play it safe?

Day after day, police officers put their lives on that very dangerous line—what is referred to as the "thin blue line"—which separates the rest of us from the thugs and hoodlums who prey on the innocent. I believe the overwhelming majority of New Yorkers appreciate the work our cops do and would like to see even more of them patrolling our neighborhoods.

And that majority doesn't care whether the officer is white or black, Hispanic or Asian. They know that cops of every race and both sexes have given their lives to protect us. Every time a cop is murdered, a city grieves. And when it happens twice in the same day, a city is stunned.

Just such an event prompted the following letter to Manhattan District Attorney Robert M. Morgenthau early one morning in October 1988:

*Last night is permanently etched in my memory as one of the worst nights I have ever had as Mayor. Two police officers were murdered in two separate incidents.*

*In the first incident, Police Officer Christopher Hoban, engaged in a drug buy-and-bust operation with his partner, was shot squarely between the eyes, with the bullet passing through his brain and exiting his skull. When I arrived at St. Luke's Hospital, Dr. Gregory Fried, the Police Department's surgeon, told me that Officer Hoban would die despite his gallant struggle against overwhelming odds. All the attending doctors realized immediately that this horrifying brain injury was so traumatic that death was imminent.*

*I did not see Officer Hoban either while he was still alive or after he died. Dr. Fried advised me it would be too shocking and unnecessary, and I agreed. I spoke with Mr. and Mrs. Hoban, his parents, who though overwhelmed with grief, displayed immense courage and resolution. Mrs. Hoban said to me that her second son, Martin, would take the police exam shortly and that Christopher, who lay dying a few feet away, was very special to her since his birth. My eyes filled with tears and I embraced her.*

Father Brian Frawley and his brother, Investigation Commissioner Kevin Frawley, came to the hospital and also helped comfort Mr. and Mrs. Hoban. Their presence in the midst of this tragedy added to the extraordinary feeling that we were all part of one family.

When Police Commissioner Ben Ward described the incident at the press conference that ensued, I found it almost impossible to talk or to describe what had taken place. I went home and, while I was having dinner around 10 P.M., I was told of a second incident involving a uniformed police officer, Michael Buczek, who had been killed immediately while answering an emergency medical call. At this moment, I do not know whether his death is drug-related or not.

In both cases, the police officers' partners were overwhelmed with extraordinary grief. In the first case, undercover Police Officer Michael Jermyn wept uncontrollably. Chief of Department Robert Johnston comforted him as I sat and listened to Chief Johnston explain that Officer Jermyn should not blame himself. He told Officer Jermyn that he had done everything he could do and his partner's death was not his fault.

Ben Ward, Bob Johnston, the other police officers in the room, and I embraced Officer Jermyn to comfort him. Dr. Fried told us later that Officer Jermyn would be counseled and that his tears could not and should not be stopped at the moment. He said that Officer Jermyn would have to work out the night's events in his own mind, struggle with his emotions, and finally accept the tragedy, which would probably take months to accomplish.

In the second case, Officer Joseph Barbato was comforted by about five of his fellow officers. He was visibly upset and his eyes were red from crying. I shook his hand and patted him on the shoulder.

Before the second press conference, I spoke with Commissioner Ward and Sterling Johnson, the Special Prosecutor for Narcotics. I asked them to support a proposal requesting all five District Attorneys in the City of New York to relinquish jurisdiction and the two U.S. Attorneys to accept jurisdiction in all drug-related murders, particularly those involving police murders, where the death penalty would be available pursuant to proposed federal legislation now on the President's desk. The maximum penalty will then be available at the perpetrator's trial.

I announced this at the press conference, saying that I believe the death penalty is a deterrent and we will be able to see whether or not that is so if, in fact, it is applied. Ben Ward added that he did question *the importance of the issue of deterrence. He argued that in some cases the penalty should be applied irrespective of the deterrence factor because of the outrageous nature of the crime. I agreed with Ben.*

*He also said that we should make sure that any such cases in the federal courts receive a calendar preference and go immediately to the top of the calendar for disposition. He is right to ask that justice not be denied through inordinate delays involving the appeals which take place in all of these cases where the death penalty is applied. I pointed out to him that we already obtain priority considerations in election cases, and we should certainly seek it in these cases.*

*To close, I request that you, the seven major law enforcement officials in this city—five state and two federal—agree that the federal law with its new death penalty provision should apply in all of these drug-related murders, particularly those involving police murders occurring after the President signs the legislation into law. I would appreciate you letting me know whether you agree with me and will, in the case of the District Attorneys, decline jurisdiction, and in the case of the U.S. Attorneys, accept jurisdiction in these cases.*

*If we take this appropriate action, the State of New York will have, after all these years, the death penalty available for appropriate cases.*

*All the best.*

Regrettably, local prosecutors did not embrace my proposal to use the federal death penalty as a deterrent. Nor has the State Legislature enacted capital punishment. So the criminals in our society still have the upper hand.

It's an upper hand they are almost certain to retain. Early on the morning of October 17, 1989, Police Officer Anthony Dwyer was chasing a suspect in the robbery of a McDonald's over the roofs of buildings in midtown Manhattan.

Details were sketchy. Apparently he'd caught up with the suspect, they wrestled, and as they did the suspect kicked Officer Dwyer. The force of the blow caused him to stagger, then fall two stories down an air shaft. At 4:50 A.M. Officer Dwyer, age twenty-three, was pronounced dead at Bellevue Hospital. He had been on the force for a mere eighteen months.

My security detail awakened me at about 4:45 A.M. I began to get dressed. Ten minutes later, they told me Officer Dwyer was dead. I told them I wanted to go to Bellevue anyway. When I arrived I joined then–First Deputy Police Commissioner Richard Condon. We consoled members of the Dwyer family and the five or six other officers who had been at the scene. Inevitably, they are badly shaken when one of their comrades goes down. But the death of Officer Anthony Dwyer raises questions that go to the very heart of what's wrong with our criminal justice system. When I got back to my office, I was told that four of the robbers had been apprehended and the identity of the others was known to the police. I was told that one of the suspects, Thomas Harris, had been convicted over a dozen times; his longest sentence had been eighteen months to three years, imposed after his second felony conviction. Moreover, after being twice sentenced to state prison after years of criminal activity, he had been paroled and later returned to prison when his parole was revoked. He had served out his sentence and had been released in December 1988.

I attended Officer Dwyer's funeral. Outside, some 5,000 police officers stood at attention. The church was not big enough to hold all of them.

I had been asked by the family to speak. As I did, I had to take frequent long pauses. The emotion I felt kept welling up in my chest. Like everyone else in the church, I was so sad and so very, very angry.

For too long, I said, we have placed the rights of criminals ahead of the rights of society. We want to make sure that prisoners have access to a law library. That prisoners have good food. That prisoners have an opportunity to exercise. That prisoners have a minimum of sixty square feet of personal space. "Today the body of Officer Dwyer lies in a coffin," I said. "He doesn't have sixty square feet of personal space."

Why, I asked, had those who caused the death of Officer Dwyer been allowed to roam the streets? Those like Thomas Harris, one of the four robbery suspects, who had a long criminal record and was, indeed, a career criminal who should have been treated as such by the criminal justice system. But the criminal justice system—the judges and the D.A.'s—had failed us, I said. "That is why we weep."

"I pray to God," I said in closing, "that another officer will not die, another officer will not be injured between now and the end of my term on December thirty-first." Enough had already fallen during my watch.

I know, of course, that it's impossible to expect that another officer will not be killed or wounded by criminals in New York City. Emboldened by a society that does not seem to fight back, they kill and wound with impunity. It is not too much to expect that, once and for all, the criminal justice system will come to its sense and realize its moral

152

obligation to be far tougher on those who terrorize our society and kill the watchmen at the gate.

# To Steven McDonald

On Saturday afternoon, July 12, 1986, New York City Police Officer Steven McDonald was on anti-crime patrol in Central Park. He and his partner observed three young men who they thought might be suspects in a robbery ring. They approached them, and as Steven began to question the suspects, one pulled a .22 caliber handgun and shot him three times—once in the arm, once above the eyes, and once in the neck.

He was rushed to the city's Metropolitan Hospital a few blocks away. As afternoon became evening and plans were made to transfer him to Bellevue Hospital, First Deputy Mayor Stanley Brezenoff called me in the Hamptons, where I was visiting friends for the weekend. "Should I come back, Stan?" I asked. "The doctors tell me he's not going to make it," Stan said. "If the worst comes to pass, I'll call you."

I'm glad to say that the doctors' prognosis was wrong. I'm sure they're glad, too. Thanks to outstanding medical care and an unbelievable will to live, Steven McDonald has lived through many days and nights since July 12, 1986. He and his wife, Patti Ann, are truly profiles in courage.

When I returned to the city the next morning, I immediately went to visit Steven at Bellevue. His condition had stabilized, but it was clear that the damage done to his spinal cord would leave him a quadriplegic for the rest of his life. Tears came to my eyes as I spoke with his mother and father, surrounded by twenty-five of his cousins. I was amazed that, notwithstanding the enormous injury he'd sustained, their spirits were strong.

Moved to tears by their strength and their belief in God, I placed a telephone call from the hospital to His Eminence John Cardinal O'Connor. "Your Eminence," I said, "I am at Bellevue, where I have met the family of a remarkable young police officer who is fighting for his life.

"Although I am sure you are very busy, it would mean a great deal to him and to members of his family, who are very religious, if you came over." The Cardinal came immediately, in the first of many visits both he and I would make in the months that Steven remained in the hospital.

Steven is still paralyzed. But he's made unbelievable progress. He travels everywhere in his motorized wheelchair. His wife, Patti Ann, as young as she is, has been called on to speak publicly on many occasions. Although she had never spoken in public before her husband's injury, she has never had a misstep in conveying her feelings in the most sensitive way.

I was particularly touched by the fact that, during my campaign for a fourth term as Mayor, Steven and Patti told David Garth, my media advisor, that they would like to do a television commercial for me.

"We're speaking to you," Patti said in opening the commercial, "because Ed Koch is our friend. And because he deserves to be Mayor again."

"Ed Koch is a mayor who's good for our cops and our kids too," Steven then said. "He's a mayor who knows that the things that unite us outweigh the things that divide us. He hurts when we hurt. He smiles when we smile. He leads when others won't."

"Ed Koch has been a good mayor and a good friend," Patti concluded.

Over the years David Garth has made a large number of very powerful, very effective campaign ads. But I don't think any were as powerful or effective as the one with Steven and Patti. And best of all, it wasn't an ad written by Ed Koch, David Garth, or some Madison Avenue media mogul. It was written by Steven and Patti McDonald. It's something I will never forget.

The day after the primary election, Steven, Patti, and their son, Conor, who is now two and a half years old, came to City Hall to visit and console me after my defeat. I told them not to worry about me. I did not feel dejected or distressed in any way.

Indeed, I said that I felt liberated by no longer having the enormous burden of the mayoralty sitting on my shoulders. I knew I had handled the load better than anyone else. I also knew that the next mayor might not do it as well and would have enormous problems because of the city's declining economy. While I wish David Dinkins well, I believe that I will be missed.

Steven responded to my feelings as a friend would. He understood. But he had a question for me. "Aren't you worried about the drug lords from Colombia?" he asked. "They are killing people and they could kill you as well. Don't you worry about it?"

"No," I said. "I am a fatalist by nature and I believe that the day of my death is already inscribed in the book of life. However, I don't believe that one should test God, so I'm certainly not going to throw myself in front of a truck to test the theory."

He agreed.

After he left my office, Brian Mulhern, a police detective who is also a close friend of Steven's, gave me a note which Steven had written by placing a pen between his teeth. His note, addressed to "My Captain," read, "Before they ever take your life they'll have to take mine. I love you."

My response read as follows:

*It was so nice of you, Patti, and Conor to come and visit me at City Hall the day after the election. I really appreciated your thoughtfulness.*

*Brian gave me your note after you left. It was very touching, and I want you to know that I have the same feeling about the three of you that you expressed about me. I do love you.*

*All the best.*

What more can I say? Steven and Patti have overcome tremendous hardship with unbelievable courage. They are models to us all.

# PART

# 6

# MINDING THE STORE

―――――――――――

## On Loyalty

No other city government does as much or does it as well as the City of New York. But we do make mistakes. And when we do, the press is sure to pounce, particularly on the commissioner in charge of the agency that made the mistake. Editorial calls for heads to roll are usually not far behind.

I pride myself on the fact that I stand shoulder to shoulder with commissioners who are under siege. Most mayors would cut their losses, give in to the clamor, and demand a letter of resignation. Not me. Unless the commissioner has been demonstrably derelict in performing his or her duties, I'll stand with my colleague.

In return, I expect commissioners to do the best job they can and to remain loyal to my administration and, yes, to me. During my third term, one of my best commissioners was Bill Grinker, head of the Human Resources Administration. Notwithstanding the fact that HRA faces some of the toughest, most intractable issues, like his predecessors at HRA—or maybe because of it—Bill was the subject of constant scrutiny and criticism by the press. He handled the problems and pressures well, and I believe the services delivered by his agency today are better than when he first took the job.

Like the rest of us, though, Bill's not perfect. In March 1989 he agreed to be interviewed for a profile by *The New York Times*. His first mistake was to consent to an interview that, he later told me, lasted between six and seven hours. No one can go that long with a reporter without making a major gaffe.

Which Bill did. "It would be nicer," he was quoted as saying, "to have a Mayor who really felt deeply about some of these issues. . . ."

When I read his comment, I was incensed. I knew that a line like that would be used by editorial writers and my opponents to try to beat my brains in. And it was. Again and again. Frankly, I couldn't believe Bill had said it, because I'd been supportive of his agency and of every idea he'd proposed as commissioner.

When I wrote the following letter, I intended it to sizzle his brain (he told me later that it had):

*I read the article in today's* New York Times, *which you surely must have found more than acceptable because it certainly gives you high marks.*

*I was distressed with some of your comments concerning me, particularly, "It would be nicer to have a Mayor who really felt deeply about some of these issues about welfare and knew them intimately." Are there issues that you have taken up with me where you found me unsympathetic in response? Is my lack of knowledge glaring? I thought I was pretty knowledgeable on most of the issues, particularly since I have to be a generalist and not a specialist.*

*With respect to my feeling deeply, was it you or me who suggested that we charge single individuals rent for being in our dormitories? Was it you or me that suggested we charge them the full cost of $900 a month? My recollection is that it was you who suggested that figure,* *while I said it was stupid and that the maximum should be 30 percent of their salary or $218 a month. And was it you or me who took the editorial and columnist bashing for this hard-hearted demand of charging rent? Did you step forward publicly and identify it as your idea or did I take the heat for you?*

*Was it your or my idea to urge the public not to give money to panhandlers? My recollection is that it was your idea. Who took the heat for that hard-hearted demand? You or me? My recollection is that it was me. Did you step forward and publicly say it was your idea?*

*It is true that when you are interviewed by some reporters you weep or apparently your eyes brim with tears. Regrettably, I don't have the time to weep. I have to make the government work. When your agency fails in its responsibility as perceived by the public to protect youngsters who are abused or molested or killed, is it you or me who takes the flak? My recollection on such occasions is that it is me. And who defends you when these things occur? My recollection is that I have stood next to you and defended you rather than saying, "Ask him, let him defend himself."*

*By the way, was it you or me who created the Harlem shelter employment center, which was so successful that it was placed in other areas as well? Did you or I require that it be placed in the women's and family shelters? I think I did.*

*I have defended you and your predecessors. I am not sure I will do it any more. I think I will let you do the weeping and explaining the next time the press asks why your agency has failed in a particular matter. I expect the language that you employed from advocates who have a political agenda. I certainly did not expect it from you since I appointed you.*

After receiving my note, Bill called me and said his comments had been taken out of context. He'd had the good sense to tape-record his interview, and he sent me a copy of the transcript. Though the *Times* has yet to run a correction, the transcript clearly demonstrated that he had been quoted out of context. All was forgiven and forgotten.

Until two months later. Someone leaked a copy of my letter to Bill Grinker to Marcia Kramer of the *Daily News*. I knew that meant trouble. One Sunday afternoon Marcia called Bill asking him for comment on the memo, which to her meant a major rift in city government. Bill called me and we agreed that when Marcia called I would say that tempers had cooled and that Bill's comment had since been put in its proper context. By 4:00 P.M., however, Marcia still hadn't called me. I knew her story was probably headed straight for the front page.

Of all the reporters in City Hall's Room 9, Marcia Kramer is one of the most aggressive. And, in this particular case, she didn't want the story to have a happy ending. Happy endings don't make headlines. If she called me for comment she knew she wouldn't have as big a story, since the issue between Bill and me had been resolved months earlier. So she didn't call.

I called George Arzt, my press secretary, asking him to call Marcia and give her my statement on the matter. He did. But guess what? Nary a word of my comment appeared in the first edition of the *News*. And only six words of it appeared in later editions. Wouldn't want to ruin a front-page story, right?

In hindsight, I believe the letter I sent to Bill is one of the best I've ever written. At the time I wrote it, I meant every single word. But as the story turned out, it proves again that you shouldn't always believe what you read in the newspaper. A few times, it's the whole truth. Many times it's only half the truth. And sometimes it doesn't resemble the truth at all.

Bill submitted his letter of resignation on October 3, 1989, two weeks after my defeat in the Democratic primary. He was very generous. "To have been able to perform my responsibilities with your continued support," he wrote, "a support born of intelligence, wit, political courage, and a deep understanding of how government works and how to make it work, is to be doubly fortunate." As is traditional, I sent him a reply:

*I have your letter in which you submit your resignation as Administrator/Commissioner effective November 19, 1989.*

*You have been one of the best commissioners, serving in one of the most difficult agencies that exists on any level of government. When you have to serve one and a half million people on a continuing basis who suffer from poverty or the effects of old age, young people who need foster care, spouses who are battered, [and] abused and sexually molested children, you are serving those most in need and doing God's work. You have done it effectively.*

*When mistakes were made by some of the tens of thousands of people who serve in that agency or, on occasion, by you yourself, you have not hesitated to stand up and accept responsibility, holding those who work for you to the highest of standards. Your job breaks lesser people physically, mentally, emotionally, spiritually, or a combination thereof. You understood that it does not help to let yourself become overwhelmed with the injustice that fills the world, but instead you did what you could to eliminate as much of that injustice as was possible within the limitations that are placed upon any agency in terms of authority and finances.*

*To refer to a particularly applicable line, you kept your head when all around you were losing theirs, and that is what leadership is all about.*

*I will tell the next mayor-elect of your offer to help in the transition period, and I am sure he will avail himself of that generous offer. All the best in your new endeavors and let's stay in touch.*

Bill Grinker did a terrific job in a trying position. If our years as colleagues proved anything, it's that none of us is perfect. And, of course, that includes me.

# On the NIMBY Syndrome

As every mayor of every city surely knows, we live in the age of NIMBY—the "Not In My Back Yard!" syndrome. Unveil plans for a new playground or a branch library and you're sure to earn the plaudits of every neighborhood newspaper, activist, and resident. But announce plans for a sanitation garage, a homeless shelter, or, as you'll see, a group home for foster infants, and the petition drives and picket lines pop up faster than the speed of light.

I understand the anxiety and anger of the protesters. A jail or a shelter, after all, isn't going to do much to improve the quality of life or property values in a neighborhood. No wonder residents feel threatened.

But a mayor is elected to serve an entire city, not just a particular neighborhood. Some municipal activities and facilities we must provide will not always have a beneficial effect, and they must be distributed as fairly as possible. Every neighborhood must carry its share of the municipal burden. No neighborhood has the right to expect it will be spared.

Running for mayor, in a sense, is a popularity contest. Running a government is not. As an elected leader, a mayor often must take positions which are unpopular in areas where he or she is most popular. It comes with the territory. The risk is that your position will lose you votes, even the margin of victory, in the next election. The reward is that you've let principles, not politics, be your guide. Knowing that made sleeping at night—and governing by day—a lot easier for me.

But once the NIMBY cry is heard, things can turn ugly in a hurry. As a mainstream Democrat, for example, I have long enjoyed widespread support in Queens, the city's second-largest borough and the home of hundreds of thousands of middle-class home owners and renters. It has been, as columnists and analysts are quick to write, "Koch Country" in all four of my elections for Mayor.

In the mid-1980s New York City faced a foster care crisis. After years of declining caseloads, the number of foster care placements ordered by the courts increased dramatically. Having shrunk our foster system for years, we suddenly had to reverse gears and expand it. We needed beds and we needed them fast.

That responsibility fell to the city's Human Resources Administration. As part of a plan to add more than a thousand new foster care beds to our system in less than a year, HRA announced that the Jewish Child Care Association would open a group home for six foster infants at 171-27 Gladwin Avenue in Queens. It quickly became one of New York City's more famous addresses.

Gladwin Avenue is a quiet, tree-lined street in the Flushing section of Queens. Its single-family homes are well kept, the lawns are beautifully maintained, and you wouldn't be surprised to see Beaver Cleaver bicycling his way home to Ward and June after school. It's an all-American, picture-perfect neighborhood.

But in 1986 it revealed a not-so-perfect side. Late one April evening fire broke out at 171-27 Gladwin Avenue. Fortunately, no infants had been placed in the home yet, and no one was injured.

No, the fire wasn't caused by faulty wiring or a lightning bolt. It was deliberately and maliciously set by people who wanted to drive the foster home out of their neighborhood. It was not the kind of act I as Mayor could tolerate, notwithstanding the political support I'd enjoyed in the neighborhood. I responded in a column in the *Staten Island Advance,* which had chastised me on this issue in its editorial pages:

On the evening of April 20, fire broke out at 171-27 Gladwin Avenue. Fortunately, no one was hurt because no one was home. The fire was a form of terrorism. We won't be deterred by terrorism. We have people to care for, services to deliver, a city to run. As Mayor, that's what you expect me to do. Nothing will stop me from doing it.

A bad attitude has sprung up. Everyone says the city should do more for foster children, the homeless, the mentally ill and that we ought to build more housing, resource recovery plants, prisons, and tow pounds. But every time we try to open a facility for one of these purposes, in the neighborhood where it's to be located goes up a loud and clear, "Not in my back yard!"

The simple fact is that if we're going to deliver the services you expect, we have to open such facilities. Our policy can't be and won't be that some neighborhoods will have city facilities, some will not. Every neighborhood, every borough must bear a fair share.

Whether it's the house at 171-27 Gladwin Avenue after it's been repaired or another house, HRA will open a group foster home in Flushing. We'll also open homes in other neighborhoods. If necessary, we'll post police officers around the clock.

I hope it won't be necessary. Ultimately, I'm sure the overwhelming majority of decent people who live in Flushing will realize that six infant foster children won't destroy their neighborhood. If they open their arms to these infants, a story that began as a near tragedy will have a happy ending.

The commentary on how we responded to the events in Flushing has been supportive. Except for the *Advance*. "If Mr. Koch had listened more closely to the crowd" which gathered the afternoon following the fire, the *Advance* wrote recently, "he might have heard another explanation. These people, like millions of others in New York, don't trust city government to do what it says it will do. It is mistrust that is at the root."

Mistrust? I disagree. Since August, the residents of this Flushing neighborhood have been kept fully informed of the plans proposed for the house. And they've had input. When the first plan met with opposition, it was modified. When that modification met with opposition, the plan was withdrawn and a new plan submitted. That, too, met with opposition.

"No, no, no"—that's what we heard no matter what we proposed. How many "no's" were we supposed to hear before we concluded that "no" was all we would hear?

And if "no" was all we could expect to hear, would the *Advance* have preferred that we cancel our plans altogether? I hope not. Because if it's suggesting that any time we hear "no" to a project we ought to abandon it, then we should abandon our plans for resource recovery plants. I don't think the *Advance* wants that.

But there's a larger, more important point. Nothing can excuse what happened at 171-27 Gladwin Avenue. Nothing. Setting fire to the house was an attempt to intimidate the city. If the *Advance* is going to explain away what happened there as a result of mistrust in city government, will it also try to explain away the taking of hostages in Tehran or the bombing of an embassy in Beirut as a result of mistrust in the United States government? Of course not. Terrorism can never be explained away; it can never be excused.

Ultimately, five people were brought to trial for the firebombing at 171-27 Gladwin Avenue. In 1988, I'm pleased to say, they were found guilty by a jury of their peers. But as they moved toward sentencing, I was disturbed to learn that the Honorable William D. Friedman, a Supreme Court justice in Queens who was presiding over their trial, seemed to be more upset with how the city had acted on Gladwin Avenue than with the defendants. So I wrote him the following letter:

*Upon reading your reported statements in the pre-sentence conference proceedings in the cases of* People v. Rita Amato, Philip Amato, and James Raffa, *and* People v. Michael Scotto and Ugo Serrone *concerning the City's actions, I obtained and read the minutes of those proceedings.*

*These defendants stand convicted of firebombing a house that was to be used by the City to house babies that had been abused. In the pre-sentence proceedings on August 30 you stated that the City's actions in proceeding with our plan to house "boarder babies" in that house were "not admirable" and "may have contributed in a great extent to what happened here." Additionally, you stated, referring to the defendants, that "so-called good people found themselves being pushed against a wall. . . ."*

*Although you stated that the City's actions did not "justify" the defendants' criminal conduct, you have clearly stated that it is your belief that the City's policies and actions were improper and that they contributed to the defendants' resort to criminal conduct.*

*Your stated position is both factually incorrect and, in my opinion, inappropriate for a judicial officer to express.*

The City has an obligation to provide for the housing of "boarder babies" and has no alternative but to use residential dwellings for that purpose. The selection of the Queens residence for this purpose was discussed by City officials with the community at community board meetings, and the issue of the price that the City was paying for the residence was investigated by the Department of Investigation, which concluded there was no impropriety. My administration made a decision to utilize this particular residence to fulfill its public responsibilities and to satisfy an urgent need to provide the necessary housing for the babies.

Governments often encounter a "not in my back yard" response from communities when seeking to find sites for governmental facilities which everyone agrees are desired and needed. Such has been the case with jails, drug treatment facilities, homeless shelters, sanitation facilities, and homes for boarder babies. Yet these facilities must be placed in someone's back yard, and every community must accept its share of them.

When an individual or group disagrees with government's policies or actions, there is a democratic process within which those actions or policies can be challenged. In a civilized democratic society, criminal conduct is not an acceptable method of challenging the actions of the government.

While the defendants' disagreement with the governmental action may bear on the motive for their crimes, it all the more enforces the need for a stiff sentence if others are to be deterred from challenging governmental action through criminal means. But of what relevance was your opinion of the propriety of the government's action? As a judicial officer, it is your sworn oath and duty to uphold the laws. In doing so, your agreement or disagreement with the governmental policy or action which the defendants state they were challenging by their criminal acts is irrelevant.

All the best.

In his sentencing decision, I am pleased to report, Judge Friedman did the right thing. Three of those found guilty were sentenced to jail and the other two were sentenced to community service work. They were also ordered to pay the city more than $40,000 in restitution for damage done to the house on Gladwin Avenue.

"It is clear that you are not the usual persons found in the criminal justice system," Judge Friedman said at the sentencing. "However, your convictions must result in discouraging others from following down your paths of destruction and self-destruction." Hear! Hear!

And yes, today there is a group home for foster infants at 171-27 Gladwin Avenue. As I promised the day following the fire, we would spare no effort and no cost to rebuild and reopen the facility on that exact spot. I kept the promise. And despite the fears raised back in 1986, the home hasn't ruined the neighborhood. To the contrary—it's helping improve the lives of foster infants.

## On the Fiscal Crisis

I have always believed that tough problems bring out the best in people. I certainly had an opportunity to test that theory within days of taking office as Mayor.

"Massive Fiscal Mess Greets Koch," read the headline in *Newsday* in early January. New Yorkers had better "fasten [their] seatbelts," advised Felix Rohatyn of the investment firm of Lazard Frères in a memo which reached my desk just ten days after my inauguration, because the city was heading into a "storm as dangerous and unpredictable as any it had weathered since 1975." By 1979, he warned, bankruptcy would be "a real possibility."

Ed Koch "is going to be the Joan of Arc of this city," Rohatyn told reporters. They then reminded him that Joan had been burned at the stake. "Yes," he answered, "but she saved France."

Well, I'm pleased to report that with the help of a lot of people—former Governor Hugh Carey, our congressional delegation, the municipal unions, city managers and workers, local elected officials, and the private business community—I did indeed prevent bankruptcy and restore the city's fiscal integrity. Even better, unlike poor Joan I survived to tell the tale.

Success, it's often said, has many fathers. Failure does not. Had Rohatyn's predictions come true and the city gone into bankruptcy, one person and one person only would have been blamed. Me. Since that didn't happen, of course, everyone wanted their fair share of the glory. Certainly many were entitled to share credit for the success. Including me.

I'm afraid Abe Beame, my predecessor and the 104th Mayor of the

City of New York, didn't agree. My relationship with Mayor Beame has not been a particularly good one. I bear some of the responsibility for not showing what he considered to be the deference and courtesies due him as a former mayor. I truly believe he thinks the city was "saved" before he left office and I became Mayor. That simply isn't true.

In August 1984, I began to solicit contributions for my campaign for a third term in 1985. Mayor Beame received one of the mass-produced fund-raising letters. And it made him angry. Very angry.

I "respectfully request that you remove my name from your mailing list," he wrote to my campaign organization. "This will relieve your campaign of an expenditure of 20 cents for postage and relieve me of the annoyance of once again hearing, in Mayor Koch's words, how he inherited a 'nearly bankrupt' city in 1978, and how he 'rescued the city from bankruptcy.' The record is clear that New York City had already avoided the threat of bankruptcy long before Mayor Koch took office."

I replied:

*I read your letter of September 13, 1984. If your name was inadvertently put on my 1985 campaign mailing list, I will make sure it is removed, as you requested.*

*With respect to your comments about New York City's fiscal condition when I became Mayor, let me refresh your memory.*

*When I took office our credit rating had been suspended, we had no access to the public markets for even short-term notes, unemployment was 40 percent above the national average, and in the fiscal year preceding my election we incurred a deficit of over $1 billion.*

*Things were so bad that* The Wall Street Journal *suggested that we declare bankruptcy, financial guru Felix Rohatyn warned that the City was about to enter "a fiscal storm as dangerous and unpredictable as any it had weathered since 1975," and Moody's, six weeks before I took office, declared that the City's "financial position is so precarious as not to preclude the possibility of bankruptcy. . . ." The headline writers were no more optimistic. Greeting my introduction into office were such headlines as "Massive Fiscal Mess Greets Koch" (Newsday), "Fiscal Gale Threatens to Blow City Away" (the* Daily News), *and "Giving Up the Game" (*The Wall Street Journal). *Not exactly consistent with your characterization of a city "well on the road to recovery." Do you know a lot of other cities on that road for which* The Wall Street Journal *advocates bankruptcy twice within six weeks, or for* *which Moody's declares "the general obligation pledge of the City to these notes is of minimum value in assuring payment"? I can't think of any.*

*You won't find such headlines today. Now the headlines read "City Ends Fiscal Year with $497 Million Surplus" (The New York Times) or "Big Apple Shines in the World's Markets" (Business Week). Our credit ratings have been restored, we have had five years of truly balanced budgets, unemployment has been below the national average for the past two years in a row, and our notes now carry Moody's highest rating. We've also gained over 200,000 new jobs. What a contrast!*

*Do you know what Standard & Poor's cited in 1981 as part of the rationale for restoring the City's credit rating? "A change in the attitude of City management." And they noted, "Management effectiveness improved noticeably in the Office of the Mayor. . . ." The Citizen's Budget Commission gave me its award for High Civic Service in June of 1981 for "effective leadership in restoring fiscal stability to the City of New York." I could go on and on, but is it really necessary?*

*I trust this letter refreshes your memory. After reading it you may even want to reconsider your request to remove your name from my mailing list. If you do, I can assure you that you will be most welcome.*

In early 1988, Mayor Beame was at it again, telling *New York Newsday* that he had put the city back on the road to recovery and had left me with "a $200 million cash surplus."

His statement surprised me. As a certified public accountant, he should have been the first to acknowledge that calling the $200 million cash on hand in the bank a "surplus" is a deception when, as was true in 1978, the city was already over $1 billion in debt. Moreover, in a city which at the time had a budget of $12 billion a year, $200 million in the bank wouldn't even cover one week's expenses. What a foolish statement for a former mayor and a CPA to make.

My comments, or lack thereof, about the fiscal practices of John V. Lindsay, the 103rd Mayor of the City of New York, were also cause for controversy. Following my reelection in 1985, I took a vacation in Japan. "Is Mayor Lindsay, who brought the city to bankruptcy, still alive?" an elderly man asked me at a Tokyo press conference.

"I have a rule when overseas," I replied. "I don't criticize former New York mayors. But I will tell you he is alive."

That angered *The New York Times.* "Mr. Koch knows better than anyone that John V. Lindsay was no more responsible for the New York fiscal crisis than Mayor Wagner or Comptroller and then Mayor Beame," it wrote while I was away. "His Japan gibe needlessly dishonors two excellent city administrations—Mr. Lindsay's and his own."

I, of course, responded:

*I read with amusement your November 22 editorial entitled "Postcards from Ed Koch—Two Mayors."*

*From that editorial, I am forced to conclude that no mayor should be held responsible for what takes place during his administration. I hope that you will not diverge from that position during my term in office, although I am afraid you already have. Do you really believe that John Lindsay had no responsibility for the condition of the city at the time he passed the reins of government on to Beame?*

*Surely at this point in time you must conclude that both he and Beame had nearly spent us into bankruptcy. If that is true, why is it unreasonable for people to say so, even me? . . .*

*You refer to the blame of others including me as a member of Congress. You are right. I have publicly stated and referred to myself as "Mayor Culpa" for having voted for programs in the Congress which added to the city spending. I neither knew nor cared at the time how those wonderful programs would be paid for and by whom. Indeed, I have summed up my responsibility by saying that if I had the power I would punish every member of Congress who participated in those days, and perhaps even today, with some of their mandates imposed on cities by having them serve one year as mayor. Has John Lindsay ever admitted an error relating to the finances of this city? If he has, I am unaware of it.*

*Notwithstanding this carping comment, I am grateful that you included my administration as one of the excellent ones. This letter is not intended for publication but rather for your understanding of my thoughts. I do not feel a collegial responsibility to bury the errors of my predecessor. To do that would have meant that we would not have learned from those errors so as not to repeat them.*

*All the best.*

It's worth noting that while the *Times* had taken me to task for failing to give credit where it believed it was due, a few months earlier the *Times* had failed to give me credit where I felt it was due.

"The city surely owes gratitude to the officials who shaped a sound rescue package and those who shepherded it through a suspicious

Congress," it wrote in an editorial entitled "City to Nation: Thanks, with Interest." Then followed a list of people who indeed deserved credit: Governor Carey, Vice President Rockefeller, Senators Javits and Moynihan, union leaders Barry Feinstein and Victor Gotbaum, and, yes, Mayor Beame.

But nowhere did the editorial mention me. So I wrote the *Times* the following letter:

*I read* The New York Times *editorial of May 2 entitled, "City to Nation: Thanks, with Interest."*

*I imagine it was the same way when the early revolutionaries who participated in the overthrow of the Czar and had a major role in that battle fell into disfavor with the Chairman of the Communist Party and saw their names and history eliminated from the Soviet encyclopedia, becoming a nonperson.*

*Is it possible that all that took place beginning with January 1, 1978, when the City had a billion-dollar deficit and was on the edge of bankruptcy occurred without any participation on my part? Would it all have occurred without me? And if we had gone into bankruptcy, would I have escaped comment in your editorials? Would you have fastened the blame on those whose names you now cite in your editorial as having "shaped a sound rescue package and . . . shepherded it through a suspicious Congress"?*

*Perhaps like some of those earlier revolutionaries, someday I too will be rehabilitated and once again appear in a comparable encyclopedia. All the best.*

"You are not—yet—the Trotsky of the New York revolution," replied Max Frankel of the *Times*. "You are the Khrushchev who never did get himself painted into the murals about old Petrograd." The editorial's focus, he explained, had been on those who'd secured the federal bailout package, not on those "who managed the recovery— among whom you surely rank first." Anyway, he added, "we always tremble for fear of misspelling your name." It was a terrific rejoinder.

Throughout the worst of our city's financial troubles, I was confident of my ability and the city's ability to put our fiscal house back in order. So confident, in fact, that I made a bet with Lee Iacocca.

As a member of Congress, I'd opposed federal loan guarantees for the Lockheed Corporation to help it out of bankruptcy. They were provided anyway. When I became Mayor and urged loan guarantees for the city, I was attacked for being inconsistent. "If they weren't good for Lockheed, why are they good for New York?" my critics asked.

There was, in fact, no inconsistency. Lockheed is a private, for-profit corporation. The City of New York is not. If Lockheed is unable to compete in a free market system and goes bankrupt, that's the way the free market is supposed to work. Just ask the thousands of small-business people who shut their doors every year.

A city is different. It can't eliminate the delivery of basic services, close its doors, or move elsewhere. When a badly run or uncompetitive company fails, that's capitalism. When a city fails, it's a catastrophe.

My view did not prevail. Congress authorized loan guarantees for the Chrysler Corporation. Giving them, I said, was "ridiculous," just as it had been ridiculous to give them to Lockheed. "I heard your statement on network TV that a loan guarantee for Chrysler is ridiculous," Lee Iacocca wrote to me. "Let's put our money where our mouth is. I'll bet you a box of Monte Cristos that we pay off our guaranteed loans before New York City does. Agreed?"

Agreed. I wrote to Lee Iacocca in August 1980:

*First, let me say I wish you the very best. I ride in a Chrysler so I want you to be around when I need spare parts. I did not intend to put you down. I just said that if the federal government paid the cost of Medicaid and welfare instead of requiring New York City to bear the burden we could lend you money.*

*I'm not going to bet you a box of Cuban cigars. I don't smoke and you shouldn't either. Instead, I'll bet you a bushel of apples.*

*All the best.*

The City of New York did pay off its loans ahead of schedule. But Lee Iacocca and the Chrysler Corporation got there first, paying theirs off in 1983.

A bet is a bet. So one evening when I went to a dinner in honor of Iacocca, I presented him with a pewter bowl containing six apples from the farm of District Attorney Bob Morgenthau. He graciously accepted the gift, looked at the six apples and the pewter bowl, and said, "In New York City, I guess, this is what's called a bushel of apples."

We've come a long way since the dark days of January 1978. New York City is stable and strong again. "In the last decade," reported Moody's less than one hundred days before I left City Hall in 1989, "New York City has made significant improvements in its credit position. The current Mayor's administration has implemented strong budget and management control systems, which have enabled officials to react quickly and appropriately to changes in both revenue and expenditure estimates."

We're so strong, in fact, that even the Reagan administration—the most anti-urban presidency since Herbert Hoover's—was impressed by what we'd done. In October 1988 its Secretary of Labor, Ann McLaughlin, praised our city as an example of an "urban renaissance" that should serve "as a model for the rest of the United States."

Understandably, the secretary's comments pleased me, and I wrote to tell her so:

*I just read the Associated Press story in which you referred to New York City's economy as a model for the nation. It was very generous of you, as the Secretary of Labor, to cite the City of New York in such glowing terms.*

*You are right. There is "enormous creativity within this City." As the Chief Executive of New York City, I am extremely proud that the efforts of the public and private sectors have produced what you now refer to as a city in the midst of an "urban renaissance." . . .*

*Our economy has rebounded strongly from the problems of a decade ago. Between 1969 and 1977, the City had lost 600,000 private sector jobs. Since 1978, we have regained more than 325,000 such jobs. When I became Mayor, the unemployment rate was higher than the national average. By contrast, our unemployment rate in the first half of 1988 averaged 4.5 percent—the lowest rate in eighteen years—lower than the national average.*

*All groups and all areas of our population are sharing in the benefits of this improved environment, including our black and Hispanic communities, where unemployment rates are below the national average. And the boroughs of the Bronx, Brooklyn, Queens, and Staten Island outpaced Manhattan in their rate of job growth between 1983 and 1987, thereby providing opportunities in all our neighborhoods.*

*I am constantly trumpeting the City's successes, but, regrettably, it always sounds too much like blowing my own horn. It is wonderful to have your imprimatur. I would be very appreciative if you would provide me with a copy of your entire speech.*

*All the best.*

I am proud of what my administration has accomplished in providing this city once again with fiscal integrity. All along I had a secret trick—a mayor just has to learn how to say the word *no*. Once you do, you have to be willing and ready to say it. I was.

And I tried always to remember what my mother used to tell me when I was growing up: "Don't spend what you don't have, and live within your means." Good advice in or out of government.

# On Baseball

The closest I come to athletics is spending half an hour every morning on a treadmill at the gym before I head to City Hall. And that's not really sport. For me, it's a form of masochism—and a form of sadism as well if I happen to be in the mood to sing a few of my favorite songs from *Les Misérables*.

I've never been a jock. I've never participated in organized, competitive sports if I could help it. I've never switched on a game of the week, a tournament of champions, or a fight of the century if I could help it. Needless to say, I don't know very much about baseball.

But I do know it is one of the glories of American civilization. And with both the Mets and Yankees, New Yorkers expect their elected officials, especially their mayors, to love the game. We even have a Governor, Mario Cuomo, who, in his leaner and meaner days, played outfield for a minor-league team in the Pittsburgh Pirates' farm system, under various and sundry noms de guerre, including Glendy LaDuke, Matt Dente, and, my favorite, Lava Labretta. In my own leaner, meaner days I collected stamps and was a member of the debate team, not really the kinds of activities which warrant a nickname—good or bad.

Early on I realized that one of my responsibilities as Mayor was to attend opening-day ceremonies at Yankee Stadium and Shea Stadium. Regrettably, I was never asked to throw out the first pitch, an honor even to a nonathlete like myself. With my philatelic background, they probably feared I'd throw a spitter.

I attended Opening Day 1989 at Yankee Stadium with my new counsel Rick Schaeffer, a real aficionado. He'd been told not to get too interested in the game, since I normally left after the first inning. We didn't leave until the end of the second. "Why so late?" he asked. "Because," I said rather sheepishly, "I fell asleep."

When I first went to games, I'd stay for only the top half of the first inning. But then I realized it doesn't take a genius to know that the home team doesn't bat until the bottom half of the first. The strange thing is that even though I am so up-front about my lack of baseball expertise, the fans wouldn't boo me when I left halfway through the first. They'd applaud.

Boos, however, are part and parcel of our national pastime. A mayor can walk around the stadium before the first pitch or between innings and everyone's friendly. But at the start of the game, when the "Welcome Mr. Mayor" message is displayed on the scoreboard, you'd better close your ears and shore up the walls of Jericho. For the boos will most assuredly come tumbling down.

One day former Governor Hugh Carey and I were at a game. We were introduced on the field itself. And, as usual, the boos commenced. The Governor didn't seem to know what to do. "Doff your hat, wave it to the crowd, and bow," I said to him. "Just pretend the boos are really cheers. The crowd will love it." We did. They, of course, responded with even louder booing, but I knew the boos really masked their good will.

My baseball ignorance is legend. On opening day of the Yankees' 1979 season, Doug Johnson of WABC-TV wanted to give his viewers a graphic demonstration. He approached the box where I was sitting. "Mr. Mayor," he said, with microphone in hand and camera at the ready, "I'd like to test your baseball knowledge." "You dog," I thought to myself.

Sitting with me was David Schwartz, the son of Allen Schwartz, one of my closest friends, my former law partner, and the corporation counsel who, during my mayoralty, transformed the city's Legal Department into one of the finest law firms in the country. Allen and David are baseball savants. They know everything there is to know about ERAs, RBIs, and MVPs. Allen, in fact, seems to know everything there is to know about all sports. Just ask him.

He couldn't join me on opening day. So he asked me to bring David, who was celebrating his thirteenth birthday. Was I lucky I did. Doug began to question me.

"Mr. Mayor," he said, "what is the infield fly rule?"

Looking directly into the camera, I said, "Tell him, David."

David gave a perfect answer.

"Mr. Mayor," Doug then said, "what is a hit-and-run play?"

Again, I looked directly into the camera and said, "Tell him, David."

Again, David gave a perfect answer.

Doug asked two more questions, I took two more looks into the camera, and David gave two more perfect answers.

By now Doug Johnson, his face flushed, was clearly upset. "Don't you know anything, Mr. Mayor?" he asked.

"Sure," I said, again looking directly into the camera. "I know his name is David."

It's the last time Doug or anyone else has tested my baseball expertise.

Except for my fellow mayors. Whether ardent fans or not, whenever their hometown team is in a championship play-off against a New York team, mayors from other cities apparently feel compelled to bet on the outcome.

Frankly, it's tough on the waistline. Usually, the stakes are some kind of food. I'll wager a bushel of apples from the upstate farm of Manhattan District Attorney Robert Morgenthau. My fellow mayors will bet something reflecting their local cuisine. Over the years I've done quite well—soft-shell crabs courtesy of Mayor William Schaefer of Baltimore, steaks courtesy of Mayor Dianne Feinstein of San Francisco, and baked beans and clam chowder courtesy of Mayor Raymond Flynn of, where else, Boston. I've enjoyed every single winning wager, every single delicious bite.

In 1986 the Mets were in pursuit of a World Series ring, and I, not surprisingly, was on a diet. Since I was sure another obligatory round of mayoral betting was about to commence, I called Bay Rigby, the very talented cartoonist for the *New York Post,* and asked him to design a flag to celebrate what I was confident would be the Mets' championship season.

If the Mets won, the mayor of the vanquished city would be required to fly Bay's "I Love NY Mets—Don't Tread on Us" flag at a prominent location in his or her city. If the unexpected happened and we lost, I figured I would just have to order up another bushel of apples.

Thanks to the Mets, New Yorkers made out like baseball bandits. The Houston Astros were our first victim. In an exciting, well-managed, well-pitched, and well-played series, the Mets emerged triumphant, four games to two, winning the National League pennant.

Our flag was on its way to Houston. I sent along with it the following letter to Kathryn Whitmire, the very able mayor of Houston and very dedicated Astros fan:

*This letter accompanies my "I Love NY Mets—Don't Tread on Us"*
*flag. Pursuant to our agreement, this flag is to fly in Tranquillity Park,*
*Houston, until high noon Wednesday, October 22, 1986. At that time*
*it is to be flown back to me at City Hall in New York, insured for*
*$1,000, same-day delivery. With respect to the conditions under which*
*this flag can be flown in Tranquillity Park, this flag must be guarded*
*around the clock by at least two (2) Houston police officers or one (1)*
*Texas Ranger.*

*If this is not possible, then the flag must be flown in front of Houston*
*City Hall, where the same people who guard you must guard the flag.*
*Enjoy!*

*The Astros played the National League championship series with*
*extraordinary courage, grace, pluck, and determination. The case of the*
*Houston Astros is certainly an illustration of the validity of the old*
*aphorism: it is not whether you win or lose, it's how you play the game.*
*But, as my mother said, "Because we're not saints, it's more fun to*
*win."*

*All the best.*

Our victory flag didn't fly as many days as expected or, for that
matter, in Tranquillity Park. The citizens of Houston wouldn't stand
for it. They did display it elsewhere, but not in a prominent place. The
only other place that would have been acceptable to me is the Alamo.
And that's in a different city.

All eyes now turned north to Beantown, home of the Boston Red
Sox. As everyone knows, it was one of the best World Series ever, not
being decided until the Mets' miraculous comeback in the sixth game
when they clinched victory in the final inning. The Amazin' Mets
simply pulled off the amazing, winning their second World Series
championship. So off our victory banner flew to Boston, along with the
following letter to my friend Mayor Flynn:

*Our much-traveled victory flag is now being entrusted in your hands*
*to be flown at Boston's City Hall for one week. It recently flew in front*
*of the office of Mayor Kathryn Whitmire in Houston following the*
*National League Championship Series. In fact, it was only returned the*
*day the Amazin' Mets won the World Championship from your Red*
*Sox.*

*I look forward to receiving the crock of Boston baked beans (please*
*cook them slowly) and the crock of Boston clam chowder (I like little-*

*necks). Remember, if you are ever in need of a corned beef sandwich,*
*just give a holler and I'll send one up to you.*
  *All the best.*

Mayor Flynn was very gracious in defeat. But once a betting man, Ray Flynn apparently always is a betting man. "In case you're counting, the score between us is now tied one to one," he wrote upon receiving our victory flag. "Perhaps the rubber match might involve the Celtics over the Knicks or you joining me in an upcoming Boston or New York marathon?" To be courteous, I took him up on his invitation to join him at the next New York Marathon. He ran. I fired the cannon.

When the Mets had won it all, President and Mrs. Reagan invited the team to dinner at the White House. It promised to be a marvelous occasion. But then Larry Speakes, the President's spokesperson, misspoke. "I hope they don't do to the White House what they did to Rusty's restaurant," he told the press on the eve of the dinner. Mets fans everywhere were shocked.

I sent the following telegram to President Reagan:

SPEAKES SPEAKETH WITH A FORKED TONGUE. THE WORLD CHAMPION NEW YORK METS ARE WONDERFUL FAMILY PEOPLE. JUST THE KIND YOU AND MRS. REAGAN WOULD LOVE TO HAVE FOR DINNER. BY ALL MEANS BREAK OUT THE BEST CHINA AND SILVERWARE. SHOULD SOMEONE NOT KNOW EXACTLY WHAT FORK TO USE . . . THEY COULD ASK LARRY SPEAKES.

OUR NEW YORK METS ARE THE BEST IN THE WORLD. THEY'VE PROVEN IT. THEY'RE PROUD TO BE A NEW YORK TEAM AND THEY'RE PROUD TO BE AMERICANS. WHEN YOU RECEIVE THEM AT THE WHITE HOUSE, THEY WILL (AS THEY USED TO SAY IN WESTERN FLICKS): "DO YOU PROUD."

MAYBE LARRY SPEAKES MEANT HIS COMMENTS TO BE JOCULAR, HOWEVER, NOT EVEN THE ACROBATICS OF A GARY CARTER COULD HANDLE A WILD PITCH LIKE LARRY'S.

MR. PRESIDENT, MORE THAN SEVEN AND A HALF MILLION NEW YORKERS—METS FANS ALL—JOIN ME IN SALUTING YOU.

Regrettably, neither the Mets nor the Yankees have won a pennant since 1986. No matter how much I know or don't know about sports, I do know this much—the best series is a subway series. And I care enough about sports and my city to hope and believe that such a series will one day be. But who will the other city's mayor bet with and lose to then?

# About the Roosters on Staten Island

With so many skyscrapers and so many people, who would ever believe that New York City has a wildlife problem? Well, we do, particularly on Staten Island, the least populous of our five boroughs, with fewer people today than the island of Manhattan, just one third the size, had in 1850.

Staten Island's development began with the opening of the Verrazano-Narrows Bridge in 1964. It has boomed and bustled ever since. But it remains the most countrified of the boroughs. A thousand-acre greenbelt runs its entire length. More than a thousand horses are stabled on privately owned land.

And it's still got wildlife. Wild roosters, to be precise. One Saturday afternoon I was at Gracie Mansion reading the *Staten Island Advance.* A tale of two wild, one-eyed roosters caught my eye.

It seems that a bicycle-riding city health inspector was on his duly appointed rounds. He came upon a vacant lot in the Travis section and noticed the two roosters. Suspicious, he began to investigate. A Mrs. Joanne Mistler, owner of an adjacent parcel but not of the two roosters, came out to explain that the roosters had taken up residence in the area some seven years before. They had been born free and now lived wild.

The inspector threatened to call the ASPCA and have the roosters destroyed. "Oh no," Mrs. Mistler replied, "I'll claim them if that will keep them alive." Having tricked her, the inspector wrote out a summons against Mrs. Mistler, charging her with harboring the two fugitive one-eyed roosters. The summons carried a fine of up to $500. Mrs. Mistler refused to accept it.

The inspector pedaled off for reinforcements, returning later that afternoon with four police officers and one police lieutenant to serve the summons. Undaunted, Mrs. Mistler refused again.

By the time I read the *Advance* story, the situation had escalated. Many people called and visited Mrs. Mistler with confessions of their own. Some told her, reported the *Advance,* that they too "had wild ducks, geese, rabbits, and pheasants in their yards." Talk of circulating a petition began, and some visitors even "offered to take the law into their own hands, hiding the roosters on their own property."

After conferring with Tom Kelly, my assistant press secretary and a Staten Island resident, I decided to urge the Health Department to void the summons. It did.

"Clearly we have to train our inspectors to distinguish between barnyard fowl, which are prohibited, and wild birds, including roosters, who are a delight to see and hear scampering in the woods," I said in a statement announcing my rooster resolution. "I suspect that some of our inspectors can't even distinguish between domestic turkeys and wild turkeys."

Mrs. Mistler and one-eyed-rooster lovers everywhere were ecstatic. Mrs. Mistler even said I was "cute and very warm." With those wonderful words, I was sure the case of the carousing chanticleers was closed.

No such luck. A couple of weeks later, I received a marvelous letter from Mr. Arthur Crudo of the Sunset Hills section of Staten Island. More wild roosters were on the run.

"For the last two years," he wrote, his life had been disrupted by the "daily and incessant crowing" of several roosters which roamed wild in his neighborhood. "A rooster does not crow only at sunrise," he went on to explain. "It continues to crow all day long until dusk. An adult rooster can crow as frequently as thirty to forty times a minute. Believe me, I've counted. When you are losing sleep, what else is there to do?

"It's a regular barnyard symphony," he said of the racket being made by the three adult and four baby roosters who were making his days and nights so miserable. "Neither the cold, snow nor rain stops them. They do it year round." And, he said, "the roosters have even attacked a child and several adults on the block."

A health inspector had issued summonses to the neighbors who were feeding the Sunset Hill roosters, but the birds had found other means of sustenance. Beyond that, the inspector had said, he was powerless. "He did suggest," Mr. Crudo reported in his letter, "that we get a pellet gun, blow pipe, or slingshot to kill the roosters." All illegal, he reminded me.

The neighborhood's rooster rooters had also gotten into the act. "Neighbors on the block who like the roosters," Mr. Crudo wrote, "began to harass me and threaten me with legal action, while the head rooster protector offered to have me shot, a threat which I took very seriously." Having received "nothing but bureaucratic red tape, buck passing, and outright inaction," Mr. and Mrs. Crudo appealed to me as "our last hope." Otherwise, they feared, they might have to "move away from New York City."

Obviously, this was much more than a barnyard squabble. So I wrote the following letter to Mr. and Mrs. Crudo:

*Thank you for your letter. I want you to know I appreciate that you expressed your grievance without acrimony and invective, which usually accompanies the letters I receive concerning a complaint of this kind.*

*First of all, in regard to your saying that this situation "is strongly influencing us to move away from New York City," I urge you to reconsider such a rash statement. The problems of living here will never be solved by running away. If you move to another city, you will only find yourself living in a place with more problems—and no place like Staten Island. If you move to the country, you will only find yourself living in a place with more roosters. So, let's agree that you're going to stay here in New York and that we're going to work this problem out, O.K.? O.K.*

*Second, I do not want you to use a pellet gun, blowpipe, slingshot, or any other means to kill or harm the roosters, no matter who may have advised you to do so. We live in a city where roosters are not above the law. Neither are City officials. Neither are you. And neither are your neighbors. If you are the object of physical threats by any of them, you are entitled to protection. If you want to lodge a complaint in Criminal Court against anyone who has threatened you with violence, be assured that you will be protected by the police from any retaliation.*

*From your letter it seems that, while the roosters are clearly discommoding you and your wife and disrupting your sleep, they are a source of great amusement and enjoyment for some of your neighbors. I wonder if it is this clash of tastes between you and them—more than the noise the roosters make—that is the problem. Here, even a Mayor can offer only suggestions, not solutions.*

*I am one of those whose credo, when it comes to the Adirondacks, is "forever wild." Staten Island is not the Adirondacks, I know, and is obviously not the proper place for a mountain lion to be roaming. But how about a wild turkey? Or a rabbit? I guess what I'm trying to say is that, in your collective zeal to maintain Staten Island as a "countrified place within the city," you and some of your neighbors seem to be drawing the line differently as to just what constitutes "countrified."*

*I won't ask you to accept their point of view when I see how greatly you are being vexed by the crowing the roosters make. But until we can get this resolved, I'd ask that you see the bright side of the problem. Be proud of the fact that Staten Island is a place wild roosters think is an appropriate environment for them. The roosters aren't giving up on New York City—so how can you?*

*All the best.*

I've not heard back from Mr. and Mrs. Crudo. But I hope they've stayed in New York. Anyone who can write so wonderful a letter belongs here.

Perhaps Mother Nature intervened and the roosters have gone to roost in some other neighborhood outside of Mr. and Mrs. Crudo's earshot. I just hope they didn't end up as *poulet en casserole.*

## On a Public Figure's Lack of Privacy

The hours are long, the criticisms are ceaseless, and as soon as you've addressed one problem or overcome one crisis, two or three more are sure to arrive on your desk demanding your full attention . . . yesterday, if not sooner!

But if you like the work, there's nothing like being a high public official, especially being the Mayor of the City of New York. And if you do the job right, the reward is knowing that you are having a positive, lasting impact on the lives and futures of 7.5 million people. No wonder so many people want the job.

But there's a downside to being Mayor. For me, at least, the worst thing was that, for twelve years, I was unable to go anywhere in the five boroughs without being accompanied by five detectives and one press secretary. And even when all the day's public events were over, all I lost was the press secretary. The five detectives went wherever I went—to a movie with friends, dinner with my family, even an appointment with my barber.

The detectives on my detail were marvelous guys. Hardworking, dedicated, always with their eyes and ears out for my personal safety. But am I really at risk while what's left of my hair is being trimmed by my barber?

And then, of course, there's the presence of the press. They're constantly asking questions and making inquiries about everything you do, personal or professional. No detail is too trifling to interest them, no question too frivolous for them to ask.

A couple of weeks after I'd suffered my "trivial stroke" in the summer of 1987, I came into City Hall one morning with a bruise over one of my eyes. The ever watchful denizens of the fourth estate stationed in Room 9 in City Hall were quick to notice. It must have been a slow news day, for the theories about why the bruise had befallen me flew fast and furious. Had I been in a fight? The victim of a mugging?

"It's no big deal," I remember saying at a press conference convened to explain what happened. "Since my stroke, my doctors have advised me to take an aspirin a day to prevent blood clots. Ever since, I've had to use the bathroom to urinate more often. At around two this morning, I went into the bathroom, and as I did, I slipped and fell, bruising myself."

Like I said, no big deal. Case closed, I thought.

Not so fast. Later that afternoon one of my assistant press secretaries wandered into Room 9. "There's one question that hasn't been answered," said one reporter. "My editors uptown want an answer."

"What's that?" my press secretary asked.

"Did the Mayor slip and fall forward or backward?"

"Well," my press secretary answered, "since the bruise is on his forehead—to wit, on the front of his head—both common sense and Newtonian physics would tend to suggest that he fell forward."

"True enough," said the reporter. "But would you confirm that with the Mayor? My editors will want it officially confirmed."

Inquisitiveness, of course, is a reporter's stock-in-trade. And these days, their curiosity is being aided and abetted, and my right to privacy as a public figure eroded and ignored, by the courts.

During my years in City Hall, I kept two schedules—a "public schedule," which listed all of the day's events, such as press conferences, ribbon-cutting ceremonies, and meetings with visiting dignitaries, for which we were seeking press coverage, and a "private schedule," which listed all of the day's private meetings, my lunch and dinner plans, and any personal appointments I may have had.

Reporters received copies each afternoon of the former, but not of the latter. In late 1987, a reporter formally requested copies of both my public and my private schedules. Under the state's Freedom of Information Law (FOIL), she had a right to make the request and we had an obligation to reply. I asked Pat Mulhearn, my counsel, to assemble the requested materials, leaving out only those events on the private schedule which, in his view, had nothing to do with my duties as Mayor and were strictly personal in nature.

Pat assembled the information and sent it to the reporter—some five pounds of paper in all. The reporter wasn't satisfied. She wanted everything, including the purely personal information that had been excluded. She went to court to get it. And she won.

"Even as Mayor," I thought, "I must have some minimal rights to privacy." Not so, ruled State Supreme Court Justice Bruce Wright in his decision. "As a public person with a public trust," he wrote, the Mayor "should be accountable for his associations."

I can't say I was outraged by Judge Wright's ruling. Over the years, I'd come to expect the unusual from him. But I did feel that, in the name of liberty, Judge Wright's decision had given the press license to probe the essentially private affairs of public people and have access to our private schedules. By the way, judges and their schedules, public or private, are not subject to FOIL.

Justice Wright's ruling allowed the press to go a lot further than it had ever gone before in invading the privacy of others. As I wrote in the *Staten Island Advance* at the time:

> Open government helps ensure good government. But aren't we going too far? When does open government become Big Brother government? To its credit, the press has alerted us to the virtues of open government, the dangers of Big Brother government. But, as [Dan] Rather said, the press focuses more and more on the heat, not the light, of the world it covers. I hope these recent incidents will force the press to consider again what's news, what's not. After all, there's a thing called news and a thing called gossip. Regrettably, some reporters have lost sight of the distinction.

Thanks to Judge Wright's ruling, then, your right to know who my barber is is now firmly established as a matter of law. It's a victory, I suppose some will argue, for the First Amendment and a free press.

But when the court and the press show a callous disregard for a public official's true privacy, I think we've taken a step over the line that separates a free press from an oppressive one and are permitting a situation that tends to drive good people away from elective or appointed positions.

# PART
# 7

# GIVING AS GOOD
# AS I GET

## Joe Klein

Joe Klein is a reporter for *New York* magazine. He is an excellent writer, but a bundle of neuroses. He was incensed at my taking on Jesse Jackson in the 1988 presidential primary.

"I live in an integrated neighborhood," he said in an excited voice on the last occasion we spoke about Jackson. "You endangered the lives of my wife and child with your remarks."

"You must be crazy," I said. "You're telling me that your neighbors who are black are going to assault your wife and child because of something that I said? That is the most prejudiced remark I've heard in years."

I later learned that he moved out of the integrated neighborhood of which he'd been so proud and into a more suburban, predominantly white community.

Joe Klein covered the 1989 mayoral campaign. On occasion, he'd write something nice about me. Generally, though, he was negative, derisive, and, I believe, unfair.

At one point I twitted him on the hostile reaction he received from black leaders to a piece he'd written that was critical of the black community. I believed he'd dramatically changed his position on some matters reflected in that article, and I told him so.

Some time later, when I gave a speech at a synagogue, Joe followed me outside afterward, particularly incensed at something I'd said. He began to berate me for hypocrisy in speaking out in opposition to quotas while supporting affirmative action programs to increase minority representation in government. I had explained in my speech that if there are three applicants who are relatively equal in experience and ability and one of them is a minority, a woman, or someone from a group of people never having held the position before, I'd prefer that person for the position. I told Joe that that did not constitute a quota and didn't violate my rule that hiring should be based on merit, since all three of the relatively equal applicants had already met that test. And the Civil Service rule of one out of three allows for such considerations.

Klein wouldn't accept that. His voice became shrill, and he even compared me to the Reverend Al Sharpton. Realizing how foolish he'd been, Klein later sent me a letter. "Congratulations," he said, "you got my goat last night. It won't happen again." He then said he wanted to explain his "parting shot" comparing me to Sharpton, "lest you go off, in your inimitable fashion, and say 'Klein, he's hys-ter-i-cal.'

"My point was this," he explained. "So far, there seems to be a broad, positive reaction in the city to what I wrote this week; the only exceptions appear to be black nationalists and media hounds like Sharpton, and also you. That puts you, as I suggested, in the same boat with Sharpton.

"As for my doing a 360-degree turn," he explained, "if that means that I examined my feelings and wound up exactly where I've always been, I guess you're right." But, he insisted, "if it means to imply that my position on any of the issues discussed has changed an iota, you're mistaken." After "some callow stupidity in the late sixties," he said, his position had "remained unchanged since I covered busing in Boston in 1974."

I wrote a long letter in reply to Klein. My advisors, however, urged that I not send it. So I sent him a short note. "I have your letter," I said. "Unfortunately, I don't think you're hysterical. I just think you're irrational."

How irrational? Well, consider the long letter I'd drafted but didn't send. It was right on target:

*Getting your goat is the last thing on my mind, though given such an easy opportunity, it was hard to resist.*

*As far as our discussion is concerned, you were clearly confusing two concepts. There is no contradiction between opposition to quotas and strenuous efforts to increase minority representation. White & Case, or any other organization, would not have to resort to quotas to increase the number of minorities in its employ. Consider my appointments to the Criminal, Family, and Civil Courts. Of 186 appointments, 45 percent have been women and minorities. There has been no quota, just an intensive effort to reach out for quality candidates from all communities. I am proud that this success has come without quotas.*

*What I found particularly troublesome about your piece on race is how it trumpets certain proposals as though they had somehow been overlooked or, in some cases, as though I had not already taken a good deal of flak—some of it from you—for taking tough stands on these issues.*

*For example, you write that "programs that divide by race, even well-intentioned ones, are too costly in moral terms." Let me recall, however, your profile of me from last December 5, which opens with a highly critical account of a City Hall press conference at which we announced a program to bring small contractors into the city's construction programs. In this piece, you criticize my insistence on emphasizing that this program did not exclude companies on the basis of race. We worked hard to develop a program that would be open to all contractors but that would ultimately increase the number of minority contractors we did business with. You quote me: "Everyone knows I'm against all quotas. Racial, ethnic, religious, or gender. They're not fair. They don't work. They create an opportunity for great fraud."*

*Given your new-found pessimism about these kinds of programs, can you now tell me what's wrong with my comment? And as far as walking like a duck and quacking like a duck, as you quote David Dinkins so approvingly, the distinction that I was trying to make at the press conference was not lost on the United States Supreme Court, which ruled that programs based on a racial set-aside were unconstitutional. As a result, cities around the country have been scrambling to come up with a constitutional model for increasing minority participation in government contracting programs.*

*My point involved much more than being "technically correct," as you dismissively put it. Guess whose program they are examining? Guess whose program moves happily along? Guess who just designated five small contractors—all of whom turned out to be minorities, by the way—to develop 242 units of affordable housing around the city?*

*You prescribe a greater emphasis on assimilation of poor blacks into the middle class. Aside from me, is there another political leader you know of who has so consistently stood up for middle-class values and so vigorously defended the aspirations of the poor to join the middle class? Indeed, this was one of the points I made during my appearance at the Sutton Place synagogue.*

*Go back to your "areas of agreement" on the agenda for dealing with the problem:*

*—Education? Operation Giant Step is a city initiative that brings four year olds into school. We have established all-day kindergarten as a citywide goal. Kindergarten and first-grade programs are now being expanded into the summer months.*

*—Crime? TNT is the most effective street-level enforcement technique that has emerged nationally. And it is effective. Newsday reported recently that 80 percent of the TNT arrests made in Queens since March 1988 have resulted in convictions. You know the City can't do it alone. You acknowledge the need for a vastly increased federal interdiction effort—which, I think it is fair to say, is one of my principal themes.*

*—Personal responsibility? Maybe the toughest issue of all. But that's why this is the issue I have spoken out on most forcefully. Rudy Giuliani entirely misses the point in his comment to you. HRA already has a number of programs that seek to teach parenting skills. But this problem goes well beyond the reach of government. What can we do to encourage or even compel standards of personal responsibility? My answer has been to focus on the family, the church, and civic organizations—which all must add to what the government provides.*

*Think of the heat I have taken on a number of issues: Billie Boggs,*

188

*the squeegee men, passing by panhandlers, uniforms in the schools, etc.
Isn't there a theme of personal responsibility that links them? Yet I do
not recall your commenting favorably on any of these initiatives or
coming up with another tough one.*

*Finally, your Al Sharpton remark is rather loony. Or is that simply
your knee-jerk dismissal of any criticism of the pieces you write?*

I usually listen to my advisors when they recommend that I not send
a letter. Once again, I wish I hadn't.

# Michael Pakenham

In the months that followed the suicide of Donald Manes, the independently elected Borough President of Queens who conspired with others
to take kickbacks from collection agency contracts awarded by the
city's Parking Violations Bureau, and the conviction of Stanley Friedman, the independently elected leader of the Bronx Democratic Party
who was found guilty of racketeering, the *Daily News* apparently decided to use any trick, fair or foul, to try to bring down me and my
administration. Unfair editorial commentary that, had I not been a
public official, would most surely have been considered libelous, began
to fill its pages. Day after day after day, every effort seemed to be made
to link me directly with the corruption of others.

Leading the *News*'s charge was Michael Pakenham, its editorial page
editor. Time and time again he'd use exaggerated, inflammatory language, so much so that I became convinced he had gone out of editorial
control and was incapable of making responsible, objective judgments.

Am I being too harsh on Pakenham? You judge. In early 1988 the
city's Department of Investigation completed an undercover operation
which resulted in the arrest of thirty-six inspectors at the Department
of Health. They'd been soliciting bribes from restaurant owners. In
return, they'd look the other way when it came to violations of the
health code.

I was outraged. Diners were outraged. And of course, Michael
Pakenham and the *News* were outraged. But the *Daily News*'s editorial
on the subject went too far, expressing shock that in the course of my
numerous nights out with friends at restaurants no owner had ever

approached me about extortion by health inspectors. The implication, of course, was that I'd been approached, had been told tales of corruption, but had chosen to do nothing about it.

I was incensed:

*Your ill-informed editorial of March 26 entitled "Health Inspectors Wallow in Graft" justly deserves the scorn of your readers. It is painfully naive and unfair, and it was clearly written without checking the facts with your own reporters and certainly without questioning me.*

*You refer to the fact that I go to restaurants, and I do indeed. I probably go to a maximum of thirty different restaurants on a regular basis, not thousands as you state. You ask, "Is it possible that in those two or three thousand restaurant visits, no restaurant owner or operator ever let on to Ed Koch that he or she was being bled white by N.Y.C. Department of Health officials who were extorting them for cash payoffs?"*

*Why not lift up the phone and do the modicum of legwork you would require of any cub reporter? . . .*

*Restaurant owners are more likely to tell the* Daily News *than the Mayor about extortion attempts since they know their identities will be protected. The City Charter requires that I act on such information. Have you ever asked your reporters if they have been given such information? Were you ever given such information and have you turned it over to law enforcement officials?*

*In this administration, if you are found to be corrupt, you are pursued relentlessly by law enforcement and at my urging. Yet you would have the world believe that this administration is the most corrupt ever to have existed.*

*You know that only seven top-level officials (seven too many) have actually been indicted. Of those seven, five served in the two prior administrations. You know that because I have told you personally. Yet you convey the idea that dozens, perhaps hundreds, of my appointees have been indicted. If you want to go beyond indictments, look at what's happened to the five who engaged in unethical practices. They were compelled to leave the administration.*

*You have deliberately mixed together the scandal involving a handful of mayoral appointees with the reprehensible, age-old problem of civil service inspectors on the take. For decades, unfortunately, too many of these employees have been engaged in corrupt activities. The difference is that under my administration we pursue and prosecute them.*

*Contrast this with your own actions. One of your reporters was, while covering a sports event, paid for publicizing it. When that was exposed, did you fire the reporter? No. Would I have? You bet. On another occasion, an editor you employ had a congressman co-sign a loan on which he had to make good. Is he still with the* News? *Yes. Are your standards as high as mine? Apparently not.*

Initially, I'd thought Michael Pakenham was an intelligent man. But the longer his tenure at the *Daily News,* the more its editorial pages are afflicted with double standards and sloppy reporting.

And in this particular editorial he proceeded from an unbelievably stupid premise—to wit, that when a mayor is told of corruption he automatically looks the other way. The exact opposite is true.

When someone comes over to me and tells me a tale of corruption, my surest and only protection is not to ignore it, but as soon as I get back to my office to send a note to the Department of Investigation asking it to look into the charge. If I didn't do that, I'd open myself to the possibility that that person would later reveal that I'd closed my eyes and ears to possible corruption.

Believe me, Michael, I've never claimed to be the smartest man in the world. But I'm not that stupid. Now what about the restaurants you go to?

# Connie Chung

After so many years in the public eye, I've learned that, a few exceptions notwithstanding, it's unwise to count too much on commitments made by reporters.

During the summer of 1988 the debate over dumping treated sewage sludge in the Atlantic Ocean a hundred miles or more off the seaboard rose to the top of the public agenda. Based on the advice of my experts, I defended the practice as posing little, if any, danger to the environment.

Other experts disagreed and were successful in getting the Congress to impose a ban on ocean dumping. That ban means that the City of New York and other cities will have to spend billions of dollars in the years ahead—billions that could instead go into producing affordable housing, repairing our bridges and roadways, modernizing our hospitals, or building new schools—to find an alternative means of disposing of the millions of gallons of sludge a large city produces each and every day. But a ban is a ban and we will comply.

In October I received a telephone call from Connie Chung, then of NBC, now of CBS. She was preparing a special report on ocean dumping, she told me, and wanted to interview me. Since she also planned to interview a sea captain who'd developed a reputation as being extremely knowledgeable about sludge, I said no.

As Mayor I'm required to know a great deal about a great number of things. But I knew I didn't know enough about the nitty-gritty of sewage sludge to do public battle with a sea captain. "If you're going to interview an expert on the other side of the issue," I explained to Connie, "then you ought to talk to the expert on our side of the issue—Harvey Schultz, my Commissioner of Environmental Protection."

Harvey is a very intelligent and well spoken man. But he's not a media celebrity, and I guess Connie felt he was no match for her sea captain. She called back, imploring me to reconsider as an old friend. "Since when," I asked myself, "does talking to a reporter a couple of times on television make you an old friend? Especially since the reporter's about to portray you as a modern-day Ahab because she believes you're destroying the deep blue sea?"

I put my reservations aside, though, and consented to be interviewed. But I imposed one condition. "I'll appear and give an overview on the subject," I told Connie, "as long as you also interview Harvey. That way the expertise of your sea captain will be matched by the expertise of my commissioner." Without hesitation or reservation, she said O.K.

Lo and behold, her story appeared on the network news and Harvey was nowhere to be seen. So much for Connie's word. Just me and the sea captain. "Never again," I promised myself after viewing the segment.

I was furious. A couple of mornings later I sent a letter to Connie's executive producer.

*I am writing to complain about Connie Chung's report on ocean dumping Tuesday evening on* Summer Showcase Magazine.

*When Ms. Chung personally contacted me at home regarding this segment, I agreed to do it, but only if she included Harvey Schultz, the*

*New York City Commissioner of Environmental Protection, who is the expert in my administration on the subject. She agreed without hesitation to include Commissioner Schultz, so I agreed to be interviewed.*

*Regrettably, she called me yesterday morning to inform me that while editing the piece, you, the executive producer, deleted Commissioner Schultz's expert commentary. I conveyed my distress to her, and now I am conveying that same distress to you. I had an agreement with Ms. Chung that was violated. I accepted her personal apology, but I still informed her that this breach of journalistic ethics leaves me no choice but to decline any future interviews for* Summer Showcase Magazine.

*All the best.*

Three weeks later, the producer replied. He did not dispute that Connie had made a commitment. But for him that wasn't the point. "She should not have made such an agreement without consulting me as the responsible producer of NBC News," he wrote. "I understand your displeasure with this decision, but I hope you will appreciate my responsibility in the editorial process that resulted in the exclusion of Mr. Schultz."

I didn't appreciate it. Her producer stressed his "responsibility." Then why wasn't he "responsible" enough to keep the commitments made by his reporter in the field? I sent him another note:

*I have your letter of September 23.*

*No, I do not agree that you have the right to violate an agreement between your agent, Connie Chung, and me. My participation was based on that agreement. If you decided that you did not want to honor it, then you should have eliminated my part of the program. I consider it a gross misjudgment on your part not to have honored that agreement or, alternatively, to have eliminated my section of the program.*

The bottom line? As I've said before and I'm sure I'll say again, never trust a smiling reporter, especially one who calls on an alleged "old friendship" to save her program by trying to do you in.

# Father Lawrence Lucas

The Reverend Lawrence Lucas, pastor of the Resurrection Roman Catholic Church in Manhattan, is a theological maverick in clerical garb who strays well beyond the mainstream of the Catholic Church in America and what it's trying to accomplish.

In late 1982 the City of New York was considering plans to open a shelter for homeless men in a vacant, unused school building in Harlem. "It will mean destruction to the Harlem community," said a flier distributed by opponents to the shelter, including the Reverend Lucas. "This crazy plan will bring over 400 drug addicts, rapists, killers, and mental rejects to the Harlem community," most of whom, it said, would be "white homeless men." Describing me as the "racist Koch," the opponents said the shelter was "devised by Mayor Koch as a vindictive way of punishing the blacks for voting against him for governor."

The flier's claims, of course, were outrageous. It displayed absolutely no compassion for others, no concern for homeless people. And if anyone was introducing racism into the issue, surely it was those who had distributed the flier. Despite that, clearly the opponents had a right to demonstrate against our proposal. And they included the Reverend Lucas.

I decided it would be useful to try to calm the situation. So I agreed to a meeting with the shelter's opponents a few days before Christmas. Most of the elected officials from the area attended. Father Lucas was the spokesperson. They wouldn't listen to reason and wouldn't listen to the facts, one of which was that most, if not all, of the shelter residents would be black.

Sitting across from Father Lucas in the Blue Room of City Hall, I finally said, "No room at the inn, Father?" He became apoplectic, and they all left the meeting vowing to prevent the opening and promising my political demise. The Reverend Lucas went back to Harlem and, according to a newspaper report, said at a rally that he had had to resist the temptation during our meeting to "put two .38's in the head of something that purported to be a man," meaning me. "We don't want your butt in City Hall," he said of me to the assembled crowd. "In fact, if you asked us where, we'd like to dump it in the middle of the Harlem River loaded down with bricks."

But these comments were only the first example of how venomous a priest Father Lucas could be. Five years later, during a protest and fund-raiser against allegations of police brutality, Father Lucas spewed forth again. Calling Phil Caruso, head of the Patrolmen's Benevolent Association, a "racist clown," this man of God, reported the press, told the protesters at the fund-raiser to "pretend that when you reach into your wallets it is a 9mm [pistol] for Caruso's head."

This time I felt Father Lucas had gone too far, especially since I later learned that he had police permits to carry a pistol. He was, in my view, a dangerous man in the raiment of a priest.

I felt I had no choice but to write to His Eminence John Cardinal O'Connor:

*It is with great regret that I must write this letter to you, but it involves a serious matter concerning one of your priests, Father Lawrence Lucas, from the Church of the Resurrection.*

*I believe on a prior occasion I may have mentioned that I had a strange and troubling experience with Father Lucas in 1982. At that time we were creating a men's shelter at what was formerly Sydenham Hospital in Harlem, and there was significant community protest against the plan. Father Lucas played an activist role within the opposition to the shelter and along with others came to City Hall to discuss the issue. Legitimate protest over government actions is an expected, and I believe necessary, part of evolving government policy. It was not Father Lucas's critical statements at City Hall that caused the problem, but rather his comments as reported in the* Uptown News *shortly thereafter which were so disturbing. . . .*

*I had hoped that time had put my concerns to rest, but all the more troubling were remarks allegedly made by Father Lucas, as reported in the* Amsterdam News *on March 14 of this year, with regard to Phil Caruso. . . . It was Phil Caruso who brought the article to my attention, and while it could be passed off as the irresponsible incitements of an opinionated priest, I was also informed that Father Lucas carries a gun. So I checked with the Police Department and found that he has permits for at least four pistols ranging from a .25 caliber to a .357*

*magnum. I understand that he was issued permits based on his attesta-*
*tion that he on occasion carried large sums of money in a high-crime*
*area.*

*Where this all leads I am not sure, but I thought it was important*
*to bring it to your attention. I also wanted to let you know that I feel*
*it important enough to bring to the Police Commissioner's attention*
*as well.*

*Perhaps there is nothing you can do here, and I do not want to add*
*to your burdens, but that is why a Cardinal, like a Mayor, has broad*
*shoulders.*

*Hope to see you soon.*
*All the best.*

Cardinal O'Connor replied a few days later, reporting that he had
begun to look into the situation. In a conversation with the Cardinal,
members of his staff indicated their great distress with Father Lucas's
comments and revealed that Cardinal Cooke, gentle as he was, had
once said in responding to a complaint about Father Lucas, "We can't
shoot him," sounding as though the thought had entered his mind.

Apparently it's no longer possible to reassign miscreant priests to
out-of-the-way parishes far, far away from civilization. Just a few
months later, the Reverend Lucas was at it again. This time the issue
was the selection of a new Schools Chancellor. He was supporting a
particular candidate. But his comments went well beyond her qualifications for the post.

"Those who are killing us in our homes, falsely arresting us in the
subway, murdering us in the streets," he said at a rally, "come primarily
from the Catholic persuasion." And "those who are killing us in the
classroom," he added, "I do not have to tell you what persuasion they
come from. You just have to look at the Board of Education, and it
looks like the Knesset in Israel."

He would later claim that his comments were taken out of context.
Cardinal O'Connor, however, said that he could not justify "condoning
rhetoric that, either in or out of context, could be construed by reasonable persons as racist, anti-Semitic, and, ironically, even anti-Catholic,
regardless of the intention of the speaker." He's absolutely right.

The Reverend Lucas had given new meaning to the word *vile*. After
viewing a tape of his reference to the Knesset, I described his comments as "outrageous." Hardly tough enough rhetoric. By the way, of
the seven members of the city's Board of Education—only two of

whom are appointed by the Mayor—I believe only one was Jewish. In context or out, if his comments were not anti-Semitic, I don't know what is.

# Sydney Schanberg

One September morning in 1986, Barbara Margolis, the city's Commissioner of Protocol and a personal friend, came into my City Hall office.

"Ed, there's a group of young people from the Soviet Union and their American counterparts in the Rotunda," she explained. "They're in New York to put on a play called *The Peace Child*. Do you have time to come out and welcome them by reading a proclamation?"

"Sure," I said. Out to the Rotunda we went. Some eighteen young people, accompanied by their parents and Soviet government officials, were waiting. A crowd of reporters had their notepads at the ready.

"Welcome to New York," I said and then began to read the proclamation. As Mayor, in the course of an average year I would read a hundred or so proclamations. I didn't write any of them. But they are a necessary part of government. People love to have whatever it is they are doing supported by government in a formal way. And proclamations are sought by dozens of organizations.

The proclamation I read on that particular morning was as supportive as any of the others I'd issued. But as I read it I began to think to myself, "Just yesterday I saw the son of the *U.S. News & World Report* correspondent Nicholas Daniloff. He looked very worried about the fate of his father." Daniloff had recently been taken prisoner by the Soviet Union on the charge that he was a spy. I thought, "To allow the Soviets simply to grab up innocent Americans in order to force the return of one of their spies is intolerable. If I don't speak out about the false imprisonment of Daniloff and the outrages of the Soviet government and its violations of everything decent, I'll be conveying that I truly believe putting on a play called *The Peace Child* can actually help improve relations between the United States and the Soviet Union." (I learned only later that the very play being praised was anti-American and anti-Semitic propaganda.)

So, when I finished reading the proclamation, I spoke my mind. I said, "The Soviet government is horrendous. It's the pits." I tried to make clear that I was not holding the young people responsible for the outrages of their government. But my comments brought forth a torrent of abuse from columnists and editorial writers.

In its genteel, conservative fashion, *The New York Times* applauded my right to speak up but noted that I could have chosen a more appropriate forum. *Newsday* said the occasion was appropriate, but the phrase "It's the pits" was not. The *New York Post* congratulated me, reminding its readers that if LaGuardia had said something similar about Adolf Hitler to Nazi schoolchildren who might have visited City Hall, it would have been remembered to this day with great admiration.

Tass, the official Soviet news agency, described me as "a bellicose anti-Soviet." It said I had "poured out indecent, coarse words" on the Soviet system. "It's always a compliment," I replied, "to be denounced by Tass."

But then came Sydney Schanberg, a columnist for *New York Newsday*. In a column entitled "The Mayor Should Go Stand in the Corner," written a few days after the visit, he wrote that "the Mayor's behavior is that of a badly behaved twelve-year-old."

I prepared a response and submitted it to *Newsday*, expecting it to be published. However, Sylvan Fox, the editor of its editorial page, refused to run it as submitted, insisting that some of the language critical of Schanberg be deleted. I refused, telling him that I would not accept his censorship. Instead, I submitted the piece to the *Staten Island Advance* as one of my weekly columns.

A few days later Les Trautman, the *Advance*'s editor in chief, called to tell me that Schanberg had demanded that he not run my piece in the *Advance*. To his credit, Les refused to accede to his wishes. Schanberg then berated the *Advance* for permitting me to appear regularly in its pages as a columnist. Les Trautman told me he was amazed at Schanberg's demand and at his anger.

But the episode revealed an interesting aspect of Schanberg's journalistic standards. The First Amendment protects his right to speak his mind and to attack others. But apparently he doesn't believe that public officials have the same First Amendment right or that they should be allowed to voice their own opinions in newspaper columns. My editorial did in fact appear in the *Staten Island Advance*, prefaced by a note explaining the circumstances of its publication. Part of it follows:

I wonder what Sydney Schanberg's reaction would have been if a Soviet mayor had told a group of visiting American students that America and its government were "the pits" because of our ongoing problems with homelessness, drugs, and unemployment? Would an outraged Schanberg have rushed to attack that Russian mayor? I doubt it. Instead, we could have expected a Schanberg column expressing embarrassment at America's shortcomings and urging students to heed the Russian mayor's criticism and work to make our country a better place.

I also wonder what Schanberg's reaction would have been if those young people I met in City Hall had been not from the Soviet Union but from South Africa? Suppose I had told a group of young white South Africans—as I certainly would have done—that their oppressive government is the pits? Would Schanberg have rebuked me, or would he have praised me for seizing the moment to advance the cause of justice and democracy in South Africa?

I speak out where and when the occasion demands. I attack tyranny on both the right and the left. I will not heed the dubious advice of Sydney Schanberg and let myself be subjected to a double standard. I will not be silent while Soviet Jews, Christians and other religious groups are terorrized and imprisoned for trying to practice their faith.

I will not let myself be censored for saying to Russians what Russians are saying to each other.

Am I helping or hurting the cause of freedom in the Soviet Union when I speak the same message that Andrei Sakharov, Anatoly Scharansky and Alexander Solzhenitsyn have spoken so bravely?

I will not be brushed aside by the pendulum of political fashion. The Soviet government, like the government of South Africa, is still the pits. And I will continue to point this out until they raise themselves up to a level where their citizens and the entire world can live in freedom from fear.

Previously, Sydney Schanberg had been the metropolitan editor at *The New York Times.* He was removed from that post and named as a columnist on the *Times's* op-ed page. That ultimately ended as well. As an op-ed columnist, he became a populist, radical in perspective as well as in tone. When he finally went to *Newsday,* his radicalism grew still more pronounced.

Our already bad relationship took an even worse turn in November 1987. A State Supreme Court Justice had just ruled that "Billie Boggs," the first mentally ill homeless person involuntarily removed from the streets of New York City and admitted to a hospital for care, should be released. Shortly afterward, I'd appeared on *Face the Nation* with Norman Siegel, executive director of the New York Civil Liberties Union and Ms. Boggs's attorney, to speak about the ruling.

Siegel thought the city's program to help people like "Billie Boggs" was unconstitutional. I thought—and said—that Siegel was "nuts," pointing out what a disservice the NYCLU and Siegel were doing to Ms. Boggs by helping to deny her the medical assistance she plainly needed.

"After ten years on the job," Schanberg wrote of my exchange with Siegel, "our mayor, rather than mellowing, still seems constitutionally unable to deal with criticism other than by calling the critic a loony or a wacko or a pinko."

In response, I wrote the following letter to *Newsday*. This time, I'm pleased to report, they accepted the piece without reservation and published it without cuts:

*Schanberg takes me to task for my castigating those who have opposed our program to take into custody for hospitalization a small group of homeless on our streets. These individuals have been diagnosed by psychiatrists as gravely mentally disabled and in danger of death in the foreseeable future. We can argue about the program and its worthiness. It suffices to say that the policy has been challenged four times in court.*

*On three occasions the individuals were found by judges to be legally detainable under that definition. One case, that of Billie Boggs, is the subject of a review by the Appellate Division, the trial court having found that if she wants to return to the streets she has that right. This letter is not intended to discuss the Billie Boggs case, which I am happy to do and have done in other forums. Rather, it is to take on Sydney Schanberg.*

*First, let me give you my understanding of why he and I are clearly hostile toward one another. When I became Mayor, one of the first public events that I held at Gracie Mansion was a party to honor Dith Pran and Sydney Schanberg. Dith Pran had just been released by the Khmer Rouge in Cambodia. The two of them were lionized by the city, as they were at this party which I held in their honor. If I knew then what we all know now of how Dith Pran had come to be taken prisoner in Cambodia, I would have held the party to honor Dith Pran alone. Schanberg knows of my feelings on this. Enough said.*

*Sydney Schanberg berates me for referring to opponents as "pinkos." The fact is that I write six columns a week, and I have written two books. I have been quoted ad nauseam, every day, 365 days a year, for the last ten years. I defy Schanberg to produce any writing in which I have ever called anyone a "pinko." He cannot because I have not said it.*

*So his defense is that when I refer to a critic as an ideologue, it is, as he puts it, "A Koch code word for pinkos." Now we no longer can use the word ideologue even if we believe it applies to an individual. It is a "no-no" according to Schanberg, to be stripped from our lexicon. I would describe this columnist not only as an ideologue but more specifically as a populist. Or is such a designation also a Schanberg "no-no"?*

*He seeks the plaudits of the crowd and wants, as implied in his columns, a redistribution of wealth in this city and probably the country. Except, of course, if that redistribution were to include the Schanberg holdings as well.*

*Let's examine his career. Its high point was as a Pulitzer Prize winner for his reports on Indochina. Then he became Metropolitan Editor of* The New York Times, *one of the greatest jobs in journalism in the country. Then he was not. He was shunted to an op-ed column but remained in print in the premier paper of this country. Then he was not.*

*Whenever one in polite circles discusses Sydney Schanberg, it is as though he has two first names. The conversation always begins with "Poor Sydney." I don't think he is so poor, nor do I think he is deserving of anyone's sympathy. He has gotten away with murder and has been given preferential treatment accorded to very few. . . .*

*Schanberg and some of his friends and colleagues have been opposed to my administration for years. They thought that as a result of the corruption of Donald Manes and others, which was first uncovered in January 1986, within six months I would be brought down and they would be doing the bringing. . . . I not only survived but, according to polls, I am politically stronger than ever, and so the new cry of my critics is, as they gnash their teeth, "Yes, he is resilient." (It is said with much regret, I assure you.) How arrogantly they deny common sense on the part of the public.*

*Now let's talk about fairness not just to me but to others as well. Sydney Schanberg is one of the most unfair columnists I know. He tears people apart unmercifully and often without basis. One of the more egregious attacks, one defaming a very reputable lawyer, was his attack on Nicholas Scoppetta. Even after Schanberg knew what the facts were, he declined to report them and was bent on smearing Scoppetta in spite of them. The defense of Scoppetta was made cogently by Judge Harold Rothwax, and I won't repeat it here because it has already appeared in this paper. Schanberg should have been ashamed of himself for unfairly attacking Nick Scoppetta and injuring his family. But he wasn't and no apology was forthcoming. Immunized by pomposity and an awesome belief in his own probity, he seems never to feel the need to look into himself.*

*Finally, let me challenge Sydney Schanberg in his role as a columnist. Why doesn't he simply rely on the defense of the truth, as John Peter Zenger once did, rather than hiding behind an artificial defense? If you attack a public figure, even if what you say is totally false, if legal malice cannot be proven, there is no basis for a libel action. This is a difficult, if not impossible, standard of proof to meet, à la Westmoreland and Sharon. Schanberg restricts his victims to those in the public sector in order to hide behind this legalistic shield. He could easily show the courage of his convictions (if he has any) by waiving this defense because it must be affirmatively pleaded. By doing so, he would allow his victims to test his word solely against the truth.*

*All of us are subject to the scrutiny of history. One hundred years from now, historians will be analyzing figures in public life, government or the private sector. Their impact, positive or negative, on our society will be judged. When they examine Schanberg in his role as columnist and me in my role as Mayor, who will be perceived to have had the most positive impact on this city? If you were inclined to wager, on whom would you bet? Ever heard of a sure thing?*

*All the best.*

Schanberg never accepted my challenge. He said I'd referred to my critics as "pinkos." Yet he never offered the proof to support his charge. And, of course, I never had used the term against my critics.

But that's just the kind of "journalist" Schanberg is. Hit, run, then hide and never worry about whether what you write is true or not. And never, ever acknowledge or accept responsibility for your mistakes, deliberate or otherwise.

# Jack Newfield

Jack Newfield, now a columnist for the *Daily News*, is a powerful person. He shows up at all of the right parties, uses his column to curry favor with all of the right people, threatens his colleagues and those elected officials who don't fall into his line, and holds near and dear all of the populist theories that were rejected years ago.

But Jack has a little problem. He's a self-admitted liar. Others may value his opinion or trust his judgment, but I don't. For not only has he lied; as I wrote to *The City Sun*, he has also consistently distorted the facts:

*Jack Newfield's "Tales of the Other New York"* (The City Sun, *November 7th) is aptly titled. In the* New Webster's Dictionary, *the word "tale" is defined as "a narrative of events that have happened or are imagined to have happened; a short story, true or fictitious; a piece of information, especially gossip; a rumor; a falsehood; a lie."*

*In a letter he published in* The Village Voice *of September 28, 1972, Jack Newfield wrote: "I was there when Bella [Abzug] said at the VID [Village Independent Democrats] in 1970 that she was against the jets for Israel. And then I watched her deny she ever said it. And finally I lied, and denied she ever said it, so that she might defeat Barry Farber."*

*I leave it to the reader to decide which word in the definition of "tale" is most appropriate to Jack Newfield's style of journalism.*

*Another characteristic of Newfield's style is a failure to state his bias and hidden motives. Newfield is not simply a writer who happens to be critical of my administration. He is a longtime political opponent of mine who takes an active role in organizing efforts to unseat me. An article in the January 28, 1981,* New York Times *identified Newfield as a founding member of a "group of New Yorkers who oppose Mayor Koch's reelection this year [and who] drafted a preliminary platform yesterday in the hope that someone would volunteer to run on it."*

*When seen in this light, Newfield's brand of journalism can be properly judged for what it is. It is not surprising that his personal bias leads him to make statements that are not factually accurate. . . .*

*I strongly object to the systematic and persistent distortion of my record on race relations for the purpose of generating racial bitterness or gaining political advantage, or both. I believe that people are catching on to Jack Newfield's real motives, and that his distortions will harm only himself.*

Regrettably, some people aren't catching on at all. Recently, the *Daily News* hired Newfield as a columnist. It's ironic at best, hypocritical at worst, for Newfield, someone who consistently berated my administration for racial insensitivity, to go to work for a newspaper—the *News*—which has been found by a court of law to engage in racially discriminatory hiring and, in fact, has had to pay millions of dollars in damages to those discriminated against as well as to enter into a court-ordered remedial hiring plan. But Newfield has never been one to apply the same standards to himself that he demands of others.

He is what I have called "a politician with a press pass." Believe me, the description fits. In the 1989 mayoral race, for example, many people said Newfield was largely responsible for encouraging Joe Hynes, the State Special Prosecutor and my former Fire Commissioner, to offer himself as a candidate against me. But then Newfield apparently had a better idea, dropped Hynes, and became the driving force behind Manhattan Borough President David Dinkins's mayoral candidacy. Even then he wasn't done mayor-making. He had an even better idea, and apparently also became the driving force behind the federal prosecutor Rudy Giuliani's decision to enter the race. It was even reported that Newfield had been doing some scheduling work for the Giuliani campaign. In the end he voted for Dinkins, he said.

I don't know if Hynes is upset that Newfield dropped him for Dinkins. I don't know if Dinkins is upset that Newfield was also courting Giuliani. And I don't know if Giuliani ever worried that Newfield would drop him for someone else. But I do wonder if the *Daily News* has ever been upset that a journalist in its employ who is supposed to get paid to report the news instead spends much of his time trying to manipulate it. As I wrote to *The Nation:*

*I thought* The Nation *was more responsible than to publish the half-truths, distortions and outright lies in Jack Newfield's article "Mayor Daley Is Alive and Well in N.Y.C." (April 4). The author's style is well known to me, as is his treatment of the subject matter. So it came as no surprise to see fairness supplanted by calculated falsehood. I would have expected, however, that* The Nation *would have men-*

*tioned in its brief biography of the writer that he was an active member of the "Dump Koch in 1981" campaign committee. . . .*

*Newfield, whose style could be characterized as misstatement, omission and sleight of hand, has almost never written a piece in my nine-and-a-half years in office that was other than an attack. To present him to an unsuspecting reader as fair or as a journalist without portfolio is, at best, misleading. . . .*

*If there is any one area that could serve as a . . . test on the issue of whether an administration is under the influence of political leaders, it is the process by which a mayor appoints judges. In New York City, this is an area in which mayors have virtually unfettered discretion. As Mayor, I have appointed more than 150 individuals to terms of up to ten years on the Criminal Court, Family Court and (on an interim basis) the Civil Court. . . . Political leaders have historically held out judgeships as the principal carrot to the party faithful, party chairs, lawyers involved in the petitioning process, lawyers who volunteer to mount court challenges and lawyers who assist in Election Day operations.*

*Following my election, . . . my predecessor, Mayor Abraham Beame, drew criticism from local bar associations and the press for his midnight appointments to the bench of individuals deemed political and unqualified. Mayor Beame was acting in the tradition of big-city politics. . . . If the party bosses of New York have had the influence that Jack Newfield claims they have had over this administration, the evidence would be in my appointments to the courts.*

*My appointments have been praised by my admirers and critics alike for being based solely on the merits. Not one of the more than 150 men and women whom I have appointed has been sworn in without first having survived a rigorous and independent selection process which included review by an independent nominating committee; a screening by the City Bar Association; a personal interview with me; and a public hearing. Not one of the individuals appointed was the product of a patronage arrangement. . . . Not one applicant was ever asked his or her party enrollment. . . .*

*Does all of this sound like Mayor Daley to you? . . .*

*According to Newfield, "During the runoff Koch made a deal with the Democratic Party bosses. They all endorsed him in exchange for promises of patronage and access." Clear and simple, that is a lie. Although I was endorsed by some county leaders during the runoff election (none had supported me during the primary), there was never a quid pro quo or any other arrangement for government jobs and access.*

*Newfield writes that "Koch gave party bosses like [Meade] Esposito, Stanley Friedman . . . and the late Donald Manes of Queens control over patronage, blocs of jobs and sometimes whole city agencies." A total fabrication. The only knowledge I have of Manes ever supporting candidates for jobs at the Parking Violations Bureau is Manes's recommendation that Lester Shafran, then director of the bureau, be made First Deputy Commissioner of the Transportation Department, and that Geoffrey Lindenauer take Shafran's place as P.V.B. director. In both instances, although Shafran and Lindenauer had worked for the city for ten or more years, someone else was given the job. . . .*

*For Jack Newfield, truth is putty, to be twisted and squeezed into one fantastic shape or another. The result is an ugly self-portrait of the artist as a bitter man.*

So much for Newfield.

# Donald Trump

Donald Trump likes to make a big deal about the big deals he makes. No wonder he stirs strong emotions among people who have had dealings with him. "I wouldn't believe him," said Alair Townsend, my former Deputy Mayor for Economic Development and now publisher of *Crain's New York Business*, "if his tongue were notarized." Bravo, Alair.

Trump used to be one of my biggest supporters. Indeed, one night in the spring of 1987, at a dinner commemorating the opening of the Vietnam Veterans Memorial in lower Manhattan, he made a very, very strong statement about what a good Mayor I had been.

It didn't take him long to change his mind. At the time, the National Broadcasting Company was suggesting that it might consider offers to move its headquarters from Rockefeller Center—known throughout the broadcasting world as "30 Rock"—to another location. If the price was right, NBC said, it would even consider a move across the Hudson to the swamplands of New Jersey.

Donald Trump rode to the rescue, saying that only he could keep

NBC in New York, by developing a project known as Television City on the Upper West Side. The problem with his plan was that it wasn't only his money that he needed to develop the site. He was asking city taxpayers to dig into their pockets and provide deep tax subsidies to develop the site and, thus, to subsidize the million-dollar residential condos he was building to sell.

And when Donald Trump says deep subsidies, he does mean deep. In fact, the city subsidies he was seeking were far greater than any that had ever been provided to any private sector development in the history of the city. Donald Trump's not the kind of guy who takes no for an answer, and when I said no to his subsidy plan, he erupted. Immediately he launched into a factually inaccurate and personally offensive attack on me and my administration's position.

"If Donald Trump is squealing like a stuck pig," I said at the time, "I must have done something right." So I took my case to the people. The following column, published in June of 1987 in the *Staten Island Advance*, outlines the issues which divided us; I wanted to let it be known that, as far as I was concerned, the interests of the city would always come before the interests of Donald Trump:

Donald Trump vs. Ed Koch. The way it's being played, you'd think it was the fight of the century. But it involves more than that, not just whether the National Broadcasting Company will stay in Manhattan, but also to what degree the city treasury should subsidize economic development for specific companies.

Claiming I have "absolutely no sense of economic development," Mr. Trump charges I'm "playing Russian roulette with perhaps the most important corporation in New York over relatively small amounts of money." Ed Koch, he says, "can't hack it anymore."

Well, when it comes to economic development, I clearly can hack it. When I became Mayor there was twice as much construction under way in Morris County, New Jersey, as in all of New York City, even though Morris County had just one-eighteenth the population. Today, there's more than twenty times the construction activity here [that] there was back then. Similarly, during the 1970s New York City lost more than 600,000 jobs. Since 1978, we've gained more than 300,000 private sector jobs. Doesn't that prove we know something about economic development? Absolutely.

And I know enough about economic development to know that Mr. Trump is a great entrepreneur. I've never hesitated to say so. But I also know that more than "relatively small amounts of money" are at issue. That's why I've responded toughly. "When you're Mayor," I've said, "there are always hard choices. And those who carry the responsibility of running the city should try to resolve them in a common-sense way. Common sense does not allow me to give away the city's treasury to Donald Trump."

Strong rhetoric, right? But behind the histrionics and the hoopla, you'll find that the issue is one of protecting the city treasury. Lately, you see, Mr. Trump has been asking for a free pass to the treasury. We won't allow it. Let me tell you why.

NBC is one of the city's major employers. Its presence bolsters our deserved reputation as the communications capital of the world. Eighteen months ago it said it might relocate from Rockefeller Center to another site here or in New Jersey. Starting with a meeting with NBC at Gracie Mansion in September 1985, we reached out to discuss alternative sites and incentives to lower the cost differential between New York and New Jersey. The conversations are ongoing and, I hope, will result in NBC's recommitment to New York.

Some weeks ago Trump called for the city to grant a thirty-year full tax exemption on his entire proposed Television City project on Manhattan's West Side, not just that part for NBC's use. The exemptions would be used as a subsidy to cut NBC's rent to $15 a square foot in 1993, or well below market rates in Manhattan. According to Deputy Mayor Alair Townsend, his proposal would have meant a huge tax loss to the city—$1 billion in constant dollars. Is it any wonder we rejected his proposal?

Mr. Trump then modified his proposal. He now sought a twenty-year full exemption for the entire project at a cost of over $700 million in constant dollars, with the city sharing in the potential profits from the project.

We rejected that offer, too. Instead, I made a proposal to NBC with respect to real estate taxes and energy as good as any we have ever offered to any company anywhere in Manhattan. NBC could use that package either at Mr. Trump's site or [at] any other location including, among others, Battery Park City and the Gulf & Western sites.

Alternatively, we made NBC a proposal to provide substantial financial incentives if they choose to remain at their current Rockefeller Center site, perhaps relocating some of their studios to Queens. Why is ours the most reasonable, responsible approach? There are a number of reasons.

- We want NBC to stay in New York. We started to do that through Mr. Trump, but rather than the normal concessions one could expect between a landlord and a tenant eager to make a deal, Mr. Trump expected the city to make all the significant concessions. His competitors—Rockefeller Center and Hartz Mountain—have made concessions. As of this writing, Mr. Trump is the only one of the three landlords competing for NBC who does not have a specific proposal for NBC to examine.

- What Mr. Trump wanted was simply too expensive and would have established undesirable precedents. In 1971 a tax-exemption program was created to spur housing construction. Until 1985 luxury residential development got a partial, declining tax benefit over ten years. Two years ago we revoked this limited benefit because Manhattan's residential market was so strong.

Mr. Trump wanted a 100 percent, nondeclining benefit for twenty years—an exemption more than three times as valuable as the most generous benefit we've ever given in Manhattan and nearly twice as valuable as that currently provided to builders of low- and middle-income housing in such areas as Jamaica, East New York, or the South Bronx. And he wanted it for condos selling for $400 to $500 per square foot. Tenants living in surrounding buildings would pay full taxes while people living in Television City wouldn't pay for twenty years. Is that fair? No.

- He also wanted twenty years of no taxes for his retail space and non-NBC office space. Everybody else now building commercial space on the West Side is entitled to an eight-year declining tax break to be repaid in full after ten years. Mr. Trump's tenants or Mr. Trump, however, would get a full tax break for twenty years, which would never have to be repaid. That's ten times as valuable as the existing as-of-right benefits.

When we were in the depths of economic depression in the mid-seventies the most generous tax break we ever gave any commercial building was only a declining exemption for fifteen years. Even now, those building in our most depressed neighborhoods only get a full tax break for thirteen years. Mr. Trump asked for more.

- NBC wouldn't have paid real estate taxes for twenty or thirty years. Over thirty years, that would cost taxpayers $165 million in constant dollars. NBC is very important to New York, but I've never given a thirty-year, zero-tax deal to anybody. And never will.

A new plateau can't be set for every company considering relocation.

Where would it stop? Total revision of our tax structure for one company sets a dangerous precedent. Will we do the same for the next company? And the one after that? If so, our real estate tax base would be diminished, service delivery would be jeopardized, and tax policy would be in shambles. We'll go a long way to spur economic development. But not that far.

His proposal raises other serious concerns. It's nearly twice as large as [the one] the Board of Estimate, myself included, had previously approved for the site under the earlier Lincoln West plan. He wants to build 7,600 condos; the board had previously approved 4,300. He wants 7,300 parking spaces; the board previously approved only 3,700. He wants 1.5 million square feet of retail space; the board previously approved only 400,000. The site should be developed. But not at the density Mr. Trump proposes. To sign on now as a "partner" in Mr. Trump's potential profits would give the appearance of prejudging the zoning issue in advance of the zoning process, and that would abrogate my responsibilities as Mayor and as a member of the Board of Estimate. Private developers may make any proposals they wish to maximize their interests. But public officers have a different, broader concern. In all of the discussions we've had with NBC, one standard has been paramount: doing what was best for all the people in the City of New York.

We believe that what Mr. Trump wants would mean a massive loss of public funds exceeding any potential participation in profits the city may have received from the project and far larger than needed for him to subsidize NBC.

What's good for Television City may be what's good for Mr. Trump. But it isn't necessarily what's good for the people of the City of New York. I'll continue to do everything that's reasonable and responsible to keep NBC in New York. It's good for the city they're here. Being in New York has also been good for NBC. It can be good for NBC in the future.

The City of New York, I'm pleased to report, prevailed without giving in to Donald Trump. By year's end I was able to report that "the world's most famous peacock will continue to roost right here. The National Broadcasting Company has reached an agreement . . . that will enable the network to keep and expand its office and studio facilities at 30 Rockefeller Center. NBC's decision shows that a peacock can have both brains and beauty."

Donald Trump's West Side site still lies undeveloped. He can't do it alone; he wants huge city subsidies, which are unwarranted and would if given be a raid on the public treasury. I say Trump's next book should be called *The Art of the Steal.*

# Jim Hoge

The *Daily News* supported me twice, in 1977 and again in 1981. In 1977, in fact, it was one of only two major dailies—the other being the *New York Post*—to shock the city by endorsing my candidacy and, thereby, to give me credibility.

That was then. This is now. For years the *Daily News* has been losing millions of dollars a year, despite the fact that it has the largest circulation of all the papers in the city. A few years ago, the Tribune Company out of Chicago, which owns the *Daily News,* began to change its top management, bringing in Jim Hoge and Gil Spencer, who in turn brought in Art Browne and, ultimately, Jack Newfield.

Apparently, even before Newfield arrived the new team made a conscious decision to try to boost its fortunes by setting out to ruin my reputation. Specifically, it decided to use the corruption scandal and any other issue it could find to try to force my resignation or to prevent my reelection as Mayor. Its columnists—people like Bob Herbert; Jimmy Breslin, who has since gone on to *Newsday;* Mike McAlary, who came to the *News* from *Newsday* to replace Breslin; and, most recently, Jack Newfield from *The Village Voice*—are in the front lines of the *News*'s campaign against me. For them, the truth has no relevance.

Shortly after the corruption scandal broke in early 1986, in fact, Jimmy Breslin—a close personal friend of a number of corrupt people involved in the scandals involving the late Queens Borough President Donald Manes—appeared on *The Larry King Show* and predicted that I would be forced to resign within six months.

When I appeared on *The Larry King Show* shortly after Breslin's prediction, I had a prediction of my own to make. I would not resign, I promised, but I expected to speak at Breslin's funeral as Mayor. Neither event occurred.

Regrettably, the *Daily News* exercised absolutely no control in terms of grace, decency, or ethics as its columnists, day after day, pummeled me. I believe it was part of the *News*'s grand design to topple me. Jim

Hoge, its publisher and president, said otherwise. At a lunch he told me that the *News* had not made a decision as to whom it would endorse in the 1989 mayoral election, and that I was wrong to think it wouldn't consider endorsing me.

I was also wrong to think, he said, that he would allow his paper to be used as a vehicle against me. It was hard to believe him. Browne, for example, had been the *News*'s City Hall bureau chief before becoming city editor. In addition to covering me day to day, while he was bureau chief he also worked with two other City Hall reporters on a book entitled *I, Koch*. I thought it was unethical for him to do the book while covering me as a reporter at City Hall. People may differ with me on that, but I don't think you can do both at the same time and maintain journalistic and intellectual honesty.

Browne and his coauthors were particularly gleeful that they were able to label *I, Koch* "a decidedly unauthorized" biography of me. That's because I decided not to cooperate by granting interviews for their book. I was sure it would be a hatchet job. It was.

At lunch, Hoge also said he had expressly warned Newfield, who has never permitted journalistic ethics to stand in the way of his desire to be mayoral kingmaker, not to use his column for his personal vendettas against me or, for that matter, to advance the candidacy of whoever his current political champion was.

I really believe Hoge believed what he was saying to me, even though at the time he obviously had no real control over his columnists. Why was it obvious? Just a few days later, his columnist Mike McAlary engaged in a tasteless, unfair attack on me for speaking at the funeral of a police officer. He was so eager to pursue his political agenda— "Dump Koch"—that he totally distorted the facts.

When his column appeared, I was particularly incensed because of the commitment to fairness made just days earlier by Jim Hoge. So I sat down and wrote to Hoge. The letter which follows is not exactly the letter I ultimately sent.

My advisors felt that the sentence "You may think that you are running the paper, but I think they think they are running the paper for their own political purposes" was offensive and unnecessary. So on their recommendation, I deleted it from my final draft.

On reflection, however, I wish I had kept it in. I find that my initial responses to a hatchet job of the McAlary sort, tough as they are, are usually right on the mark and more effective. They also give me far more psychic satisfaction.

*As I told you when we had lunch, I believe that many of your columnists use their columns to try to do me in and elect their candidate—Dinkins or Giuliani. They do this with the vilest of tactics. McAlary's March 8 column is such an illustration.*

*In his column, McAlary says, "Edward I. Koch had walked to the church pulpit a few moments earlier. He started out with outrage and went straight to fingerpointing, turning a funeral into a campaign outing. He blamed public officials who do nothing about drugs. Mostly, it can be argued, he was talking about himself. 'If people that make the laws don't change them, then change the people,' the mayor said. Koch has been to dozens of cop funerals, probably more than any mayor in this city's history. He always blames the federal government for local problems and then walks away. Then another cop dies and he's back again talking about Washington, D.C."*

*If Mike had taken the time to take an even cursory look at my record, he would know I have in fact done a great deal at the local level to combat the scourge of drugs. But consulting the factual record would have prevented him from making a political point.*

*But that's not the most outrageous part of McAlary's column. I did not intend to speak at the funeral service for Officer Robert Machate. I was there to attend the funeral service, as I do for every police officer. As I entered the church, it was Robert Machate, Sr., the father of the slain officer, who came over to me and said, "Mayor, would you please speak at the service? My family and I would appreciate it." I was moved by Mr. Machate's request and did so. My comments were all extemporaneous, and I believe anyone listening to that extemporaneous statement would agree that it was appropriate. I would not withdraw a word. If you want the full statement, I will have it transcribed and send it to you. Perhaps you might even publish it. Please let me know. But I thought that the viciousness of McAlary should be brought to your attention. You may think that you are running the paper, but I think they think they are running the paper for their own political purposes.*

Tacky, tasteless, and typical McAlary. Nowhere in his column, of course, did he mention that as Mayor I always went to the funerals of New York City police officers.

And it wasn't electioneering that motivated me to go. I went out of the fundamental respect all of us owe to the memory of young men and young women who have given their lives to protect us. And I went to Officer Machate's funeral to express my support for the bereaved widow and children that young officer had left behind. For me, it was an act of simple human decency.

I didn't expect the *News* to endorse me in the 1989 Democratic primary. For months, almost every *News* columnist had not only jumped aboard the "anybody but Koch" bandwagon, but openly used their columns to give short shrift to the many accomplishments of my administration and advance the cause of David Dinkins. Occasionally a columnist like Ken Auletta or Bill Reel would lean toward Richard Ravitch.

Much to my surprise, then, shortly before the primary, I learned that a huge battle was raging at the *News* over whom it would endorse in the primary. Virtually every columnist and editorial board member wanted to endorse Dinkins. But Jim Hoge, the *News* publisher, thought I should be endorsed. Usually, the publisher of a newspaper has the final word on electoral endorsements. So I at least had a chance, slim as it was.

We were told that the endorsement was to be made on a certain date. That date came and went, however, and the *News*'s editorial page remained silent. I knew then that I had lost the battle, because the publisher would only grow weaker with any delay. Several days went by. Still there was no endorsement, and, I heard, still the battle raged.

Ultimately, the *News* endorsed Ravitch. Even at that late date in the campaign, he still enjoyed the support of only about 3 percent of the likely voters in most polls. Most observers had already declared him a sure loser, and everyone realized that, for the *News*, he was nothing more than a compromise candidate. The publisher didn't want him, most *News* columnists didn't want him, and indeed, most voters didn't want him to be mayor.

It was not exactly a profile in journalistic courage. With the Ravitch endorsement, the *Daily News* lost credibility and the publisher lost more than face. He had given up his prerogative to choose who the paper would endorse and had caved in to his employees.

From my point of view, of course, it was better to have Ravitch receive the endorsement than Dinkins. I had already been endorsed by *The New York Times*, the *New York Post*, and the *Staten Island Advance*. Only *Newsday* had endorsed Dinkins, and it was the most liberal of the city's daily editorial pages.

I didn't restrain myself when asked about the battle at the *News*. "This isn't the first time that there's been a fight between the publisher and the editorial staff of a newspaper," I told reporters. "But it is the first time a publisher has lost." I'm sure that Hoge was very angry at me. He should have been, since I was attacking the one guy at the *News* who wanted to endorse me. On the other hand, he deserved the chiding.

A few days after the primary defeat, the *News* went out of its way to praise me, as though it hadn't attacked me viciously for more than three years running in a relentless flood of editorials and columns almost as vile as anything written by *The Amsterdam News*. And *News* editorials really hurt because it's a real paper, whereas those in *The Amsterdam News* hurt not at all because a real newspaper it is not.

But my feeling that *News* columnists and editorial writers had been using the paper for political ends had proved true. I decided I should send Hoge a gentle letter:

*I read your editorial yesterday and its references to me, and I am very appreciative of the accolades.*

*I do hope and believe that when historians examine my twelve years as Mayor, they will conclude that I and the overwhelming majority of those whom I brought into government served the people of this city honestly and well. I still believe that public service, if done honestly and well, is the noblest of professions.*

*I regret that you and I have on occasion not only disagreed, which would be normal, but that there was some ill will and harshness—at least in some of my comments. Sometimes in the heat of the moment, there are comments made that you wish you could take back the moment the words pass your lips. All that is now history, and with respect to our relationship, I prefer to forget the differences and start anew.*

*All the best.*

I can only hope that New York City's next mayor will be treated less hysterically and more fairly by the *Daily News* than this mayor was. Only time will tell if the truth is still relevant on East Forty-second Street.

# PART
# 8

# MATTERS OF RACE

---

## On Jesse Jackson

In public life you are what you are publicly perceived to be. And how you are perceived is determined overwhelmingly by the press. If the press likes you, you'll be seen as generous. If it doesn't, you'll be portrayed as mean-spirited.

There's no question that over the years I have had strained relations with the black community. In my judgment, however, the strain has resulted principally not from what I have said or done but from how my opponents—many white, some black; many in the press, some not—have decided to "spin" the work and words of my administration.

Originally those who opposed me on ideological grounds tried to portray me as a barbaric reactionary because, in the 1977 mayoral campaign, I said I favored restoration of the death penalty. "That's a matter for the State Legislature and the Governor to decide," my opponents argued. "It's none of the Mayor's business." In fact, my opinion on matters over which I have no direct control is very relevant. The opinion of the Mayor of the City of New York—not just this mayor, but any mayor—is sought on every major piece of legislation which moves through the Legislature. Including the death penalty.

And since the majority of people—whether they are white, black, Hispanic, or Asian—support the death penalty, my opponents' efforts to portray me as Koch the Barbarian simply didn't fly with most New Yorkers.

Thus vanquished, the ideologues decided to shift their attack to a second charge, one much more difficult to defend against—to wit, that at best I am insensitive and at worst I am a racist. Once begun, the attack was incessant. The charge was first employed by the vilest of reporters and underground newspapers, but given the effectiveness of the "Big Lie" technique, ultimately it spread and was picked up even by decent newspapers, including *The New York Times*.

What I gave them to attack is my belief in a single standard for whites, blacks, Hispanics, and Asians. I hold all equally responsible for their actions and will not accept sociological excuses for antisocial or illegal acts.

When advocates seek to explain away the disproportionate numbers of crimes committed by blacks as the inevitable, unavoidable result of three hundred years of slavery, I object. And when they go on to argue that it is the whites, therefore, who are responsible, I say, "My grandfather owned no slaves," I say. "He was a slave himself in Poland."

I do not have a feeling of personal guilt about slavery. Certainly it is a terrible tragedy and a blot on the history of our republic. But neither I nor my ancestors contributed in any way to the tragedy. It is not my father's sin and it is not mine.

Nor do I believe that three hundred years of slavery offer a justification for reparations or a system of racial quotas or set-asides. To prefer one group over another based on race simply breeds resentment among the millions of whites who are equally poor but are excluded from preferential-treatment programs. If the point is to heal divisions, why create new ones?

Do these beliefs make me a racist? I don't think so. Nor did the policies and practices of my government. I appointed more minority commissioners and more minority judges than any of my predecessors. I appointed them not because they were black, Hispanic, Asian, or female but because they were the best qualified applicants, and I simply reached out to find them. All of which infuriated my ideological opponents. To their way of thinking, because I insisted on treating people with equal qualifications as equals, and refused to make concessions on the basis of race, I was a racist.

As I wrote to the *Daily News:*

*There are some people who believe there should be two standards: one which allows both black and white leaders to engage in intemperate, inflammatory language directed at me; and another which finds it unacceptable for me to call such critics to account. I am proud of the fact that I call both white and black leaders to account when they engage in outrageous language or behavior. If I did that only with blacks, I would be guilty of racism. But if I apply the same standard to both whites and blacks, am I the racist or are those who say that blacks should be treated differently the racists?*

*I believe in ending all discrimination based on race, religion, and sex. I am opposed to racial quotas and preferential treatment. However, many black leaders disagree with their own constituencies. Should I change my position to concur with the leaders when their constituents and I share the same point of view? Would you have me treat blacks differently in language than I do whites? I have what I believe to be common sense. That common sense requires that you speak the truth to all people in the same way without regard to race, religion, or sex. I think I do that. Do you really want me to change? I hope not.*

I will admit that there have been occasions when I have erred and not chosen my words carefully. Controversy has been sure to follow. Consider the case of Jesse Jackson. As a person, there is much to admire in the Reverend Jackson. He's come a long way from his impoverished childhood in South Carolina and has clearly established himself as a leading spokesman on behalf of black Americans, on behalf of a meaningful war against drugs, on behalf of better schools, and on behalf of improving family life.

But as a potential President of the United States, there is much to fear in Jesse Jackson. He is farther to the left than George McGovern, and far to the left is not where the overwhelming majority of the American people want to go. While many of his domestic proposals are laudable, they could bankrupt us. While he certainly seeks peace, he seems willing to weaken the nation's defense through measures that would have the effect of unilateral disarmament. While he wishes to form new alliances, he seems ready to jeopardize old ones, particularly with the State of Israel.

Each of these is a valid, substantive criticism. And I have made them in front of white audiences, Hispanic audiences, Asian audiences, and, yes, black audiences. Jackson has twice offered himself as a serious candidate for the White House. And unlike most others, I have taken him seriously both times.

Most politicians apparently believe that a Jackson presidency really isn't a serious possibility, and so they don't subject him to the same rigorous standards they'd apply to another candidate. In my view, that's not only patronizing, it's foolish, especially given his very impressive performance in 1988.

But my problems with Jackson did not begin with his second run for the White House in 1988. In fact, I'd opposed him when he ran in 1984, particularly because of his refusal to repudiate the Nation of Islam's Louis Farrakhan, a vicious anti-Semite and a racist.

The Reverend Jackson wasn't quick to forget or to forgive my opposition. In 1985, a year after his first presidential campaign, he was invited to deliver a sermon at the Cathedral of St. John the Divine in Manhattan. The setting was not surprising, for until last year it was the seat of New York's Episcopal Bishop Paul Moore, a radical clergyman who was very taken with clergymen even more radical than he.

What was unusual was the topic of the Reverend Jackson's sermon— "Housing as a Human Right." Having heard the sordid and sad tales of what it's like to live in the monstrous housing projects like Cabrini Green in Chicago, his hometown, and knowing that the Chicago city government does virtually nothing to help the homeless, I thought it was an act of gross hypocrisy for Mr. Jackson to lecture New Yorkers— residents of a city that does more for the homeless and produces more affordable housing than any other in the country—on what more we should be doing. Why wasn't Mr. Jackson bringing housing for the homeless to Chicago?

So, I took him on in the following column, which appeared in the pages of the *New York Post:*

> The Reverend Jackson is a citizen of Chicago quick to criticize the citizens of New York. The Lord has blessed him with an ability to speak,

so he can criticize eloquently. I only wish he would use his ability to check facts so that he criticized accurately.

If Mr. Jackson had checked the facts before he chastised and if, using his own standard, he had measured New York by how it "treats those in the manger," he would have found New York does more than any other city in the land. That's especially the case if the other city is Chicago, his hometown. . . .

In April 1984, our Human Resources Administration examined what the ten largest cities in the United States, including New York, were doing for the homeless.

In Chicago it found that there was one public shelter operated by the city with 100 beds. Since then we've learned that the Chicago city shelter had added 35 beds. Chicago also has a network of about 40 privately operated shelters providing about 1600 beds a night.

The U.S. Department of Housing and Urban Development estimated last year that there were between 19,400 and 20,300 homeless people in the Chicago metropolitan area.

How does New York City compare? In April 1984 we were operating 18 shelters with 6200 beds for homeless individuals. This April we're operating 19 shelters with 7400 beds. We're also temporarily housing 3465 families—or another 13,860 people—in hotels and family shelters. The Partnership for the Homeless, a private network of 106 churches and synagogues, provides another 800 beds for the homeless.

No individual and no family need go without temporary, public shelter in New York City. No one will be turned away. Does any other city in the country—including Jesse Jackson's Chicago—have the public facilities with which to make and keep this commitment? It doesn't appear so.

Since my administration began in 1978, we have rehabilitated or newly constructed 140,000 units. In fact, even with the federal government's abandonment of its traditional role in the housing marketplace, the city today is renovating 10 times the number of apartments it renovated in 1977.

Just recently, I announced a $4.4 billion program that, if approved, would add 100,000 additional units over the next five years. Clearly, the record of my administration demonstrates our commitment to better housing for all New Yorkers.

What's unfortunate about the Reverend Jackson is that he's a former presidential candidate not yet cured of the campaign bug. As a result, he goes from town to town raising issues on behalf of candidates amenable to him, but without checking the records of the incumbents he doesn't like. His flights of rhetorical fancy may be impressive. His grasp of the factual record is not.

Jesse Jackson is a citizen of Chicago. Like any major city in America, Chicago has problems waiting to be solved by those with good ideas and a strong commitment to the poor. He should take some time off from his cross-country tour and help Chicago help itself.

Jesse Jackson, of course, didn't return to Chicago in 1985. Instead, he hit the campaign trail again, in pursuit of the 1988 Democratic presidential nomination.

By the time he arrived in New York for the April primary, Jackson had already exceeded expectations. He'd won a number of Southern states on Super Tuesday, had surprised everyone by capturing the Michigan caucuses, and had amassed 704 delegates, just 36 fewer than Governor Michael Dukakis, the front-runner for the party's nomination. He was indeed a contender and, in my judgment, would become the odds-on favorite if he won a majority of New York's 255 convention delegates, which would give him the momentum that was critical at that point in the campaign.

With the New York primary less than three weeks away, reporters asked me if Jackson would do well in New York, particularly among Jewish voters. "Jews and other supporters of Israel would have to be crazy to vote for Jesse Jackson, in the same way that blacks and other supporters of black causes would be crazy to vote for George Bush," I responded.

It was Easter weekend and my comments made big news. "Koch to Jews—You've 'Got to Be Crazy to Vote for Jesse' " screamed the front-page headline of the *New York Post* the following morning. And on a what was traditionally a slow news weekend, what seemed like every newspaper, TV, and radio station across the country jumped right on the story.

Jackson's supporters didn't miss a beat. They seized the opportunity to portray me as the great divider. "It's exceedingly unfortunate that the Mayor has taken this tack," said then–Manhattan Borough President David Dinkins, who was cochairman of Jackson's New York campaign. "How dare this man declare himself king of the Jews," said Congressman Charles Rangel of Harlem. "Let us keep this campaign above any form of racial or religious bigotry or anything that incites such a reaction," said Jesse Jackson himself.

The comments of Jackson supporters didn't surprise me. The comments of some Jewish New Yorkers did. Hence the following column in *The New Republic:*

Early one Friday morning, a week after I made the remarks, I noticed an old friend who is very active in the Jewish community sitting near the police desk at City Hall, waiting to meet with my deputy mayor. After we exchanged greetings, she said, "You know, Ed, I am offended by your speaking for the Jews—that Jews would be crazy to vote for Jesse Jackson. And because of what you said, my husband and I are thinking of coming out for Jackson."

I replied, "Let's review what I said. My statement referred not only to Jews but to the supporters of Israel. Do you oppose every part of my statement?"

She said, "No, only to the use of the 'Jews.' "

I said, "If I had said that the supporters of Israel would be crazy to vote for Jackson, would that have been okay?"

She said, "Yes."

I said, "Are you opposed to my having said that blacks and supporters of black causes would be crazy to vote for George Bush?"

She said, "No, that is okay."

I said, "So the word 'black' does not distress you in that context but the word 'Jew' does upset you."

She said, "Yes."

I invited her into my office, where we continued the discussion. I said, "I want to tell you something I have never voiced before, but which I think is true. Cast your mind back to when you and I were young. Remember how overwhelmed we were with the Hitler rhetoric which made 'Jew' a pejorative word? It became so pejorative that we found another way to describe ourselves. And that word was 'Jewish.' Isn't it a fact that if anyone ever pointed to an individual in your presence and said, 'He is a Jew,' you would feel as though someone had placed a dagger in your heart?"

She said, "Yes."

I said, "But if they had said that he was 'Jewish,' would that be okay?"

She said, "Yes."

I said, "The word 'Jew' is still pejorative for many, and has been for many years. But it's not for me. I am proud to be identified as a 'Jew.' "

Another reaction to my criticism of Jackson came from Representative Charles Rangel. He is the leading black public official in the state of New York, and has tremendous clout in Washington because of his seniority on the Ways and Means Committee.

He said of me, "How dare this man declare himself king of the Jews."

My immediate response was that his statement was an outrageous insult to Jews, Catholics, and other Christians. His comment was a reference to the title posted derisively by the Romans above Christ's head on the cross. And yet there was not a single condemnation of Rangel by anyone other than me. Is it unfair to ask why?

Rangel's criticism was stated in less offensive terms by others. Ken Auletta wrote in the *Daily News*, "What is wrong is the inflammatory way Koch framed the issue. And the unspoken assumption that Jews should think and act as one, or that Jews should think only as Jews, not also as Americans. That puts Jews right back into the stereotypical ghetto in which our politics is sometimes mired."

In New York City we have 175 different religious, racial, and ethnic groups. Is it wrong for these groups to have a special interest in matters of great concern to them? Blacks are concerned with South Africa. Hispanics are against any law or constitutional amendment that would make English the official language of the United States. Many people of Irish extraction have concerns about the virtual civil war in Northern Ireland. Isn't it okay for Irish people to demand boycotts of Great Britain, and demand that we send a special U.S. envoy to Ireland? Why should any of these groups be denied the opportunity to question candidates on any of these issues?

More Jews live in New York City than in any one city in the entire world. Would they allow Mike Dukakis or Albert Gore to reject invitations to respond to issues in which Jews have a special interest? Would the NAACP allow them to duck questions pertaining to special interests in the black community? Yet Jesse Jackson turned down numerous requests to address Jewish groups. Is it unfair to ask why?

The media and the candidates have treated Jackson in a patronizing way. They have not asked him any of the tough questions. They have allowed him to obfuscate and decline to answer. I understand how much the Jackson candidacy means to black Americans, and I recognize that my pointed criticism has distressed many. But I believe Jackson is a serious candidate and must be treated seriously.

Traditionally, *The New York Times* has been the most incisive, correct, and fair of all the city's dailies. But it too took strong exception to my comments. "Blacks and Jews, blacks and Jews: it's as though they were the contenders in Tuesday's New York Primary," it wrote. "For the election to be framed that way was wrong, destructively wrong, and a big reason for that was the behavior of Ed Koch." I could, it said, "be a man of kindness, humor, rigorous fairness, and incisive intelligence. But when he errs as harshly as he has in recent days, the loss is not his alone."

I responded:

*I am writing in reply to your April 21 editorial, "What Mayor Koch Has Lost."*

*Some people perceived my rejection of Jesse Jackson's presidential candidacy and my blunt attacks on his positions and character as a rejection of the black community. It was never my intent to reject or insult the black community. The fact that this perception is not only held by some but is widespread among blacks deeply saddens me. Over time, through dialogue with this community and by a great effort on my part, I hope to assuage these feelings.*

*I am well aware that Jesse Jackson is more than a formidable candidate for the Democratic nomination. He is an important symbol of the hopes and aspirations of millions of Americans. Many people in the black community voted for him for the understandable and acceptable reason of racial pride, similar to the way many Greek-Americans voted for Mike Dukakis, or for that matter, as many Catholics voted for Al Smith or Jack Kennedy.*

*My opposition to Jesse Jackson was based on his policy positions and the record. When the candidates came to New York, I offered specific criticisms of Reverend Jackson. I was critical of his often laudable but excessive domestic spending programs and his radical views on defense. I challenged him to be specific on how he hoped to achieve peace in the Middle East without endangering the security of the State of Israel.*

*These are life-and-death issues. If I am impassioned about them, it is because of my love for this country. If I was carried away in my language and in the repetition of my attacks, it was because of what I perceived to be a danger at hand. Anyone who truly knows me realizes it had absolutely nothing to do with race.*

*Regrettably, in reporting my concerns the press ignored two of my three criticisms and chose to focus almost exclusively on my comments about Jesse Jackson and Israel. I was not the only person to have such concerns. In a recent letter to the* Times, *Stanley H. Lowell, a former chairman of the New York City Commission on Human Rights and founder of the Black-Jewish Coalition, which opposed me in 1985, wrote, "New York Jews did not vote against Jesse Jackson because he is black. They voted against him because of his views and some of his past associations. They voted against an individual. They would not have voted for him if we were white and Jewish."*

What concerns Mr. Lowell and his organization, in other words, is Jesse Jackson's stand on the issues. That is the very same thing that concerns me. I regret that my opposition and my voice sounded strident. In part, this was because no other voices were being heard on this issue.

The presidential primary presented me with a set of choices. The politically "safe" choice was to greet each of the candidates politely and to join them at a press conference indicating that, although I wouldn't make public my personal preference, I considered each to be presidential timber. Had I selected this approach, my colleagues in the Democratic Party would have been pleased; the constituencies of each candidate would not have been offended; and columnists and editorial writers would have had to write about something else over the last week. There were many public officials around the state who chose that route. I don't fault them or pretend to know their rationale, but I obviously came to a different conclusion.

In my judgment, a public official has a special responsibility to be involved in a presidential election. For quite some time, I urged Mario Cuomo to become a candidate. When he convinced me that he truly wasn't going to run, I made a judgment as to who was most able of the remaining contenders. I chose Al Gore.

I also chose to criticize Jesse Jackson's positions and credentials as a presidential contender. In a democratic society which prides itself on free speech and a free press, a presidential contest should include a vigorous debate on the record, character, and positions of those who would lead us.

*In your editorial analysis you say that my participation in presidential primary politics heightened tensions between blacks and Jews. You come to this conclusion because I forcefully challenged Jesse Jackson's positions on Israel. I regret it if racial or religious friction resulted from my comments. It was never my intent to draw political lines with racial or religious borders.*

*Rather, my full comment, which even you have edited, was* "Jews and other supporters of Israel *would be crazy to vote for Jesse Jackson."* My critics emphasize the excessiveness of the word "crazy." The foun-

*dation of their argument is that I was inciting a religious group to vote against a black candidate because he was black. As often as this quote has been repeated, rarely has it been put in the context of the remark which followed immediately thereafter. I went on to say that blacks and those opposed to apartheid would be just as crazy to vote for George Bush if he planned to continue the current administration's failed policy of constructive engagement with South Africa.*

*But as is cited by this* Times *editorial, there are ample grounds to oppose Jackson's attitude toward Israel, none of which have anything to do with his race. My decision was based on Jesse Jackson's view on Zionism (he called it "a kind of poisonous weed that is choking Judaism"), the PLO, and the creation of a Palestinian state. While Israel is very important to me, it was not my only focus.*

*It is personally distressing to have to defend myself against accusations of racial bias. This editorial correctly cites my participation as a young lawyer in the civil rights movement and could have also mentioned black candidates whom I have endorsed or actively supported. Over the years, I have enjoyed a great deal of support in the black community, despite the vocal opposition of some of its leaders. I intend to keep reaching out to that constituency and to do all that I can to reconcile any misunderstandings.*

*This has been a very painful experience for me. But I cannot sacrifice my principles in the selection of the next President of the United States because of a fear that I may alienate some of my constituents. My job is to lead and to speak the truth as I know it. I hope that those who are angry with me will understand and forgive my transgressions as they perceive them and help me to be a better Mayor. Show me when I am wrong, support me when I am right, and understand that I am just another human being seeking the truth.*

*Be assured that I realize my obligations, both as a Mayor who must represent all the people and as an individual who has invested his entire life in public service and who must be true to himself. The challenge comes in striking the right balance.*

Following the primary, however, Jesse Jackson and I did meet. It was in everybody's interest that we patch up our differences. The meeting was arranged and hosted by Governor Mario Cuomo at his offices in the World Trade Center. After about a ninety-minute conversation that included the Governor, the Reverend Jackson, Congressman Rangel, and myself, we all went out to meet the press.

Not surprisingly, neither Jackson nor I was particularly ebullient during the press conference. But we all agreed that we had had a frank and full discussion, and we announced that we would set aside our substantive differences to campaign for Michael Dukakis. I spoke after Governor Cuomo. When I had finished my comments, in a gesture of unity I turned and shook hands with Jesse Jackson, who had asked to speak last. Mike McAlary of the *Daily News* did not appreciate my gesture, saying I had stolen the handshake from an unsuspecting Jackson. I responded with the following letter to the editor of the *News:*

*I read Mike McAlary's article entitled "The Mayor Didn't Give Jackson a Fair Shake" with amusement and contempt. Here is a first-class writer turned ideologue who, instead of reporting insightfully on an incident, stoops to the lowest common denominator.*

*He attacks me for extending my hand to Jesse Jackson for a hand-shake at a press conference. It was intended to convey that at least for the time being we had put aside our political differences to elect Michael Dukakis. He describes my extending my hand as "beggarlike," and then he quotes Charlie Rangel, who is considered to be the most important publicly elected black official in the City of New York because of his position on the House Ways and Means Committee, as saying, "This is a very crummy thing to do."*

*Let us assume that instead of my speaking immediately after the Governor, as was requested by Jesse Jackson, who wanted to speak last, it was he who spoke second and extended a handshake to me. I suspect that McAlary would have whooped it up in his column and called it "a statesmanlike act," and Rangel would have said this was "a saintly thing to do."*

*My meeting with Jesse Jackson had one purpose and one purpose only—to put our joint energies and leadership qualities, whatever they may be, at the service of Michael Dukakis to help ensure his election. There are, apparently, many people willing to take their direction from Jesse Jackson on whom to vote for, as demonstrated by the New York primary.*

*But I daresay, based upon the fact that in 1985, when I was last reelected, I got 78 percent of the vote, the highest in the history of the City of New York for Mayor, and carried every Assembly district in this city—black, Hispanic, and white—that there are at least some people who look to me for direction. Indeed, I tend to have greater impact on the independent voter and those who vote Republican than I do on* the more radical Democrats who turn out in disproportionate numbers to vote in the Democratic primary.

Jesse Jackson is far more radical ideologically than I am and attracts those people. I am a moderate liberal, and I suspect that those, particularly in the suburbs as well as in the city itself, tend more to agree with me than with him. But that does not suit McAlary's purposes because I suspect his ideology is closer to Jackson's than to mine. That is his right. But without the support of those who philosophically identify with Jackson and those who philosophically identify with me, Dukakis has no chance of winning. Both Jackson and I know that, which is why we came together in Governor Mario Cuomo's office.

It is distressing that Charlie Rangel would have said, as reported by McAlary, that "Koch is mentally and politically crippled." McAlary prints it as though that were an acceptable statement. Assume for a moment that a deputy mayor in my office had said something comparable about Jesse Jackson. Would there have been demands immediately made for me to repudiate that statement and maybe even fire such a member of my staff? Or at the very least bar him from future political involvement? You bet. Is there one word of critical commentary appearing anywhere directed at Charlie Rangel for such a vile comment? The answer, regrettably, is no.

Finally, let me say something about a handshake. It is simply a social grace. It does not necessarily convey and certainly did not convey in this case that all is forgiven and all is forgotten. It was simply an expression of agreement on the issue of the day—Dukakis. My disagreement with Jesse Jackson on a number of issues, ranging from his position on the Mideast to unilateral disarmament to increasing social programs that are not affordable, remains undiminished. However, we agree on many more issues than we disagree on and are probably closer on those other programs than are Dukakis and Bentsen.

Also, as it relates to black/Jewish relationships, I made it very clear to Jesse Jackson that I was not there to discuss them. If he wanted to take up the issues which divided him from the Jewish community because of his philosophical positions, I told him that he has to do it not with me or other individual Jews, but would have to take it up with Jewish organizations like the Council of Presidents. Using McAlary's definition of a handshake—as opposed to mine, a social grace—I doubt that I can ever shake hands with McAlary again, since he would think that doing so would be conveying that I was forgiving and forgetting, which I am not.

Do I regret taking on Jesse Jackson in 1988? Well, I regret the tone of my comments. My stridency unnecessarily upset many people.

But I do not regret the substance of my attacks. I was right on target, and without question, my remarks were appropriate for discussion in the midst of a hotly contested election to choose the next President of the United States, who in the next four years would be making decisions on the very issues I had raised.

"If I am not for myself, who will be?" the great Rabbi Hillel asked almost two thousand years ago. "If I am only for myself, who am I? And if not now, when?" If no one else would speak up, I felt compelled to do so.

Undoubtedly, I paid a huge price in 1989 for what I had done in 1988. An unprecedented 89 percent of the blacks voting in the Democratic primary voted for the black candidate and did so with relish. Every action has a reaction, both in physics and in politics.

# On Bensonhurst

At around 9 P.M. on Wednesday evening, August 23, 1989, a terrible crime was committed on the streets of Bensonhurst, a predominantly white neighborhood in Brooklyn. Along with four friends, a young black man named Yusuf Hawkins, age sixteen, had come by subway to Bensonhurst from his home several miles away in East New York to take a look at a used 1982 Pontiac one of his friends wanted to buy.

As they walked toward the owner's home, the group was set upon by a mob of between ten and thirty young white men in their late teens and early twenties. Most were armed with baseball bats. At least one had a gun.

"Let's club the nigger," an unidentified source at the NYPD reported someone in the mob as saying during the attack. "No, let's not club him," said another. "Let's shoot one." Four shots were fired. Two struck Yusuf in the chest. He died a short time later at Maimonides Medical Center.

"The vicious racial murder of Yusuf Hawkins is a crime that is chilling to all New Yorkers," I said in a statement I dictated and released the next morning. "We are all united in revulsion at this crime and in the conviction that we cannot tolerate the kind of violence that ended in the death of this young man.

"At this moment of great emotion, we must recall certain basic truths. The truth that all individuals are entitled to be judged on their own merits, not on their skin color, their religious beliefs, or their origins. The truth that communities or groups of people are not to blame for the crimes of individuals. And, finally, the truth that people who commit murder—especially a murder on racial grounds—must be caught, arrested, and, if convicted, punished to the full extent of the law, no matter what their age is."

It was reported later that the murder of Yusuf Hawkins was a case of mistaken identity. The mob had actually been after someone else, another young black man who had dared to date a Bensonhurst girl. "Bensonhurst girls don't do that," said these Bensonhurst boys. Even if it took a murder to hold their sexist "turf." Unbelievable!

A case of mistaken identity, of course, doesn't explain and can't excuse a racially motivated murder. Nothing can, especially to the parents of the victim. Nothing can take away their pain or their anger.

And no penalty is too strong for those found guilty of committing so brutal a crime. Personally, I am a longtime supporter of capital punishment. It certainly would be appropriate in this case.

In the days that followed the murder of Yusuf Hawkins, a number of militant black activists called for a protest march through Bensonhurst. Undoubtedly many of those who joined the march did so out of anger as well as sorrow over the death. But others intended to exploit the killing and to use it to shame an entire community for the wrongful deeds of a few of its members. When I heard of the plans for the march, I was certain it would exacerbate an already tense situation.

The television pictures shown the Sunday evening of the march confirmed my worst fears. As the thirty marchers, almost all of them black, walked through Bensonhurst, crowds of neighborhood residents lined the sidewalks, separated from the protesters by a thin line of police officers. "Nigger go home!" was yelled again and again and again. Teenagers held watermelons over their heads as a symbolic insult to the marchers. It was so vile, so awful.

The next morning, a Monday, at City Hall, reporters asked if I had seen the TV reports and what I thought. "I believe the people who engaged in taunting are doing the city a great disservice when they engage in vile epithets or signage," I replied. "Those people have to be condemned. Communities ought not be condemned. You cannot brand a community that way.

"While you have a right to march," I continued, "if you're interested in quieting the passion, then you're not quieting the passion by marching into Bensonhurst. There is nothing wrong or illegal about a protest march. The question is do you want to be helpful to reduce the tensions or do you want to escalate the tensions? At this particular moment, if you want to lower the passions the thing to do is to find the people who committed the vile acts, make sure that their trials are expeditious, speedy, and that when and if the evidence is there, and they're convicted, they go to jail for a long period of time."

My comments were not well received by the city's editorial writers. "Mayor Edward Koch," said *The New York Times*, "has always had a troubling propensity for sending the wrong message. He did that again Monday." My remarks, said the *Daily News*, "sound like coded pandering to the basest instincts of some of his constituents."

Nor were my comments well received by some of my closest friends in government. Gordon Davis is now an attorney in private practice. But in my first term I had appointed him as Parks Commissioner, making him the first black to hold the position. He performed superbly, and in my third term, I asked him to become Chairman of the Planning Commission. He declined, saying he was tired after so many years in government and wanted to return to private practice to recharge his batteries and restore his personal finances.

After I'd made my comments about the marches through Bensonhurst, Gordon called Diane Coffey, my chief of staff. He was very upset by what I had said. In the years since he had left city service, on occasion Gordon had disagreed with things I had said and done. Indeed, he had been distressed by my comments about Jesse Jackson in 1988.

On such occasions he could have done what others have done and attacked me publicly. That most certainly would have generated headlines. Instead, he always offered his counsel privately. I will always appreciate that, and it's one reason we've remained such good friends.

After he spoke with Diane, I called Gordon. I tried to make my case, pointing out that all but one of the marches had been provocative, more interested in sullying a community than condemning a murder. The one helpful march had been conducted by the parish priest in Bensonhurst to the site of the murder, where a wreath was laid. Other marches had not been helpful. One march had even led to a violent confrontation between police and demonstrators at the foot of the Brooklyn Bridge. Forty-four officers had to be treated for injuries. The marches weren't healing the city, I told Gordon, but threatening to divide it.

The next morning, Gordon sent me a note. Included with it were a copy of Dr. King's "Letter from Birmingham City Jail" and a copy of Taylor Branch's newly published *Parting the Waters*. "I send these," Gordon wrote, "in the same spirit that you called me, which is the hope that each of us in our way will be guided in these circumstances to do our best and to be true to our beliefs."

I was very moved by his note and sent him a reply:

*Thanks for your note, Martin Luther King, Jr.'s very compelling "Letter from Birmingham City Jail," and the Taylor Branch book, which I know has been very well received. I am not at all put off by your sending the material to me.*

*I want to reiterate that I don't believe marches are bad. You and I have participated in them. We have condemned bigotry and denounced racism; we have fought for racial justice in the sixties and even since then as the need sadly persists.*

*I cannot stress enough that as Mayor I will never tolerate racial injustice under any circumstances. I will seek with all my power to eradicate it. In this case, though, with Yusuf Hawkins's death several days past and many expressions of anger and sympathy already manifested in his community, in Bensonhurst, and around the city, I believed that another march was not helpful in restoring calm. I believed this particularly since the leaders of the march were not condemning the murder but rather the Bensonhurst community by referring to it as Reverend Timothy Mitchell did as "Johannesburg."*

*We unfortunately disagree on what the best way is to achieve racial peace. The marches created additional anger, resulting in hateful and inexcusable rhetoric from those watching. In some cases, the marches resulted in physical injury, as evidenced in the march to the Brooklyn Bridge, where forty-four police officers were injured. The marchers threw bricks and bottles and injured David Scott, Chief of Patrol, who happens to be black, by throwing a bottle in his face. Shouldn't we proceed in another way to achieve our common goal in the most productive way? I believe that the march of the priests to the site of the crime without engaging in provocative rhetoric directed at the community was helpful.*

*You will be interested to know that after the funeral I had a telephone conversation with Mr. Moses Stewart. I suggested to him that he, David Dinkins, and I take an unannounced walk through Bensonhurst and visit, in particular, the site where his son was murdered. I wanted to do it without any additional security other than my usual staff, and without press. He told me that he thought it was a good idea, but he was going to discuss it with Al Sharpton, who is one of his advisors. Unfortunately, Al Sharpton advised him against it. When I spoke with Mr. Sharpton, he said, "Mr. Stewart is a Muslim and doesn't like David Dinkins." So much for David's calming effect.*

*In any event, I hope that you are not angry with me, but, obviously, I am distressed that you are disappointed. As we continue our exchange of ideas through our conversations and correspondence, I hope that we will ultimately sort things out.*

*All the best to you and Peggy.*

Some, including a *Daily News* editorial, said my comments were "pandering" intended to solidify my support among white ethnic communities. With the mayoral election just a few weeks away, I "wasn't about to antagonize any of those voters," said Bob Herbert of the *News*, "racist or otherwise." My comments, in fact, didn't help my campaign, but hurt it.

For example, a couple of days before the election, Steve Solarz, the very influential Congressman from Brooklyn, told a member of my staff that he'd planned to endorse me. After my comments and the controversy surrounding them, he changed his mind. Our friendship of more than twenty years ended that day. My friendship with Chuck Schumer, also a Congressman, ended the same way and for the same reason.

Following the marches, my comments, and the attacks upon them, Hazel Dukes of the NAACP and Roscoe Brown, Jr., president of the city's Bronx Community College, asked for and were granted a meeting with John Cardinal O'Connor. Both supported David Dinkins, and I suspect the purpose of their meeting was probably to have the Cardinal and other participants express support for the marches and, thereby, implicitly criticize me.

But Bishop Francis J. Mugavero of Brooklyn, also a participant in the meeting, dashed their hopes. The Bishop, reported the *Times*, "said that while every citizen had a right to march, 'you have to wonder what was accomplished by going into a community.' . . . Like Mr. Koch,

Bishop Mugavero said he was worried about the possibility of condemning an entire community."

Interestingly, the only newspaper to cover the Bishop's comments was *The New York Times.* And although my comments had received a barrage of criticism, no paper raised its voice to criticize the Bishop for his.

Throughout the episode I perceived that an editorial decision had been made by all of the city's newspapers not to criticize any demonstration by blacks if its ostensible purpose was opposition to racism. Every protest, of course, marched under that banner.

Those who organized and led the marches were left unidentified. The implication was that they were marching for a good cause and, therefore, were good people. But who were the leaders? Were they just average citizens so outraged by the murder that they'd felt compelled to step forward and protest? Or were they not-so-average citizens with a hidden agenda?

Well, one of the leaders was the Reverend Lawrence Lucas. He's the Catholic priest with four gun permits who has made anti-Semitic and, strangely enough, anti-Catholic remarks on several occasions. He is plain bonkers.

Then there was Viola Plummer, again unidentified in the news stories about the Brooklyn Bridge confrontation. She had been convicted in 1985 for giving false identification to the police following her arrest as one of the "New York Eight," a group which planned a series of armored-car robberies and prison breaks. At the time of the arrests, police confiscated three sawed-off shotguns, an Uzi submachine gun, several 9mm automatic pistols, two explosive devices made of five pounds of dynamite, the floor plans of a dozen banks, and a machine for making bullets. Not exactly pacifists.

Also leading the march on the Brooklyn Bridge was Jitu Weusi, a former Brooklyn public school teacher and currently a community activist and otherwise unidentified by the media. In 1969 he had gone on WBAI radio under the name of Leslie Campbell to read a poem: "Hey, Jew boy, with that yarmulke on your head, you pale-faced Jew boy, I wish you were dead." Mr. Weusi, reported the Anti-Defamation League, had described the poem's sentiments as "beautiful" and "true."

The league had also charged him with having written, under a pen name, an article entitled "The Unholy Sons of Shylock." When forced to resign as an advisor to the mayoral campaign of David Dinkins, Mr. Weusi denied the charges. "I harbor no anti-Semitic views now," he said, "nor have I in the past."

And then there was Sonny Carson, another self-styled activist also forced to resign from the Dinkins campaign. Though no newspaper reported it at the time of the march on the Brooklyn Bridge, Carson previously had been convicted of both attempted murder and kidnapping.

Carson left the Dinkins camp after it was revealed that he'd received $9,500 in campaign funds following the march. Some said it was paid to him to prevent other marches that might lead to violence and adversely affect the Dinkins campaign. Carson couldn't document how most of it had been spent, saying he wouldn't "allow anybody to insult me about a measly few dollars." In a packed press conference the day he resigned, Carson said "just so that you don't ask the question, I'm anti-white. Don't limit my anti-ing to just one little group of people. I think you'd insult me if you tried to do that."

Lucas, Plummer, Weusi, Carson—these were the "average" citizens who led a protest march on the Brooklyn Bridge which resulted in the injury of forty-four police officers. And not a word was written at the time about their backgrounds—not by *The New York Times,* not by *New York Newsday,* not by the *Daily News,* and not by the *New York Post.* They were portrayed as just ordinary folk; apparently, their revolutionary ambitions and, in some cases, criminal backgrounds were deemed unimportant by reporters, editors, and columnists. But I believe they are important and, indeed, were the very reason why a march on the bridge billed as a nonviolent protest against racism turned violent.

Having failed to tell us who the leaders were, *The New York Times* went a step further, turning over part of its op-ed page to the Reverend Herbert Daughtry of the House of the Lord Pentecostal Church in Brooklyn, another radical activist in a cleric's collar. "New York is a powder keg. African Americans have had enough. We have boycotted, marched, demonstrated, begged, and prayed," he wrote in the *Times.* "Something has to give. A change must come. No people can be expected to continue to absorb this kind of pain and not explode. If it is not the ballot," he promised, two days before the violence on the Brooklyn Bridge, "I fear it will be the bullet."

Ironically, in the aftermath of the Howard Beach incident in December 1986, I had convened a meeting in the Blue Room of City Hall with leaders of the black community. I had hoped that we might be able to identify ways to ensure that that horrendous incident did not further exacerbate racial tensions. Originally, the Reverends Daughtry and Sharpton had not been invited to the meeting. But Jesse Jackson called and asked me to invite them. At his request I did.

The morning of the meeting, however, Mr. Sharpton stood outside and referred to those who accepted my invitation as "coons." Mr. Daughtry did not attend at all. So much for their idea of working together to achieve reconciliation.

Why, I wonder, do we extol such people, either by not identifying their backgrounds in news stories or by soliciting their editorial opinions? They are not just "average citizens." They are self-styled and very committed anti-white, anti-Semitic, and/or anti-police activists. In some cases, they're all three. They want confrontation and riots, not cooperation and peace, among the city's 175 racial, ethnic, and religious groups. Do they deserve to be extolled? I think not.

## To the Father of Yusuf Hawkins

Yusuf Hawkins's father, Moses Stewart, invited me to attend Yusuf's wake at the Lawrence H. Woodward Funeral Home in Bedford-Stuyvesant. When I arrived at the home, a crowd of some 150 people was standing outside. They were angry and they booed me as I entered.

I was met at the door and escorted to the room where Yusuf's parents were receiving visitors by the Reverend Al Sharpton and C. Vernon Mason, an attorney. Over the years I have had my differences with Mr. Sharpton and Mr. Mason. But on this occasion the two of them were extremely courteous to me.

"I am so sorry," I said to Mr. Stewart, a black Muslim and a follower of Minister Louis Farrakhan, when I entered the room. He took me to view Yusuf's body. "So young, so terrible," I thought as I stood next to his coffin.

"Mayor," Mr. Stewart said afterward, "I have been asked by the Reverend Jesse Jackson"—who had paid his respects to the family about a half hour before—"to use Yusuf's death to help elect David Dinkins" as Mayor. He went on, "I told him I will not do that."

I said to him, "Can I hug you?"

"Of course," he answered.

I left shortly thereafter, escorted by Mr. Stewart to my car. The crowd outside was still angry and again booed me. They ran after my car, which, to avoid them, had to back out of the street.

For me, Mr. Stewart will always be an example of what it means to show grace under pressure. I will always be grateful for his courtesy and his dignity. I thought I should tell him that and thank him, so I wrote the following letter:

*No one can feel the pain that parents feel when they suffer the loss of a child, particularly when that loss has occurred as a result of a brutal, racially motivated murder. You have suffered an enormous tragedy and one that has affected every New Yorker.*

*Throughout these explosive weeks when you have been goaded by many and others may have sought to use you, you have suffered your pain in an exemplary way, spurning the arousal of base passions. As you told me when I spoke with you at Yusuf's wake, you would not allow your grief and tragedy to be used for political purposes.*

*I just wanted you to know how much I appreciate the kindness and consideration that you have extended to me when you were the person who deserved the kindness and consideration of everyone in this city. I hope that I have responded in a way that was acceptable to you.*

*I want you to know that it was Yusuf's death that stirred me to think about what we could do to memorialize all victims of racial bias. Today, we announced plans for the Project for an Open City, a monument dedicated to racial harmony that will be built in the Brooklyn Botanic Gardens. I hope public funds are available for this monument. There will be a fund-raising committee to solicit support from corporations, Foundations, and civic groups. I have decided to start the fund-raising by donating some of the money remaining in my campaign treasury. I hope that much of the money will be raised in our public schools, where the lesson of Yusuf's death can be part of a program to teach children tolerance and allow them to become a part of the monument by paying for it with small coins.*

*All the best.*

*P.S. If I can help you in getting a job, I'd like to do that. Have you followed up on the bus company offer to talk with you?*

Despite Mr. Stewart's wishes, the murder of Yusuf Hawkins was used politically in the mayoral campaign. Occurring less than three weeks before New Yorkers went to the polls, it created a firestorm and mobilized the entire black community.

On election day, overwhelmingly, New York City's black voters cast their ballots for David Dinkins. Until that night in Bensonhurst, opinion polls had suggested that David would get no more than 80 or 85 percent of the black vote.

Did it cost me the election? Some say yes. I don't. When all of the votes were counted, it was clear that David Dinkins had received impressive across-the-board support from all New Yorkers. According to a *Daily News* exit poll, 28 percent of the white, 89 percent of the black, 54 percent of the Hispanic, 56 percent of the Asian, and 23 percent of the Jewish vote went to Mr. Dinkins. Dick Ravitch won 4.6 percent of all votes cast, Jay Goldin won 2.7 percent, I won 42 percent, and David Dinkins won 50.7 percent.

"I'm not praising Koch," Mr. Stewart told *The New York Times* a few weeks after the election. "But I can't take it away from him. He offered me the services of his office and those he knows. Money for the funeral. Police protection. A job interview. He called my aunt and sent flowers to my mother in the hospital. He offered those things that any person in any kind of political status who really cared would have offered. No one else did that, except Al Sharpton and Louis Farrakhan. Dinkins didn't even say to me, 'Mr. Stewart or Miss Hawkins, I am going to do this or that to see that your son's death is not in vain.' Dinkins came to me to campaign."

I wish Mr. Stewart and his family well in all that they do. They have already suffered enough.


# On Howard Beach


I have often said that when a white assaults a black, it is almost always assumed to be and is reported as a racially motivated bias attack. But when a black assaults a white, it rarely shows up on the police blotter as a bias incident.

There will be no newspaper columns denouncing the black-on-white incident as a sign that the city is divided, no marches by whites into the black neighborhood where the crime may have occurred, no denunciations of all black New Yorkers as "racist," no calls for a special prosecutor to ensure that the attacker is speedily apprehended and brought to justice.

In this day and age, white-on-black crime is considered to be societal pathology; black-on-white crime, nothing out of the ordinary. One type of brutality is treated very harshly, the other not. My own view—one for which I have been attacked venomously—is that the same standards ought to apply in both types of cases.

A brutal crime motivated solely by the race, ethnicity, religion, or sexual orientation of the victim sears souls and threatens to divide whole cities permanently.

It was the weekend before Christmas 1986. And all hell was about to break loose in Howard Beach, Queens. Three black men from Brooklyn—Michael Griffith, age twenty-three, Cedric Sandiford, thirty-seven, and Timothy Grimes, nineteen—were walking very early that Sunday morning through the deserted streets of the predominantly white, middle-class neighborhood.

Their car had broken down a few blocks away and they were searching for a telephone to call for assistance. They tried a neighborhood pizza parlor but were told it had no phone. They sat down, ordered some pizza, and tried to figure out what to do next.

They left the pizzeria ten minutes later. As they did, an angry mob of nine to twelve white punks—armed with baseball bats and clubs—set upon them. "Niggers, you don't belong here!" one of the mob yelled as they pummeled the three men. They fled and a chase through the streets of Howard Beach ensued. It would end in murder.

Seeking to escape the mob, Michael Griffith ducked through a hole in a fence and tried to run across the busy six-lane Belt Parkway at the northern edge of the neighborhood. As he did, he was struck by a car speeding west. He probably died instantly.

"All crimes are terrible, but crimes involving racial bigotry are the absolute worst," I told reporters at a press conference later that afternoon to announce that I had authorized a $10,000 reward in the Howard Beach case. "This incident can only be talked about as rivaling the kind of lynching party that took place in the Deep South."

Indeed, the attack brought back memories of events I'd personally witnessed during the Freedom Summer of 1964 when I went to the small Southern town of Laurel, Mississippi, to defend white and black students who'd been arrested trying to integrate a lunch counter. They were also part of a voter registration drive.

One afternoon, a fellow lawyer and I left the courthouse to go to the County Clerk's office. As we crossed the street, a group of white farmers started following us, loudly clapping their hands and threatening us.

"We're in trouble," my colleague whispered. "We have to make a mad dash back to the courthouse." We made it back safely, but it was one of the scariest moments of my life.

My experience in Mississippi, of course, paled by comparison with the horror faced by these young men in Howard Beach. And in the days and weeks that followed, I knew it was imperative for me, as the city's highest elected official, to set a tone of moral leadership and to send a signal sure and swift that such bestial, brutal acts of racial violence simply would not be condoned in our city.

Shortly after the attack, I spoke before a predominantly black church—the Morning Star Baptist Church in St. Albans, Queens—to reassure people that those who had engaged in this kind of crime would be apprehended, prosecuted, and, if found guilty, punished to the maximum extent of the law. Though the congregation was understandably very distressed, I received a very warm reception.

That wasn't the case at a predominantly white church—Our Lady of Grace Catholic Church in Howard Beach—which I visited the same day. I had hoped to use the occasion to encourage the decent citizens of the neighborhood—the vast majority of those living there, I was sure—to stand up together against such senseless, stupid violence and to let them know that I would do all I could to ensure that the actions of a few would not taint an entire community.

Tensions were high, people were angry. For days the residents of Howard Beach had been under a media microscope, their community and their neighbors sullied by association with the terrible events of that Sunday morning. As I left the church one woman yelled to me that she wished she could cut out my tongue and throw my body into nearby Jamaica Bay. Both they and I knew that, no matter what I said or how decent were the people who lived there, henceforth the name Howard Beach would be synonymous with racial bigotry.

Such an incident is among the most difficult and trying faced by any public official. Your mind struggles to find the right words and the right gestures to provide the leadership that will keep the city from breaking apart into a hundred angry and armed camps.

What was particularly disturbing to me was the role played by columnists in the aftermath of the Howard Beach attack. They were quick to condemn anyone, including myself, who tried to come forward with a gesture that might contribute to healing the scars and calming the tensions. "We can trace most of what has gone wrong in the Howard Beach case until now," wrote Murray Kempton in *Newsday*, "to the occupational incapacity of all parties to shut up when they ought to."

"How silly and insipid," I thought when I read his column. "He wants us to act as though what happened didn't happen. But that will only make sure it happens again."

So I wrote the following letter to *Newsday:*

*Normally columnists let loose their loudest yelps on politicians and public officials foolish enough to try to muzzle the press. Apparently eager to prove that at least one old dog can learn new tricks, however, Murray Kempton's January 18th* Newsday *column barked up a different tree. He wants to muzzle the politicians.*

*"We can trace most of what has gone wrong in the Howard Beach case until now," he writes, "to the occupational incapacity of all parties to shut up when they ought to."*

*Really?*

*I wonder if the family of Michael Griffith, who died as a result of the reprehensible and racially motivated attack on him and two companions in Howard Beach, would agree with Murray that "most of what has gone wrong" is too much talking in the aftermath. I don't think so.*

*Nor do I think the family of Jeffrey McCarthy would agree with Murray that there's been too much talking going on. Especially after he was kicked, beaten, and bloodied in Jamaica by a mob of black punks to the chant of "Howard Beach, Howard Beach."*

*Where Murray spots an "occupational incapacity," I find a personal responsibility. Every citizen has an obligation to speak out against racism, prejudice, and violence. As Mayor, I have a special obligation to denounce the despicable acts of the mobs who attacked in one case Michael Griffith and his companions and in another case Jeffrey McCarthy. Would Murray Kempton prefer that I had been silent? Murray, I make no apologies—silence in the face of racism would only embolden the racists.*

I also faced my share of out-of-town critics. On Christmas Eve, *The Clarion-Ledger* of Jackson, Mississippi, reported that five of that state's mayors had objected to my comments. "That Jew bastard," it quoted

Mayor W. W. Godbold of Brookhaven as saying of my comments. "I believe Jews like him to get in this office don't know the hell what they are talking about. . . . The trouble we had in the fifties wouldn't have happened unless people like him came down here and stirred things up."

I replied:

*I am sorry that you misunderstood my comments concerning racial attacks in the Deep South. My references were to those incidents which took place before 1965 and the civil rights riots that occurred as a result of racial attacks in the Deep South.*

*I find it difficult to understand your reference to racial incidents where you say, "To the best of my knowledge, we in the South have never had the conflicts throughout the South that exist and have existed in your City, whether it be racial, gangster, or union related." Have you forgotten the deaths of the three civil rights workers—Chaney, Goodman, and Schwerner—which occurred in Mississippi in 1964? I haven't because I was in Jackson, Mississippi, when the bodies were found buried under a dam to conceal them after they had been brutally tortured. Have you forgotten your two senators, Bilbo and Rankin? I haven't because I remember their outrageous racial invective.*

*There is no question but that the South and the country as a whole have vastly improved racial relations, notwithstanding the fact that on occasion, as it happened recently in New York City, there will be those who will engage in racial violence. We have apprehended the alleged perpetrators of the most recent incident—an attack by white youths upon three black men resulting in the death of one black man. All of the forces of law will see to it that we impose upon conviction the most severe penalty available under the law.*

*I do hope that you were misquoted in today's paper when you referred to me as a "Jew bastard." See the enclosed reference which appeared in the* New York Post. *I would assume you did not make the statement, but even if you did, I will turn the other cheek particularly in this season of the year.*

*All the best.*

In a follow-up interview, Mayor Godbold told a reporter he had not intended to slur all Jews. "I have some very good friends who are Jewish," he said. "I was saying it to Mr. Koch only, to him personally." I kept my cheek turned.

243

But I was distressed to learn that Mayor Charles Evers of Fayetteville, Mississippi, had also been upset by my comments. Mayor Evers is the brother of Medgar Evers, the black civil rights leader slain in Mississippi in the sixties. I felt I needed to write him myself:

*I do hope that you are not offended by anything that I have said, because what I said related to events that took place in the Old South.*
*If there is one person in this country who knows what took place in the Old South, it would be the brother of Medgar Evers.*
*All the best.*

Ultimately, three young men from Howard Beach—Jon Lester, age eighteen, Scott Kern, nineteen, and Jason Ladone, seventeen—were convicted of manslaughter and assault resulting in the death of Michael Griffith on the Belt Parkway that Sunday morning. "There's no hate in my heart," said Griffith's mother at the 1988 sentencing of one of the three young men. "We're all mothers. In a case like this, no one wins."

She was right. But in a case like this, if justice is to be done, the punishment must be very stiff, not just so that the guilty will pay for their crimes, but also to deter others from engaging in the same kinds of racist acts. With that in mind, I wrote the following letter to State Supreme Court Justice Thomas A. Demakos, the sentencing judge in the Howard Beach case:

*From time to time, in significant criminal cases, I feel compelled to voice my opinion on the appropriate sentences to be meted out. I am sure you are aware of my reaction to the Howard Beach incident, and my subsequent reaction to the verdict. I know that when you impose sentence on Scott Kern, Jon Lester, and Jason Ladone, you will have weighed many factors. Permit me to add my views in the hope that they assist you in arriving at a fair and just decision.*
*I was appalled when I learned of the Howard Beach tragedy. I still am. It disturbs me not only that incidents of racial violence continue to occur in its wake, but that many of the aggressors are our young people, who, despite our efforts toward racial equality and harmony over the past twenty-five years, too often remain bigoted and prejudiced.*
*I know that some individuals who urge lenient sentences for the three teenagers convicted point to their relatively young ages, arguing that lengthy incarceration will be ruinous to them and their families.*

*Despite the surface appeal of such an argument, it remains that the defendants caused the death of one man, and seriously injured another, solely because of their color. That is a heinous act, regardless of the ages of the wrongdoers. The jury plainly agreed, finding these three defendants guilty of second degree manslaughter and first degree assault, and finding two of them guilty of conspiracy as well. These are crimes that deserve to be punished by the maximum penalty for all three defendants.*

*The Howard Beach incident has brought shame to this city, and it is more shameful still that racial incidents continue in its aftermath. I therefore urge you to impose a sentence that is commensurate with the egregiousness of the crimes committed by the defendants, and appropriate to this society's goal of eliminating racial violence by deterring such crimes with whatever lawful means are at its disposal. In my view the appropriate sentence is incarceration for the maximum amount of time permitted by law.*

*I would be remiss if I did not compliment your handling of such a lengthy, emotionally charged trial. To my mind, one quality of an outstanding jurist is the ability to maintain control over his or her court under the most trying conditions, and it is clear you did so here. I know that everyone involved in this tragic case put in a tremendous amount of time and effort, including the attorneys on both sides and the jury, to ensure a fair trial and a carefully reasoned verdict. Those efforts are to be applauded by all decent and caring New Yorkers—who are the vast majority in our city, I would wager—and do not go unappreciated in this time of anguish.*

Altogether, Judge Demakos received some 1,500 letters on the sentence. Only two urged the maximum penalty. One was from Special Prosecutor Charles J. Hynes, who was prosecuting the case and, therefore, didn't need to send a letter. The other was from me.

All the other letters urged leniency. "What disturbs me about all of these letters is that there is no sense of remorse," Justice Demakos said from the bench. Almost every writer tried to "treat this case as a political and unwarranted conviction of the community of Howard Beach. This is not a conviction of a community," he said. Justice Demakos then sentenced Jon Lester to ten to thirty years. He would later sentence Scott Kern to six to eighteen years, Jason Ladone to five to fifteen years.

What happened in Howard Beach will scar the memory of every

New Yorker for years to come. But we should not indict an entire community or an entire city because of the bestial and brutal actions of a few of its residents. "I personally believe it would be wrong to hold up Howard Beach and its citizenry as illustrative of racism," I told the press following the sentencing of Jon Lester. "You could find punks in every part of this town. Every white community, every black community, every Hispanic community has punks in it. To hold up a particular area as racist because of the actions of a few punks, in my judgment, is unfair."

There are some, of course, who have argued that what happened in Howard Beach is proof that New York is a racist city. "Just look," they say, "at the number of bias incidents reported to the New York Police Department each year: 235 in 1986, 463 in 1987, 550 in 1988." What they don't say, however, is that we know how many bias incidents there are in a particular year in our city only because, in 1980, I directed the NYPD to begin reporting such crimes. No other city in the country did that before this city did.

In a given year, some 550,000 felonies are committed in New York City. But as a result of my 1980 directive, special attention is paid and special priority is given to the relatively small number of bias-related crimes.

Is New York, then, more "racist" than Los Angeles or Chicago, Boston or Baltimore, Miami or Houston? Well, until they begin reporting bias crimes the way New York City does, we'll never know. But if you look at the more segregated housing patterns in any of those cities, it would be hard to believe they have less racial tension than one finds in New York.

And, in a sense, the question misses the real issue. One bias crime of the sort that occurred in Howard Beach is one bias crime too many. Ideally, parents would raise their children in such a way that when they grow up they would not be tempted to engage in the outrageous kinds of behavior those dozen white punks engaged in early one Sunday morning. "Children have to be taught to hate," goes the song in the musical *South Pacific*. It is the responsibility of parents to make sure they are not.

Regrettably, we do not live in an ideal world, and there are sure to be parents who fail in this responsibility. Some young people—white young people, black young people, Hispanic young people, and Asian young people—inevitably will grow up to be racists.

Those who do must be deterred. For years I have supported legisla-

tion in Albany that would double the penalties against those who are found guilty of bias crimes. But for years the Assembly has passed the bill and the Senate has refused to support it unless bias crimes against gay men and lesbian women are removed from the protections of the bill.

If there is one lesson and one lesson only that we should learn from the tragedy that occurred in Howard Beach, it is that we are well past the time when that bill should have become law. Those who violently act out their bigotry should receive the harsh punishment they deserve.


# On Bias Crimes


During the past twelve years, I've spoken out on many occasions against racism practiced by whites. Never a demur from those listening. Over those same twelve years, I've also spoken out against racism practiced by blacks. Many demurs and often bitter denunciations follow whenever I make such statements.

Some contend that there is no such thing as black racism. Shortly after the murder of Yusuf Hawkins, *The New York Times* ran a story about a discussion between the Reverend Herbert B. Daughtry, a prominent and militant black Brooklyn clergyman, and the Reverend Charles S. Fermeglia, a parish priest in Bensonhurst. During their conversation, Mr. Daughtry absolutely denied that there is such a thing as black racism, astonishing Mr. Fermeglia. Mr. Daughtry's position is quite common, I've found, among militant blacks and their militant white supporters.

During the 1989 mayoral campaign, for example, Sonny Carson, a black activist then working for the Dinkins campaign, was accused of anti-Semitism. In his defense, Carson stated he was not anti-Semitic but "anti-white." This is hardly a new position for Carson. After the Howard Beach incident in 1986, he said at a press conference, "There are a lot of tires around this city. People who feel they can continue to disrespect the black community, they are in for a surprise very soon."

I responded in an article for the *New York Post:*

[Carson's] reference to the practice of some South African blacks of placing tires around the necks of other blacks suspected of collaborating with the white regime and setting them afire can only be interpreted as a threat of further violence and should be denounced.

In New York City there appear to be many more instances of bias crimes being committed by whites against blacks than vice versa. However, in order to understand the full significance of the statistics, it is important to examine how we define a bias crime: the NYPD makes the determination, and normally a crime is not considered bias-related unless a racial epithet is used or there is other clear and obvious evidence of bias.

For example, on December 24, 1987, a white cabdriver and a Hispanic were involved in an auto accident in Manhattan. As they exchanged information, a group of black males gathered and attacked the cabdriver. When an Emergency Medical Service ambulance arrived at the scene, one assailant asked an EMS employee if she was "trying to help the white guy." Another yelled "Howard Beach" as he punched and kicked the cabdriver. The NYPD labeled it a bias incident.

On the other hand, in late October at least thirty women, virtually all of them white, were attacked on Manhattan's Upper West Side by a group of up to ten teenage girls and three teenage boys, all of them black. Each victim was pricked in the arm, forehead, or neck by a sharp object, possibly a hypodermic needle, giving rise to the fear that the needles might have been carrying the HIV virus, thereby making the victims vulnerable to AIDS.

"We don't see any evidence of bias," said Assistant Police Chief Mario Selvaggi. "There was no conversation between the perpetrators and the victims." Since by definition a bias incident must be accompanied by some bias epithet, technically Chief Selvaggi was right.

Hold it. All the attackers were black. Virtually all of the victims were white. If a group of women in Harlem, all of them black, had been pricked by a group of teenagers, all of them white, does anyone doubt that the Harlem community would have denounced the incidents as racist and that the Police Department would have had similar or second thoughts?

Had I even ventured the day the attacks were reported to suggest publicly that they might be bias incidents, I would have been denounced at best as insensitive, at worst as a racist. Despite any evidence that may be offered to the contrary, the consensus among opinion makers seems to be that "bias" is an acceptable characterization only when the crime is white on black. When it's black on white, it's robbery.

After a few days, interestingly, the NYPD ultimately decided that the thirty or so attacks were bias incidents. Since virtually all of the victims were white and all of the attackers were black, the police concluded that the victims had been selected on the basis of race. Surprisingly, one of the thirty victims reacted in a way that could have the effect of excusing other bias incidents committed by blacks on whites. "I've been praying for them because I think there are certain conditions in this city which cause rage," she said. "They need help learning how to express their anger constructively, . . . to improve their lives and not hurt others."

By contrast, the "wilding" case, in which a group of black and Hispanic youths brutally assaulted and raped a white female jogger in Central Park, was not labeled a bias incident because no racial epithets were used and because a Hispanic male was also the victim of an assault by this same group. As in all cases, I accepted the police characterization of this event. Nevertheless, many people held a strong suspicion that there was some racial motivation behind that crime.

If a young black woman was savagely attacked in Central Park by ten white kids, what would the Reverend Daughtry and others who often attack the police for brutality say? I believe they wouldn't have hesitated to call it a bias attack, a racist incident, and wouldn't have hesitated to call for marches through the neighborhood where the white attackers lived.

In truth, the whole subject of bias-related crimes, because it is such an emotionally charged issue, requires particular care and subtlety. To be sure, there are some crimes that are clearly bias-related and some that clearly are not. But many crimes involve motives that are mixed and hard to determine. A particular robbery may be principally an economic crime, but the choice of the victim or the extent of violence may have to do with race, even if no one can prove it.

The issue of bias-related crime, however, should not blind us to two important facts. First, the vast majority of the victims of crimes perpetrated by blacks and Hispanics are blacks and Hispanics. Second, a disproportionate share of violent crime is committed by minorities.

These facts are sometimes hard to discuss rationally. *The New York Times* caused an uproar, for example, when it published an editorial entitled "Fear of Blacks, Fear of Crime," which noted that blacks, who make up 12 percent of the population, committed robbery at a rate of ten times that of whites, who are 86 percent of the population. Its editorial was attacked by many as stereotyping young black males. But if the facts supported the *Times*'s contention, was it really a stereotype?

A 1988 U.S. Department of Justice "Report to the Nation on Crime and Justice" concluded that a 1985 crime survey "shows that most violent offenders"—involved in such crimes as robbery, rape, and assault—"are perceived to be white males. But," it went on to report, "black males are perceived to be violent offenders in numbers disproportionate to their share of the population."

And that perception reflects reality. According to the Justice Department's report, whites committed an estimated 347,970 robberies in 1987; blacks, some 524,430. Indeed, further analysis suggests that in 1987 blacks were committing 10.8 times more robberies than could be expected from their share of the population. We can, as some militants suggest, ignore those facts. But they are still facts.

The reasons for the phenomenon are complex. But I believe a central cause is the fact there has been a more severe breakdown in family structure and values in minority communities than in white communities. Senator Daniel Patrick Moynihan was pilloried by liberals twenty-five years ago when he first began to write about changes in the structure of the black family. Even today, his insight is still resisted by many people, particularly when it is linked to a belief in personal responsibility.

"Mr. Koch insists that social conditions do not breed crime but that parents and genes do," wrote *The New York Observer* in the aftermath of the Central Park attack. "That argument not only clears him of his responsibility for the conditions but it also feeds the flames of racism—and his comments often do." This statement prompted the following letter:

*Your latest editorial, "Atrocity in the Park," is your lowest blow, and believe me, it is hard for you to get any lower. To attack me for polarizing this City and to accuse me of having said that crime is caused by "parents and genes" is an utter fabrication on your part and an attempt to introduce polarization and racism and lay it off on me. How dare you?*

*My position is that there is no direct causal relationship between poverty and criminal acts. Most people who are poor, black or white, do not commit crimes. And crimes are committed not only by the poor but also by the rich. I do indeed believe that there is parental responsibility for the conduct of a child. However, I also believe that no matter what some parents will do with respect to particular children they will be incapable of preventing criminal conduct. Nevertheless, overall, ethics and morality are inculcated by the family and the church and should be encouraged.*

*You attack me as feeding "the flames of racism" when I am probably one of the few major public officials who has stated that this crime which took place in Central Park has nothing to do with race. It is the act of wanton, feral youths who are totally amoral without even a sense of remorse after they were apprehended and who can only be compared to the youths described in . . . Clockwork Orange. Furthermore, as you undoubtedly know, when Donald Trump took his ad denouncing me for urging that there be no "hatred" and announcing that he indeed encouraged hate, I was one of the few public officials, if not the only one, to denounce him for such a bitter thought.*

*You may dislike me and my ideology, and under the current law you are able to engage in almost any slander and libel without legal liability, but surely there must be some shred of professional obligation on the part of your editorial staff to tell the truth. Apparently not. How sad!*

And then there are militants in both the black and white communities who are so obsessed with white-on-black bias incidents that they are unable or even unwilling to be outraged by a crime that does not involve a racial element but is just as brutal and just as senseless.

Consider the brutal episode that took place in Brooklyn's Prospect Park on August 26, 1987, which I described and discussed in a column in the *New York Voice:*

December is usually a month to spend with family and friends, reflecting on the year about to end, imagining the prospects for the year just around the corner, and, for many of us, renewing our faith in our Creator.

But not December 1986. Suddenly our quiet reflections and joyous celebrations were interrupted by cruel and senseless racial violence. In Howard Beach, a group of twelve young white punks allegedly attacked three black men who'd appeared in their neighborhood, chasing one onto a highway, where he was struck dead by a car.

Initially I was shocked and shamed that some New Yorkers would engage in such barbaric, hateful acts. My faith was restored when the overwhelming majority of New Yorkers condemned these acts as abhorrent and their practitioners as criminals. All decent New Yorkers expressed outrage.

Eight months later, though, we may have cause to wonder where all the outrage went, what silenced the voice of decent New Yorkers. Early on Wednesday morning, August 26, two homeless people—twenty-six-year-old Bernadette Crowley and twenty-three-year-old Gerard Grayson—were asleep in Brooklyn's Prospect Park. When they went to bed that night, they didn't know how rude, how violent a wake-up call they'd get.

As they lay sleeping, four Brooklyn teenagers—James McDermott, Steven Loesch, Sean Sullivan, and Louis Palanca—allegedly poured gasoline over their bodies, struck a match, and tried to set the two afire. Gerard received burns on his arms and ankles. Bernadette ended up in the hospital, burns covering 7 percent of her body.

There's no excuse for what happened in Prospect Park. Today the young men stand charged with attempted murder. If they're found guilty, they should receive the maximum sentence.

But most people seem to think that what happened there is nothing to get excited about. Absolutely wrong. Indeed, the burning of these two people is so inhuman an act that it passes understanding. And I haven't been afraid to say so.

Regrettably, I seem to be one of the few to say so. Reaction to Howard Beach was loud and clear. Ministers, priests, rabbis, activists, public officials, and editorial writers all joined in, as they should have, expressing outrage. Not so following the Prospect Park incident.

Consider the comments of attorney C. Vernon Mason. He agrees that what happened in Prospect Park should be condemned. But he thinks I went too far. "It is totally unnecessary, unfair, and insensitive," he said recently, "to try to compare some sick individuals with the kind of racially motivated incidents that have occurred too often in this city."

Following Howard Beach, Mr. Mason and others marched, picketed, demanded that a special prosecutor be appointed to handle the case, and predicted a "long hot summer." Now, if the four young men alleged to have committed this crime had tried to set fire to two homeless people who were black instead of white, wouldn't he have led marches, pickets, issued calls for a special prosecutor, made predictions of a "long hot summer," even a winter, in the aftermath of Prospect Park? Most certainly.

Then why hasn't he or others been similarly outraged? Is it because both the victims and alleged perpetrators are of the same race—all six of the people involved in the incident were white—making it impossible to view the incident as racial? Does violence as a matter of public concern only count if it can be seen in racial terms? Isn't that unacceptable?

Just look at the similarities between these two incidents. Without question those who tried to burn these two people were sick. But racists are sick, too. Is it unnecessary, unfair, insensitive, then, to compare the two incidents?

Not at all. It's just accurate, just common sense. The attackers in Howard Beach had suffered no harm, no provocation from those they attacked. They just wanted to harass some blacks. So too with the attackers in Prospect Park. They just wanted to harass some "bums."

Both attacks occurred merely because the attackers didn't like a particular type of person, just like some people like to beat up Jews merely because they're Jews, beat up gays merely because they're gays, or beat up people of one ethnic origin merely because they're not of the attacker's ethnic origin. Both attacks were senseless, both attacks were sick, both attacks should be condemned with equal vigor.

I agree with Mr. Mason that white on black crime of the sort that occurred in Howard Beach "matters." So does black on white crime of the sort that occurred in Jamaica, Queens. But black on black crime or white on white crime? Well, since the crime can't be cast in racial terms, apparently he and others by their silence are suggesting we not get as upset.

It's an unacceptable double standard—one kind of outrage exhibited when the perpetrator of a crime is of one race, the victim of another; another kind of response when the perpetrator and victim are both of the same race. But wasn't a criminal justice system that was built on a double standard precisely what helped keep black Americans in bondage for so long? We rejoiced when that system was torn down during the fifties and sixties. Let's not try to revive it now.

If ours is to be a civilized society, we can't consider acts of senseless violence between people of different races to be of such greater consequence than acts of senseless violence between people of the same race as to have silence apply in the latter. Whether you're black and assaulted by a white, white and assaulted by a black, or assaulted by someone of your own race, an assailant's race doesn't make the blow easier to bear. What infuriates the victim and should infuriate us is the evil act, not the color, creed, or ethnic origin of the actor.

A criminal justice system with eyes wide open to some crimes, but that winks at others, dispenses unequal justice. No matter the race of the criminal or of the victim, crime in all its forms and against all its victims must be condemned. What happened in Prospect Park is as horrendous, as appalling as what happened in Howard Beach. We are equal in the eyes of our Creator. Let's not be unequal in the eyes of our laws.

Crime is the number-one issue for all citizens in this city, whatever their race. And crimes driven by bias are among the worst of all the crimes which concern every decent person. But if we refuse to look honestly at those crimes—whether they are white-on-black or black-on-white—we will never, ever be able to work together honestly and openly to root out the problem.

We must speak the truth about crime, no matter how much it may hurt. Remember, after all, that it was Dr. King who preached, "Know the truth and it shall make you free." It was true when he preached it and it's true today.

# PART
# 9

# PARTING SHOTS

___

## To George Bush

President George Bush and I served together for a short time in Congress when I first went there in 1968. He went on to become Ambassador to the People's Republic of China, CIA Director, Vice President, and, ultimately, the forty-first President of the United States. Though I disagree with his philosophy of government, he is a very decent man.

Presidents of the United States often visit New York. As Mayor, I made it a custom to open the doors of Gracie Mansion—an eighteenth-century mansion with spacious lawns and a beautiful garden overlooking the East River which serves as the Mayor's official residence—to visiting Presidents. Upon his election, I extended the same invitation to President and Mrs. Bush:

*Congratulations on your enormous victory. You have every right to be very proud of having turned a seventeen-point deficit at the beginning of the race into a smashing victory. There will be many postmortems, but the bottom line is that the voters decided they preferred you and your policies over the Democratic candidate and his policies.*

*So much for politics. I am writing to continue a tradition I began with President Carter, by inviting you to stay at Gracie Mansion, the Mayor's official residence, whenever you are in New York City. On one occasion President and Mrs. Reagan were considering it, but they had to decline when they were told that the management at the Waldorf had placed their initials on the towels in their suite! I certainly understood their reluctance to spurn that hospitable and gracious act on the part of the Waldorf. I can't have your initials placed on the towels, but I can offer you the hospitality of the City of New York. I not only want to extend the invitation to you as our President, but also because we have known one another for years and served in the Congress together. In addition, whenever President Reagan came to the city for a nonpolitical event, his office asked that I meet him at the heliport and accompany him to his hotel. I always perceived that as a great honor, and I would be delighted to accompany you whenever you are in New York.*

*You might recall that when you were the Director of the CIA and I was a Congressman, you called to alert me to the fact that either the Uruguayan or the Chilean Secret Service had put a contract out on my life. I remember your advice. You said, "Ed, be careful this weekend." I was and I survived. I am now told by the feds that the Colombian drug cartel has put a contract out on my life. I remember your advice and try to be careful, but I have become a fatalist over the years, so I give it little thought.*

*I want to assure you of the fact that I am anxious to do whatever I can to help you become a great President. I have said that publicly and will do whatever I can to help you make this country better for all of us. That does not mean that we should end all constructive criticism. But it does mean that we should not seek to create problems for you on a political basis, at least not until you announce you are running for a second term.*

*My very best to you and with great affection for Barbara.*

President Bush replied, saying he expected "we won't get to New York near as much as Barbara and I would like, but maybe we can hit your bid." Even though I'm not from Texas, I knew what he meant— "Maybe, but don't count on it." Regrettably, he didn't stay at Gracie Mansion while I was Mayor.

Over the years, I have had the privilege to get to know Mrs. Bush. Prior to Bush's inauguration as President, I was invited to meet with him in the West Wing of the White House. When I arrived, he told me that he and Barbara were celebrating their fortieth wedding anniversary. He called her while I was there and he put me on the phone. We had a lovely conversation.

"I know, Barbara, that I will never call George anything other than Mr. President," I said. "But may I still call you Barbara?" She said, "Of course, Ed." And I always have called her by her first name.

She gets to New York more than the President does. And on every occasion I saw her, my customary greeting was to kiss her on the cheek. I didn't feel I was overstepping good manners. And she didn't seem to mind.

Until I happened to meet her at an event at the United Nations. "Now, no more kissing, Ed," she said. I thought she was kidding, so I took her hand and kissed it. The incident occurred at around the time she'd taken the hand of Prime Minister Margaret Thatcher's husband and, as a joke, kissed it. The photograph of that incident was flashed around the world.

The next time I saw her, at a reception for the Coro Foundation, she made it clear in no uncertain terms that she did not want me to kiss her. I realized for the first time that she was under instructions not to allow me to do so. Allowing a Democratic candidate to kiss the cheek or hand of a Republican First Lady might be misunderstood as an endorsement. So I assume she was told no more kisses for me.

The next time we met was at a luncheon hosted by the Association for a Better New York. As I approached her, she held up her hands as if a vampire were advancing on her. I realized that the no-kiss policy was for real. I went back to City Hall and announced that because it might be misunderstood, there would be no further episodes of public kissing involving Barbara Bush and me. I treated it as a joke. So did the press.

The denouement came after I lost the primary election. Barbara was the guest of honor at an Appeal of Conscience dinner at the Pierre Hotel. I moved through the receiving line, and when I came to Mrs.

Bush, I held out my hand to shake hers. "Come on, Ed," she said, "give me a kiss." I immediately obliged. All it took was my little defeat for us to become kissing cousins again.

The next evening she was guest of honor at the Alfred E. Smith dinner hosted by His Eminence John Cardinal O'Connor. She was extremely generous toward me in her remarks, using the phrase that I hope people will always associate with me— "How'm I doing, Ed?" "Fine," I replied. And later we kissed again. She is special.

# To David Garth

I was only the third mayor in the history of New York City to win three four-year terms. Both Fiorello LaGuardia and Robert Wagner had decided not to seek a fourth term because of precipitous declines in their popularity. In early 1989 my public approval rating was at an all-time low. In fact, David Garth, my campaign advisor, told me that early in the year only 17 percent of New Yorkers approved of the job I was doing.

I decided nevertheless to seek reelection. A lot of people thought I was foolish to run. "You don't need the aggravation, Ed," went the general argument. "Let someone else put up with the headaches. You've had twelve years. You've done enough."

I'd also endured four years of relentless and, oftentimes, unfair criticism from reporters and columnists, particularly—but not only—at the *Daily News*. Like my first and second terms, my third term ended with an impressive list of accomplishments: a campaign financing bill, a $5.1 billion housing program, a no-smoking bill, reductions in both class sizes and dropout rates in the city's schools, an ambitious citywide program to crack down on drug dealers, and economic growth in all five boroughs.

However, led by the *Daily News*, the city's newspapers nevertheless launched an "all warts-no credit" approach to covering my administration. They ignored what we'd accomplished and paid attention only to problems we hadn't solved. Some of it was motivated by ideology, some of it by a desire to sell newspapers, and, in the case of the *Daily News*, some of it by the hope that it would hasten my political demise.

Despite all of the criticism and all of the abuse I received at the hands of frequently inaccurate and sometimes ideologically motivated reporters, I personally believed I was the best-qualified of all the mayoral candidates, particularly as the local economy slowed and the city's fiscal situation deteriorated. I was not going to give up without a fight.

But it was not to be. I was not able to overcome the attacks from the press and lost the Democratic primary to David Dinkins. At 11:15 on Tuesday evening, September 12, 1989, I came down to the ballroom at the Sheraton Centre Hotel to thank my supporters, meet with the press, and speak with New Yorkers watching the eleven o'clock news. I spoke extemporaneously:

I just called David Dinkins and I wished him all success and I told him I am ready to serve, to help him to become the next mayor. He asked that we all join him tomorrow, not this evening, on the steps of City Hall. I told him for myself that that's what we will do to help plan the campaign for his victory so that he can become the 106th Mayor of the City of New York.

He won the race and he won it fairly and squarely and by a large margin. I think it's something like 42 to 50 percent. That's a substantial victory. This is my twenty-fifth election and I've lost three counting the one tonight, which means I've won twenty-two. So I know what it is both to win and to lose. And I'm not going to use the trite line because it's too trite.

But the fact is that my concern, in all honesty, is more about you. I have had twelve glorious years as Mayor. So I know that we ran a tremendous race, coming from nowhere—17 percent was the low point—to near victory, but not victory.

I obviously would have preferred winning, but I'm not distressed to the extent that the supporters are, because you've given it everything and for nothing other than the satisfaction of seeing someone you believe in win. I want you not to feel sorry for me. Believe me, there is life after the mayoralty. And let me just immediately say, so there will be no misunderstanding, I am not running for Governor.

With all of our problems, and we have many—and every one of them will be overcome, whether it's a strain in racial relations or a matter of dealing with drugs or AIDS or homelessness—all of the issues which we all raised in our campaigns, the four candidates basically agreed upon. The four of us had common goals, differences in how to reach them.

They will all be overcome because of the expertise that exists in this city and the decency that exists in this city and the fact that whites and blacks and Hispanics and Asians want a common good life for all of us. And that desire and the need to root out the bigots in our society and to uplift the poor, that common agenda is what the next mayor, David Dinkins, will seek to implement. We, all of us—you and the volunteers who did so much for me—I want you to do the same for David Dinkins.

Notwithstanding the electoral outcome, I still believe that I was the best-qualified of all the candidates in 1989. I'd made the tough choices necessary to prevent bankruptcy in 1978. And I believe I was the best person running in terms of being able to make similarly tough decisions over the next four years. I had had twelve wonderful years in City Hall presiding over one of the best municipal governments in the history of this city. I hope and I believe that, with the passage of time and the cooling of passions, historians will conclude the same.

When you've run for political office as often as I have, you'd better have a lot of friends. Fortunately, I have. As a result of their hard work, their financial contributions, and, most important, their emotional support, I've won almost all of the campaigns I've entered. To all of them I say, "Thank you."

But there are a few particularly close friends who deserve special thanks for what they've done for me. One is David Garth. He has been a friend of mine since 1977, when he took on my first campaign for mayor and made it possible for me to win. We have continued that friendship—personal and professional—up to the present time.

There is no better friend to have during a difficult time than David Garth. That is when he is most supportive. There is no better friend to have when you are at the top than David Garth. That is when he is most critical and constructive.

My unsuccessful 1989 campaign for a fourth term as Mayor of the City of New York will be the last political campaign I will ever be involved in as a candidate. While David has often said he doesn't want to run political campaigns ever again, the truth is that I don't believe he can avoid them—and for two very good reasons. First, people will continually be knocking on his door asking him to take their campaign. Second, his personality is such that I don't think he'll be able to refuse when the excitement of the next major election comes around.

My recommendation is that the next Democratic candidate for President sign him up. He is the best. This is what I wrote him the day after the 1989 Democratic primary:

*Our relationship has always been unique. You agreed to take my campaign when it had no hope of success in 1977 and again in 1989 under similar circumstances. In the first campaign, we were victorious. In the recent election, our victory was greater and sweeter, even if not so at the polls.*

*We ran a campaign that every other candidate must envy and one which you and I will always be proud of. From a textbook and moral point of view, it was perfect. The fact that we lost had nothing to do with the campaign. My longevity in office combined with an enormous change in the demographics made it, in my judgment, impossible to win. I have no regrets, nor should you.*

*I feel as though a tremendous burden has been lifted from my shoulders. I wish the next Mayor the very best, because I do so love this City. I won't in any way be critical of the Mayor when he seeks to carry out the burdens of this office, which I know so well. I'll just be thinking that many New Yorkers will be saying to themselves, "Koch did it better and really cared about me. We miss him." Just kidding. I honestly hope that the next Mayor's record excels mine, but I'm arrogant enough to think it won't.*

*All the best and many, many thanks.*

Another very good friend in 1989 was Paul Crotty, my campaign manager and, along with David Garth, my final campaign's leading light. Previously he had served as both my finance commissioner and my housing commissioner. He did an outstanding job in both capacities. But where he really proved his mettle was in Campaign '89.

I have never met anyone who combines intelligence, decency, and ability, without ever compromising his leadership and his principles, the way Paul Crotty does. He is courageous and a rock to stand beside and hold on to, and you know he will stand with you no matter how rough the going at the moment. This was my post-campaign letter to him:

*You are a special person, and I will always be appreciative of what you did for me. . . .*

*If there were a need for an imprimatur attesting to your uniqueness, it would be that David Garth has the same high opinion of you as I do. And there are only two other people he really likes—me and himself!*

*All the best.*

A third very good friend in 1989 was John Cardinal O'Connor. After the results had come in on primary night and I had delivered my concession speech to my friends and supporters at the Sheraton Centre, I returned to Gracie Mansion at around midnight. About five or ten minutes later, there was a knock on the front door. It was His Eminence, dropping by just to see how I was doing. The next day I sent him a thank-you note:

*It was so wonderful of you to come to Gracie Mansion last night after the election to comfort me. I am very appreciative.*

*I know that you and many others worry that I might be in a blue funk. But as I told you last night, I feel as though a tremendous burden has been lifted from my shoulders. While the responsibility of caring for and leading 7.5 million New Yorkers is certainly exhilarating, it also creates great anxiety. I know that I did the best job I could, so I have no regrets or remorse. I feel only elation and appreciation to God for having permitted me to serve the people of this city.*

*I hope that we will have many more occasions to talk and occasionally to sup together. Let's have dinner at the Mansion as many times as possible before the end of the year!*

*All the best and, again, many thanks.*

His visit was a remarkable gesture by a remarkable man. And I do mean remarkable.

# To David Dinkins

No one is born mayor. And no matter how good you may have been in what you did before walking up the steps of City Hall and into its northwest corner office, being elected mayor imposes responsibilites of a scope and number hard to have imagined the day you tossed your candidate's hat in the ring.

Simply put, the responsibilities are awesome, the challenges endless. If you're human, inevitably you'll have occasional doubts about your ability to perform. I know I did. But I did not let them deter me from trying to be the best mayor this city's ever had.

I know David Dinkins, my successor, has the same ambition and probably some of the same doubts. As he took office and I left, I thought a little mayor-to-mayor advice might be welcome. Hence the following letter:

*Dear David,*

*When you and I recently appeared together before a large crowd out in Brighton Beach, I began by telling the people, "I want to thank everyone out there who voted for me. I appreciate it." Then, I added, "I also want to thank everyone who didn't—you liberated me."*

*Well, David, now that I'm liberated I'd like to share with you some of my thoughts about the job I had and you now have. Of course, your experiences as Mayor will be different from mine, but some things never change.*

*When I first was elected twelve years ago, I had no conception of what it meant to run the City of New York. After all, I had been a Congressman, a very good Congressman, but I had jurisdiction over only eighteen people—half of them in New York and half in Washington. Now I had jurisdiction over some 7 million people in a city on the brink of bankruptcy, totally defeated in spirit, leaderless. Suddenly thrust upon me was a colossal job. I not only had to provide the leadership and the hope and the spirit to rally New York, I also had to begin to make decisions about many things with which I was really unfamiliar.*

*I wasn't frightened by this. I've always had sufficient confidence in myself to believe that if a job could be done, I could do it. And if it couldn't be done, it wasn't my fault: It just couldn't be done. But no matter how much confidence you have, being Mayor of New York is a job you have to grow into.*

*I believe that my greatest strength as Mayor has been a willingness to make tough decisions. You cannot defer them. You cannot linger over them when time is of the essence. If you can't make decisions, you really can't be a successful mayor. But that ability doesn't come naturally. You begin to grow into this job when you realize that tough decisions have to be made—and you have the guts to make them.*

*I learned that early on. In my first term as Mayor, I had to decide whether or not to balance the budget in three years, instead of the four-year period the law allowed. If I did that, I knew it would inflict greater pain upon the City through a greater reduction in services than the law required. But if we didn't balance the budget, we would not be able to raise money through the issuance of general obligation bonds that would allow us to restore our infrastructure: our streets, our* bridges, our school buildings. The rule of thumb in the market was that we could not get back in until three years after a balanced budget had been achieved. And therefore, if I wanted to bring the City back as quickly as possible, then I should shorten the time for a balanced budget by at least one year.

I held a major meeting, and both proponents and opponents had their say. The fiscal people, OMB, were all for drastic cuts in services; that's their nature. Fiscal people can be sadistic. The operational people were more disposed to retain as many services as possible and spread the cuts over the two-year period. They are, by nature, more for spreading the pain.

Well, we took a vote, and the results were split right down the middle, fifty-fifty. . . .

But the decision was mine. I went home and I thought about it. I decided that it was in the best interests of the City to balance the budget and get back into the markets as quickly as possible. It was probably the best decision I made in those early years. One, it got the City back into the markets in record time. And secondly, it also created in the financial world—and New York is the international center of finance—a confidence in me that was not there before.

Sometimes, though, you can make the right decision and still have regrets. The biggest disappointment to me in my three terms was the reaction to the closing of Sydenham Hospital in Harlem. It had to be done. It was a hospital providing far less than satisfactory medical services and costing far more than any hospital in the system when we had no money to spare. The closing saved us $9 million annually. But more important, it said that we were not going to be wasteful anymore.

Still, the way things worked out was sad. It probably caused the most damage in my relationship with blacks. For them, it was symbolic. It was the end of an era when they could somehow or other get their way by just a simple appeal to the Mayor.

Among the toughest decisions you will have to make right from the start, David, are those that involve how this city will use its financial resources. There has to be a just and intelligent use of the monies we have. The City of New York cannot be in the business of redistribution of wealth. A mayor cannot throw the middle class to the wolves by saying that only the poorest of the poor should have their needs and concerns addressed with the limited funds we have available. And that is the sort of decision that is never easy to make.

You'll find you grow into the job in many ways. In my case, I was this kid who was born in the Bronx. I was never a brilliant student. I was never a jock. I'm an ordinary guy. In fact, when I first became Mayor, I was a retiring, shy person. And suddenly I was thrust into the spotlight.

In those days, the mood in New York was despondent. The City was so without spirit that I realized I had to adopt a personal demeanor that would elevate attitudes throughout New York. I set out to project a spirit and optimism that would be infectious. We were without hope, and I wanted to give the City hope. Being Mayor forces you to adopt many personalities, David—for your own sake and the sake of the City.

I also had to develop some defenses against the people a Mayor comes in contact with each day, and you will too. I'm not terribly good at small talk. It bores me. I don't like to chat inanities with people I don't know. But still, I had to come up with a way of breezing through a crowd of people and conveying that I was interested in them, that they meant something to me; and at the same time I didn't want to sit or stand around and talk to everybody individually. So my defense was to use a slogan—"How'm I doing?" I believe it was brilliant, frankly, because it got people to talk and made it easy for me. I could go through a room very quickly. A mayor has to develop a slogan or some sort of public persona or else he will be clawed to death.

Still, there are some social obligations a mayor has to put up with for the good of the City. Dinner parties have never been my favorite form of recreation. But I've had hundreds of dinners here at Gracie Mansion because I decided early on that it was in the interests of the City. It was important for me to meet all the people who were the leaders of the financial, cultural, scientific, and industrial worlds within the City of New York so they would have confidence in the City. That was why I gave those dinners, and after a while I found that I enjoyed them and had become a pretty good host.

Most people, I decided, are bored at dinners that are all chit-chat. So I developed a way of focusing the table's attention on a question. It could be AIDS, abortion, some racial issue, Israel. Anything really gripping. I asked people to offer their opinions, and most of the time I had to encourage them because they were not accustomed to this kind of dinner party. But it worked, and my dinners were rarely boring. Sometimes you'll have to go out of your way, David, to get people to tell you what they really think. Learning these little tricks of the trade is another way you grow into the job as Mayor.

Of course, having the dinners at Gracie Mansion helped. In the beginning I thought I would feel very lonely at the Mansion because there were so many rooms and I would just rattle around. I had never lived in a private home before becoming Mayor. All my life I had only lived in apartments; my own apartment was just three rooms—a bedroom, a living room, a sort of galley kitchen, and a nice terrace. My thought was that I would spend my time in this apartment and would only use the Mansion for ceremonial occasions. But that's not the real world. In the real world, just as you can grow into a job, you can grow into a house. And I think I did both.

Gracie Mansion is an extraordinary place. Not in my wildest dreams did I ever believe I would end up living there, until by a miracle it actually happened. I never got totally used to it. You're never really alone—bodyguards, staff constantly hover around you. Still, the Mansion has a special wonder of its own. Every time I enter the courtyard in the car, it's like entering a castle. But when I leave it on December 31, I decided, I will probably never come back, even if I'm invited. It's a closed book in my life, and a book that is just beginning to open for you. My advice to you, David, is enjoy it. I did. I have no regrets, no sadness about leaving the Mansion, but I suspect if I were to come back it would be painful.

A mayor, however, has to learn to withstand some pain. The most searing pain of my twelve years was learning I had been betrayed by people who were corrupt. I could not have imagined Donnie Manes to be one of them. He had to have been sick. I don't explain corruption (or violence) away by saying, "Well, the guy is sick and therefore we have to understand." To understand is to forgive and I'm not forgiving of corruption. I want people punished. And I would have wanted Donnie Manes to be punished if he had lived. But still there's no question in my mind that he had to have been seriously mentally ill. He was a guy with a golden future. One of the brightest minds on the Board of Estimate, in a position of enormous power as Queens Borough President and Democratic county leader. And, surely, he would have been a candidate for Mayor in the future. In fact, if I had been elected governor in 1982, I might very well have endorsed him to replace me as Mayor. His corruption, in terms of his family, his friends, and the City itself, was so enormous that it was the worst. To this day we don't know where the money he stole went. He was my greatest disappointment.

I also never thought Stanley Friedman was corrupt. I know that he ultimately was disclosed to be a crook; there's no question about that *in my mind. But Stanley had a reputation for going right up to the edge. He saw his opportunities and he took them—yet always within the law. But he fell over the edge; he broke the law. Still, I believe his sentencing was vindictive. He didn't deserve nineteen years. They came down hard on Stanley because they were trying to get me.*

*I was always the big fish. It's incredible that I came through this period of time because everybody, including Friedman, must have been squeezed. They must have been told, "We'll reduce your sentence." "We'll give you no sentence." "Give us Koch, and we'll help you."*

*But there was nothing to give.*

*Still it was a rough time. I was despondent. I must confess, on several occasions when I was alone, I wept. It was hard to get myself out of bed in the morning. Every day in the papers there would be a repetition of an earlier story or maybe a new one. The editorials in the* Daily News *were just maniacal in their frenzy. On occasion I would choke up and say to myself, "How could this happen in my administration?" I mean, I'm as honest as the day is long. And everybody knows that. How could this have happened to me? How can I be blamed for these people— mostly people I had no authority over, like Manes, or Friedman, or Biaggi, or Esposito?*

*I felt almost like Job. I never thought of resigning, but I was pretty sure I wouldn't run again at the end of my third term. I tried to keep all my anger, all my sorrowful feelings to myself. Undoubtedly, not sharing these anxieties weighed me down. . . . Did all this contribute to my stroke? Who knows? But I paid a price.*

*I took plenty of abuse—and you will too, David. You are the big fish now, and no matter how careful you are in choosing the people around you, they can screw up. They're normal and make mistakes, and sometimes those mistakes become grotesque and blown out of proportion under the scrutiny of the press. I always tried to stand by my commissioners, even when they made a mistake—assuming it was an honest error. I took a lot of heat. But the commissioners appreciated what I did.*

*As Mayor, you'll have to be on guard, David. People will try to take advantage of you. Government, I always say, is not for my friends. Let me explain what I mean. Donald Trump—who for the most part has struck me as a miserable person, and who doesn't like me either—may not know it, but he agreed with me when he said, "Ed Koch never helps his friends." Well, he was just giving a different spin to what I'm trying to say. The mere fact that you're my friend doesn't mean that you* *should be in government; or if you're seeking to do business with government, and happen to be my friend, that you should have a lower standard applied to you. On the contrary, a higher standard should be applied to you. Trump obviously considered himself to be my friend at one time, and because of that, or because he gave or raised $70,000 for one of my mayoral campaigns, he expected something in return. He never got it. And he thought that was disloyal.*

*I'm very loyal to people. That doesn't mean I forgive them their incompetence or permit them to use me. That's not the kind of loyalty a mayor can allow himself to have. When your friends are in government or seek governmental assistance, they must be held to higher standards than ordinary citizens who are similarly situated. If they try to presume on your friendship, that's disloyalty on their part.*

*A mayor must learn to be resilient, David, to roll with the punches and then get on with the job. I bounced back. I made up my mind midway through all the corruption agony that I wasn't going to give up. "No," I told myself, "I'm not going to run away. I'm going to run for a fourth term."*

*And I'm glad I did. I have no regrets about the election. History will judge me and my administration, just as it will judge every Mayor. And while there were many painful moments, being Mayor of New York is probably the most fulfilling and exciting job in the world. More exciting than even the President's job, because even he doesn't have to make the number of decisions the Mayor of New York makes nearly every day. His decisions involve war and peace; mine the quality of everyday life.*

*Some of the decisions were tough, some were easy. There were good days and bad, highs and lows. But I loved every moment of it. I looked at a tape the other night. It was of one of the first interviews I gave after being elected in 1977. As I see myself, I looked the same as I do today. I don't think I have changed that much. I'm going out a young man, just twelve years older. The interviewers now look older.*

*Part of the reason for that, David, brings me to my last piece of advice (at least for now): always give as good as you get. By that I mean, a mayor cannot compromise his own principles. No matter who tries to pressure or intimidate him. And they'll try. Because remember, even though the saying goes that you can't fight City Hall, you can be sure someone will always be trying. And that's the way it should be.*

*All the best.*

And now I am once again a private citizen, watching with great interest as any private citizen should what happens at City Hall, but knowing, even feeling relieved, that it is someone else's problem, someone else's challenge.

I have already embarked on a host of new careers—as a columnist, a lawyer, a professor, a consultant, a lecturer, and yes, an author. I worked twelve to fourteen hours a day as Mayor. The hours have been just as long and just as much fun since leaving City Hall.

For twelve years I gave it my all. I know David Dinkins will too. Like his one hundred and five predecessors as Mayor, he will need all our help and our prayers. I know New Yorkers will be generous with both. I will no longer get 3 A.M. telephone calls to tell me of some disaster or catastrophe. David will. God bless him. He will need God's help and our support.

# ACKNOWLEDGMENTS

Putting this book together required culling through thousands of letters, trying to select those which best reflected the wide variety of issues, big and small, I have addressed over the past twelve years. A lot of research had to be done to prepare the headnotes which explain why each letter was sent and what happened when it was. I could not have done it alone.

I was lucky to have as one of my press secretaries Leland T. Jones. He is a good writer and a marvelous researcher, and he has been an intelligent and tireless advocate for the work of my administration. Every weekend for the past year, Lee and I would have a two-hour session at Gracie Mansion on a Saturday or a Sunday morning. Donating both his time and his talents to the project, he would listen, ask questions, and then take down my dictation in longhand. Vivienne Goldberg, Esther Nazario, and Dawn Mayo helped with the typing. Ariel Beard, Thomas Dillon, Jennifer Kimball, George Medici, and Carmen Recinos helped with the research.

I was also lucky to have Jenny Cox as my editor. She is a personal friend of mine. Jenny has great judgment and a marvelous way of getting things done. I never felt that I was being pushed or led, yet her persuasive insights were always worthy of accommodation and greatly enhanced the book.

Many thanks, and, of course, all the best.

# INDEX

Project HELP and, 109–10, 112
rehabilitated buildings program for,
    6–7
religious institutions and, 68–70,
    71–73
shelters for, see shelters, homeless
homosexual rights, see gay rights
Honduras, 22, 29, 30
    American soldiers in, 27
Hong Kong, 55–58
Hoover, Herbert, 17, 18, 172
Horne, Lena, 60
Hotel Bryant, 7
House of the Lord Pentecostal Church,
    236
housing, 101–2, 163, 258
    gay rights and, 113
    Jackson's sermon on, 220–21
    minority contractors and, 188
Houston Astros, 175–76
Howard Beach incident, 236–37,
    239–47, 251, 252, 253, 254
Hudson River, 131
Human Resources Administration
    (HRA), 61, 158, 188
    foster infant home and, 162, 164
    homeless and, 107, 109, 221
Human Rights Commission, 23
Hungary, 18
Hynes, Charles J., 204, 245

*I, Koch* (Browne, Collins and
    Goodwin), 212
Iacocca, Lee, 170–71
International League for Human
    Rights, 54
International PEN, 99–100
International Red Cross, 26, 27, 54
intravenous drug users, 125, 126
    needle exchange program and, 119–23
IRA, 94
Iran, 86, 93
Iraq, 93
Ireland:
    Great Britain and, 45–48, 88, 224
    Koch's visit to, 44–48
Irish-American voters, 46, 47, 48
*Irish Echo*, 48
Israel, State of, 83–86
    Farrakhan and, 88
    Jackson's candidacy and, 40, 220,
        222, 223, 225, 226, 227

Jewish Defense League and, 94
Knesset of, 83, 94, 196
press coverage of, 97–100
U.N. and, 78, 92–93, 96, 97
West Bank of, 91–93, 97, 98, 99,
    100
world opinion of, 96–97

Jackson, Jesse, 19, 26, 36, 45, 217–30,
    237
    Koch's *Post* column on, 220–22
    Koch's public criticisms of, 40, 41,
        88, 185–86, 219–27, 230, 232
    Ortega and, 26
jails and prisons, 10, 12, 20, 161, 163,
    165
    Koch's Alaska proposal for, 13–15
Jamaica Arms, 8
Japan, drug laws in, 9
Javits, Jacob, 170
Jermyn, Michael, 150
Jewish Child Care Association, 162
Jewish Defense League (JDL), 93–96
Jews, Judaism, 18
    blood libel against, 81–83
    Conservative, 84–85
    Herodian (assimilationist), 96
    Holocaust and, see Nazi Germany
    Israel and, see Israel, State of
    Jackson's candidacy and, 223–27
    Law of Return and, 84–86
    line of descent and, 84
    mayoral election and, 239
    Old Testament and, 70–71
    Orthodox, 84, 85
    Polish, 31
    presidential election and, 222–27,
        229
    Reform, 84–85
    Sabbath restrictions and, 86
    see also anti-Semitism
Jiang Zemin, 49
jobs, see employment
Joffrey, Robert, 60
jogger, assault on, 249, 250, 251
John Paul II, Pope, 33
Johnson, Doug, 174–75
Johnson, Sterling, 150
Johnston, Robert, 150
Joseph, Stephen, 61
    needle exchange program and, 120,
        121, 122

Poland, 18, 34
  anti-Semitism in, 31–34
Police Department:
  bias crime and, 246, 248, 249
  fiscal crisis and, 102
police officers, 102
  funerals of, Koch's attendance at,
    146, 148, 152, 212–14
  homeless and, 107, 111–12
  murder of, 142, 143–44, 146, 147–53
  racism or brutality charges against,
    148–49, 195
*Politics* (Koch), 99
poor, 19, 44
  crime and, 141, 250–51
  working, 5, 7, 9
  *see also* homeless
pregnant women, alcoholic beverage
    warning signs and, 1–3
*Prensa, La* (Managua), 23
presidential election (1988), 18, 19, 20,
    40, 230
  *see also individual candidates*
press, 182–83
Pressler, Larry, 27–28
Pressman, Gabe, 102, 103
press secretaries, 181, 182
Price, Leontyne, 60
Prim, Benny, 121
prisons, *see* jails and prisons
privacy, 181–83
Project for an Open City, 238
Project HELP, 109–10, 112
Prospect Park attempted murder,
    251–54
public assistance, *see* welfare
public figures, privacy and, 181–83
public financing law, 135

Quinones, Nathan, 127, 128
quota systems, 186–88, 218, 219

racism, 17, 19, 141, 217–54
  black, 247–48
  crimes based on, *see* bias crime
  death penalty and, 143
  Farrakhan and, 88, 89, 90
  Harlem shelter and, 194
  in hiring, 204
  Lucas and, 194, 196
  police officers charged with, 148–49
  quotas and, 186–88, 218, 219

in South Africa, *see* South Africa,
    apartheid government of
  special interests and, 224
  violent action and, 43–44
Raffa, James, 164
Rangel, Charles, 39–43
  Koch-Jackson meeting and, 227, 228,
    229
  Koch's criticisms of Jackson and,
    222, 223–24
Rankin, John, 243
Rather, Dan, 183
Ravitch, Richard, 135, 214, 239
Reagan, Nancy, 177, 256
Reagan, Ronald, 58, 124, 131, 141,
    172, 256
  Arafat and, 78, 79
  homeless and, 109
  Koch's invitation to, 256
  Mets' visit to, 177
  Nicaragua and, 21–31
  Reed and, 79–80
  South Africa and, 41
Red Cross, International, 26, 27, 54
Reed, Joseph V., 77–81
Reel, Bill, 214
Reform Jews, 84–85
religious discrimination, 17, 19, 219,
    222, 240
  bias crime and, 115, 116
  quotas and, 186–88
  *see also* anti-Semitism
religious institutions, homeless and,
    68–70, 71–73
religious special-interest groups, 224
reporters, 182–83
Republican Party, 17, 18
resource recovery plants, 163
restaurants, 134–35
  health inspector scandal and, 189–91
Resurrection Roman Catholic Church,
    194
Rigby, Bay, 175
Ringling Bros., Barnum & Bailey
    Circus, 102
Robb, Charles, 20, 22, 28
Roberts, Sam, 129
Rochman, Barbara, 1–3
Rockefeller, David, 79
Rockefeller, Nelson, 170
*Roe* v. *Wade*, 3
Rohatyn, Felix, 166, 167

in Nicaragua, 26
Wallenberg and, 34–36
Soweto, 43
Speakes, Larry, 177
special interest groups, 224
Spencer, Gil, 211
sports, 173
squeegee men, 189
Sri Lanka, 97–98
SRO (single-room-occupancy) buildings,
72–73
Standard & Poor's, 101, 168
Staten Island, roosters on, 178–81
*Staten Island Advance,* 178
Koch endorsed by, 214
*Staten Island Advance,* Koch's columns
in:
on Big Brother government, 183
on the death penalty, 142–45
on Gladwin Avenue firebombing,
162–64
on having fun, 104
on his stroke, 61–66
on Ireland, 46–47
on Schanberg, 198–99
on Television City proposal, 207–10
state officials and employees,
conflict-of-interest rules for, 135
Stewart, James R., 11–13
Stewart, Moses, 234, 237–39
striped bass, 131–35
subway strike, 102
Sullivan, Leon H., 89–91
Sullivan, Sean, 252
Sullivan Principles, 89
*Summer Showcase Magazine,* 192–93
"Sundae in New York," 59
Supreme Court, U.S.:
death penalty and, 142
on racial quotas, 188
Sydenham Hospital, 195, 264
synagogues, homeless and, 68–70, 71–73

Talent Bank, 135–40
Talese, Gay, 99
Talmud, 82, 84
Tanenbaum, Marc, 68–69, 70
Tass, 198
Tegucigalpa, 22
Television City proposal, 206–11
Teresa, Mother, 61–68
*Terrible Joe Moran,* 59

terrorists:
Gladwin Avenue, 161–66
Jewish Defense League, 93–96
Palestine Liberation Organization,
78–80
Thatcher, Margaret, 257
Hong Kong and, 55–58
Koch's remarks on Ireland and, 46
Thornton, John, 48
Tiananmen Square, 49–55
Tiananmen Square Corner proposal,
51–52
Tibet, 98
TNT program, 188
Townsend, Alair, 65
Koch's comment on, 3–4
Trump and, 206, 208
traitors, 144
Trautman, Les, 198
Tribune Company, 211
Trump, Donald, 267–68
Central Park attack and, 251
Television City proposal of, 206–11
Turbas Divinas, Las, 23, 25
Tutsi, 92

unemployment, *see* employment
United Nations:
Center for Human Rights of, 81–82
Israel and, 78, 92–93, 96, 97
Reed and, 77–81
Security Council of, 92–93
Wallenberg memorial and, 35
United States Conference of Mayors,
11, 13
*Uptown News,* 195–96
Uruguay, 21
*U.S. News and World Report,* 197
Utah prison proposal, 13–15

Vancier, Victor, 95
Velez, Rose, 142, 145
Vera, Luis, 142
*Village Voice,* 203, 211

Wagner, Robert, 169, 258
Walesa, Lech, 32, 33–34
Wallace, George, 43
Wallenberg, Raoul, 34–36
roadway named after, 35
*Wall Street Journal,* 93, 167